Heinkel He ___

Karl-Heinz Regnat

MIDLAND
An imprint of
Ian Allan Publishing

Heinkel He 111

ISBN 1 85780 184 9

First published 2000 in Germany by
Bernard & Graefe Verlag, Bonn

Translation from original German text
by Ted Oliver

English language edition published 2004 by
Midland Publishing
4 Watling Drive, Hinckley, LE10 3EY, England
Tel: 01455 254 490 Fax: 01455 254 495
E-mail: midlandbooks@compuserve.com

Midland Publishing is an imprint of
Ian Allan Publishing Ltd

Worldwide distribution (except North America):
Midland Counties Publications
4 Watling Drive, Hinckley, LE10 3EY, England
Telephone: 01455 254 450 Fax: 01455 233 737
E-mail: midlandbooks@compuserve.com
www.midlandcountiessuperstore.com

North American trade distribution:
Specialty Press Publishers & Wholesalers Inc.
39966 Grand Avenue, North Branch, MN 55056
Tel: 651 277 1400 Fax: 651 277 1203
Toll free telephone: 800 895 4585
www.specialtypress.com

Design concept and layout

Printed in England by
Ian Allan Printing Ltd
Riverdene Business Park, Molesey Road,
Hersham, Surrey, KT12 4RG

Contents

Introduction 3

Chapters

1 **A New Generation** 6

2 **In Commercial Service** 12

3 **In Uniform** 26

4 **Progressive Development:** The He 111A- to P-Series 28

5 **The Technical Details of the He 111H** 38

6 **A 'One-Off':** The He 111Z Zwilling (Twin) 70

7 **He 111 Production & Prototypes** . . 74

8 **In War Service:** A Pictorial History . . 80

9 **Modelling The He 111** 86

Sources and Acknowledgements 95

Personalities

Prof. Dr.-Ing. Ernst Heinkel: The Man and the Designer

The son of Flaschnermeister (master-plumber or tinsmith) Karl Heinkel and his wife Catharine, Ernst Heinkel first saw the light of day on 24th January 1888 in Grunbach (Remstal) in Württemberg. After completing his schooling, he began his Maschinenbau (mechanical engineering) studies at the Königliche (Royal) Technische Hochschule in Stuttgart.

As early as 1910 he undertook construction of his first aircraft design – a biplane modelled on the French Henri Farman biplane. On 9th July 1911 Ernst Heinkel piloted it solo on its maiden flight, but his luck lasted only a few days. After several successive flights without mishap, Heinkel crashed on 19th July, writing off his flimsy machine and suffering severe injuries that resulted in a sojourn in hospital. As a result of these setbacks, and after much deliberation, he decided not to pursue his studies, much to the disappointment of his parents.

In the period that followed he took up a post as designer at the Luftverkehrsgesellschaft (LVG) aircraft manufacturing company in Berlin-Johannisthal. However, in December 1912 the restless Heinkel relinquished this position and moved to the Albatros Flugzeugbau as a Department Engineer. With his knowledge he was able to progress rapidly, and, after only a short time, he advanced to the combined position of Chief Designer and Director in June 1913. However, hardly had another year passed when, in May 1914, Heinkel turned to a new employer, the Brandenburgische Flugzeugwerke, where he became Chief Designer and Technical Director.

In the meantime the events at Sarajevo had escalated into the First World War. Heinkel's activities at the renamed Hansa-Brandenburg firm resulted in the design of several seaplanes for military purposes. Shortly before the end of the war he was awarded the EK II (Eisernes Kreuz, or Iron Cross Second Class) for special services in the aircraft field.

The post-war years were difficult for all those engaged in aircraft manufacture; every initiative in this sphere was subject to the stringent conditions imposed by the Treaty of Versailles, and several hurdles had to be overcome, often with cunning. Thus during the period 1919-20 Heinkel opened a vehicle repair workshop in Grunbach, but then in 1921 he saw a new opportunity, and took up a position at the Caspar Flugzeugwerke. In May 1922, by which time the restrictions imposed by the Treaty of Versailles had been relaxed, permitting a somewhat more positive outlook for aircraft manufacture, Heinkel again 'shouldered his bags', and this time the restless Swabian decided to establish his own enterprise in the form of a small and seemingly innocuous Konstruktionsbüro (Design Office). Then on 1st December that year he was able to turn his long-nurtured dream into reality when the Ernst Heinkel Flugzeugwerke in Warnemünde was established.

His spectacular career as an aircraft manufacturer began here in Halle 3 of the former Seeflieger-Versuchskommando (Naval Aviation Test Detachment). The aircraft that were developed here, together with the aircraft catapults that were developed in parallel as a 'second string', enabled Heinkel to strengthen the foundations of his reputation as a designer and employer. In the years that followed he strove continuously to obtain export orders in order to secure the survival of his young enterprise. In pursuance of this goal, he extended his 'feelers' towards Sweden, the Soviet Union, and even to distant Japan. Besides exporting his products, he entered into licensing agreements, and by the end of the 1920s his originally modest enterprise had changed to become one of the most significant German aviation concerns.

Following the establishment of his company in 1922, more than 40 types of aircraft made their appearance, and from the final assembly lines emerged a wide spectrum of designs, from fighters, basic trainers and reconnaissance aircraft to passenger, mail and freight carriers. His craving to enter new technical territory, and his quest to push his aircraft to attain ever high speeds, led to numerous often revolutionary innovations.

Ernst Heinkel with the first aircraft he built, modelled on the Henri Farman biplane. Heinkel suffered severe injuries when the machine crashed on 19th July 1911.

The first aircraft of his own design from the Albatros Flugzeugwerke was this monoplane.

The beginnings of Heinkel's life-long work: the Werk Warnemünde buildings in July 1922.

As early as 1932 Heinkel began to use flush riveting, resulting in virtually no drag. Six years later the brothers Karl and Otto Butter, who worked for Heinkel, perfected the pop-riveting method, which enabled difficult-to-access components to be comparatively easily riveted, solving a long-standing problem. However, this new technique, which accelerated production, was, for whatever reason, not recognised by the rather conservative-minded decision-makers in the RLM (Reichsluftfahrtministerium, the German Air Ministry). In 1939, therefore, Heinkel was granted permission to export this technology to the USA, or enter into licence agreements there, and the experiences gained resulted in a more positive attitude towards it in Germany.

In the 1930s a number of fast Heinkel aircraft appeared: the He 70 Blitz (Lightning) in 1932; the He 111 fast civil airliner in 1935; and the superfast He 100, which on 30th March 1939 captured the FAI-recognised World Speed Record for Germany with a speed of 746.606km/h (463.93mph); however, this performance was soon overtaken by the Messerschmitt company. In that same year, on 20th June, the world's first pure liquid rocket-propelled aircraft, the He 176, accomplished its first flight. On 27th August, just a few days before the outbreak of the Second World War, Heinkel was able to add another feather to his cap by accomplishing a further hitherto unattained performance in the successful maiden flight of the He 178, the first turbojet-powered aircraft in aviation history. Naturally, Heinkel would never have been able to accomplish such achievements alone; over time he had attracted several gifted individuals into his team, among them outstanding designers, scientists and engineers such as Dipl.-Ing. Karl Schwärzler, the Günter brothers and, not least, Wernher von Braun and the physicist Dr. Hans-Joachim Pabst von Ohain, who opened the door to new forms of propulsion.

Also, as Hugo Junkers had done, Ernst Heinkel placed considerable value on aeronautical research, which was seen as a driving force for all future progress in this sphere. The aerodynamically optimised He 111 was responsible for a real manufacturing boom, and the original production centres were soon 'bursting at the seams'. The result was the erection of several subsidiary factories, each with advanced social facilities. In addition, in April 1941 Heinkel acquired the vacant Hirth Motorenwerke in Stuttgart-Zuffenhausen (which had been managed by the RLM following the death of Hellmuth Hirth on 1st July 1938). This facility was to become the centre for development of what was then the most up-to-date jet-propulsion powerplant technology. On 1st April 1943 all the separate Heinkel facilities were consolidated into Ernst Heinkel AG in Rostock.

This took place at a time when the war was already in an advanced but progressively unfavourable state for Germany. Growing enmity with Nazi Gauleiter (District Leader) Hildebrand, as well as intrigues from other quarters, not to mention the catastrophe of the He 177, led to Heinkel's removal from the company leadership. From then on he was concerned solely with matters related to aircraft design, while wartime events increasingly brought an end to his endeavours as one after another his factories fell victim to the streams of Allied bombers.

The end of the war in May 1945 brought the total collapse of the Heinkel concern, as it did for the other sectors of the armaments industry. The Soviets confiscated the Heinkel Werk Marienehe, and everything that was still usable was dismantled and transported to the Soviet Union. The plant buildings in the Bleicherstraße, Rostock, were blown up, and those in the Werftstraße were converted into a Socialist enterprise. The Heinkel Werk Oranienburg was likewise completely dismantled by the Soviets and transported to the USSR, and the same fate was suffered by the Werk Waltersdorf near Berlin, which was subordinate to the Werk Zuffenhausen. Of the entire former enterprise, only the Stuttgart-Zuffenhausen element remained intact. Fortunately it was not destroyed and served as the basis for a new post-war beginning. This, however, was not in the realm of aviation, as that activity would have required Allied approval, having been forbidden nationwide. Heinkel's new start was in 1950 with the production of small cabin and motorrollers.

During the time that the overall aircraft manufacturing ban had applied in Germany, Heinkel's rival, Prof. Willy Messerschmitt, had pursued his passion in Spain. Others did likewise on the North and South American continents, or else involuntarily in Soviet design bureaus. However, 1955 proved a year of sal-

Two personalities who became a part of aviation history: Ernst Heinkel and his chief designer Karl Schwärzler, who was with him from the very beginning.

vation for Heinkel and his team of aircraft specialists, as the Allied manufacturing restrictions were lifted, and he began once more to design aero-engines and aircraft. Activities began in 1957 with licence manufacture of the French Fouga CM 170 Magister, which was required for the new Luftwaffe. Heinkel Flugzeugbau GmbH also participated in joint projects such as the licence-built Lockheed F-104G Starfighter and the Fiat G.91. With his He 031 Florett (Fencing foil) supersonic jet fighter, Heinkel, together with his former colleague Siegfried Günter, won the study contest initiated by the German Ministry of Defence.

On 24th January 1958 the still agile and competitive Swabian celebrated his 70th birthday. He could certainly look back not only on a Stürmisches Leben (A Stormy Life) – the title of his memoirs – but also a life of considerable achievement; as a designer, industrialist and individual he had secured a permanent place in aviation history. Just one week later, on 30th January, Prof. Dr.-Ing. Ernst Heinkel passed away as the result of cerebral apoplexy, and on 4th February he was buried in the cemetery of his native Grunbach.

The Triumvirate: Karl Schwärzler and the Günter Twins

The Günter brothers were no less responsible for the success of the Heinkel Werke, a success brought about principally by Chief Designer Dipl.-Ing. Karl Schwärzler and the two brothers, who shared the leadership of the Project Office. There follows a brief account of their lives and achievements.

Karl Schwärzler

Born on 26th January 1901, after his schooling and technical education Karl Schwärzler joined the Caspar Werke. Not long afterwards, both he and Heinkel left Caspar and, following the establishment of the Heinkel concern in 1922, Schwärzler led the Design Office. His creativity during the 1920s led to a considerable number of aircraft designs, as well as various types of shipborne catapults that were used to assist the take-off of mail-carrying aircraft. By the end of the Second World War Dipl.-Ing. Karl Schwärzler was still influencing the range of Heinkel-produced aircraft, and stayed at Heinkel's side into the 1950s. In 1958 he was primarily engaged on the development of the first German jet-propelled VTOL aircraft, the VJ 101. He died at the age of 73 on 12th April 1974.

Siegfried Günter

Together with his twin brother Walter, Siegfried Günter was born on 8th December 1899 in Keula, Thuringia. At the end of his schooling, and while almost still a child, he served as an artilleryman in the First World War. In 1920 he began his engineering studies at the TU (Technical University) in Hanover, and successfully completed his studies in 1926. On 16th January 1931 he joined the Heinkel firm, his brother following at the beginning of July that year, and neither of them ever regretted taking the step. At first the twins worked under the Projektbüro Chief, Hans Reglin, and Siegfried was responsible for the design of various major components of the He 49 and He 51 aircraft. When Hans Reglin and fellow designer Dipl.-Ing. Reinhold Mewes left, the two Günter brothers took over joint leadership of the Project Office. Following the death of Walter in 1937, Siegfried assumed this responsibility alone, and under his leadership the following designs made their appearance: He 49, He 51, He 70, He 100, He 111 (commercial and bomber versions), He 114, He 115, He 119, He 177 and He 219.

The end of the Second World War also put paid to his activities at the Heinkel firm. He was now under the command of the Americans, for whom he had to compile aerodynamic reports. In October 1946 the Soviets 'courted' him, and he thereafter became one of several thousand specialists who more or less voluntarily entered the services of the Soviet Union. His field of activity encompassed theoretical work on high-speed projects, and during his Russian 'adventure' he is said – according to various accounts in aviation literature – to have worked on the MiG 15 fighter. However, allegations of this nature he vehemently denied, and it was only in July 1954 that he returned to the Soviet Zone of (East) Germany.

His destiny again led him to Ernst Heinkel, where he assumed his old post of head of the Project Office, remaining there until Heinkel's death. In 1957, with his Florett fighter, Heinkel won a contest for a fighter specification issued the previous year. As new Defence Ministry guidelines were issued, the He 231 was drawn up to served as the basis for the VJ 101A. On 7th December 1957 the Entwicklungsring Süd (Development Ring South) was established, and Siegfried Günter was appointed head of the Development Office. Under his leadership the concept for the lift and thrust engines of the He 212 was originated, and in March 1962 the He 211 airliner project was first made public.

Siegfried Günter passed away on 20th June 1969, 32 years after the accidental death of his twin brother Walter.

Walter Günter

Born on 8th December 1899, Siegfried's twin brother Walter, after finishing his schooling, also saw military service in the First World War, after which he commenced a course of studies, but, unlike his brother, he began to progressively neglect them. Instead, he preferred to use his time designing for the Bäumer-Aero firm, where he worked intensively and exercised a significant influence on this aircraft manufacturer's designs. The design of the Bäumer-Aero Sausewind (Harum-scarum) drew attention to the brothers, and Walter opted to join his twin at Heinkel a short while later.

When he joined the firm, on 1st July 1931, Walter was initially occupied with a conventional wind-tunnel, and in the period that followed he developed a new method for high-speed measurements. Thereafter Heinkel entrusted him with responsibility for the design of a competition entry for the international 1932 Europaflug, and this development soon made a name for itself under the designation He 64. His subsequent career, albeit shorter than that of his brother, included the design of the following aircraft: He 64, the retractable undercarriage of the He 70, He 74 in both low- and high-wing configuration, He 116, He 118, He 120 project, He 176 and He 178.

Both brothers assumed joint leadership of the Heinkel Project Office in 1933, but after working together for only four years Walter Günter died as a result of a car accident on 21st September 1937. Severely injured, he was removed from the wreckage of the car, but it was of no avail.

Ernst Heinkel (left) and the Günter twins, Siegfried (centre) and Walter (right).

Chapter One

A New Generation

Lufthansa and its Aircraft Fleets of the 1920s and 1930s

The confusion which was prevalent amongst German airline companies, which almost led to liquidation, took on increasingly unpredictable forms in the 1920s. So unsatisfactory was the situation that the Government without doubt had to bear partial responsibility, having wasted its 'horn of plenty' subsidy funds that would certainly have been of more use elsewhere.

The two rival airlines, Aero Lloyd and Junkers Luftverkehr, were engaged in competition, supported by public funds, that brought both of them almost to the brink of ruin. The financial situation at Aero Lloyd was so precarious that the annual depreciation of its aircraft fleet could no longer be undertaken. At Junkers Luftverkehr, the situation was hardly more reassuring. In order to force the heads of the two companies to the negotiating table, the Reich Government resorted to an invariably effective method: it simply shut off monetary support, a means of pressure that in this case proved predictably successful.

Towards the end of 1925 the desired agreement had been thrashed out and lay ready for ratification, and 6th January 1926 proved to be the historic date on which the 'forced marriage' took place between Aero Lloyd and Junkers Luftverkehr, from which emerged the so-called Einheitsgesellschaft (combined company), Deutsche Luft Hansa AG. So much for the 'birth pangs' of what is still today the largest German airline, Lufthansa. The joint-stock company was established with a basic capital of RM 50,000. Responsibility for sales was held by former Aero Lloyd Director Otto Merkel, while Martin Wronsky, also a member of the Board, was in charge of politically oriented air travel matters. The management trio was completed by Erhard Milch, who assumed responsibility for the technical requirements of the company; much was soon to be heard of this controversial personality, whose meteoric career advancement was not long in coming.

The legacy of varied aircraft types brought together by the forcibly united companies was partly very antiquated and consisted of no fewer than 19 different types of aircraft, totalling 146 machines. These were made up as follows:

Number	Aircraft type
4	AEG J II
1	AEG N I
2	Albatros L 58
3	Dornier Komet I
10	Dornier Komet III
4	Dornier Wal
5	Focke-Wulf A 16
1	Focke-Wulf GL 18
19	Fokker-Grulich F II
10	Junkers A 20
50	Junkers F 13
18	Junkers G 24
1	LVG CH 2
1	LVG C V
3	Rumpler C 1
10	Sablatnig P III
3	Udet U 8
1	Udet U 11

The new organisation disposed of many of these partly very uneconomic aircraft types. In 1932 the legendary Ju 52 'Tante Ju' ('Aunty Ju') entered the fleet and remained in service until the bitter end in 1945. A year later the He 70 joined the inventory, and in 1936 came the He 111, of which at least 12 examples flew with DLH. Before recounting the history of the He 70, which eventually led to the He 111, the following table lists most of the new-generation aircraft that, together with the He 70 (1933-38) and He 111 (1936-40), comprised the Lufthansa fleet (see the table on the opposite page).

The He 70: A Revolution in Aircraft Design

Heinkel's fast He 70, aerodynamically superbly configured and elegant in appearance, offered the observer the typical characteristics of a new generation of Heinkel aircraft. High speed is certainly not a matter of wizardry, but is founded on sober scientific knowledge, and with this knowledge the He 70's designer, Siegfried Günter, created a European challenge to the US Lockheed Orion. In order to achieve the hitherto impossible, the incorporation of technical innovation was unavoidable. In 1932 this American aircraft, with its maximum speed of 350km/h (217mph) and cruising speed of 260km/h (162mph), achieved a previously unattained level in passenger transport. German designs in this category only flew at an average cruising speed of 200km/h (124mph), and the news of the arrival of the Orion was viewed with great uneasiness by European airlines. German aircraft firms viewed the situation in a similar light, since they had hitherto produced nothing comparable. The Swiss national airline, Swissair, purchased two examples of the Orion 9B powered by the Wright R-1820 Cyclone radial, and used them on various European routes until 1935. Although it was only short-lived, the Orion could not fail but have an effect on its competitors.

In Germany, Lufthansa took the initiative and formulated a specification for a fast passenger aircraft that was intended to counter the threat from the other side of the Atlantic. The then Lufthansa Director, Dipl.-Ing. Erich Schatzki, initially placed the development order with the Junkers concern, but, as it soon turned out, this was a misguided decision since Junkers aircraft, although superb, robust and mostly well-performing designs, were anything but 'racehorses'. At this time there were also internal company problems that strongly hindered the progress of work on the resulting new Ju 60 product. It soon became obvious that the new aircraft would in no way be able to fulfil the demands required of it, which led Erich Schatzki to ask Ernst Heinkel if his firm would be able to realise such an aircraft in the shortest possible space of time. In February 1932 Heinkel received a construction contract.

The technical basis for this fast aircraft lay in the He 65, which was already under development, powered by a Pratt & Whitney Hornet radial and having a retractable undercarriage. Performance calculations indicated a maximum speed of 285km/h (177mph) and a cruising speed of 238km/h (148mph), thus below the figures for the Lockheed Orion. Although the He 65 represented a design that undoubtedly pointed in the right direction, it could only serve as a basis. In recognition of this fact, in May 1932 Heinkel allowed the He 65 to 'die' and handed over leadership of the project to Siegfried Günter, for what would be the most advanced Heinkel aircraft to date. Within four weeks Heinkel was able to submit to Lufthansa new design plans for the projected aircraft.

New territory was being opened that had to be crossed with some risk, and which could lead to the failure of the whole project.

On the propulsion side, for example, the so-called 'hot-cooling' method was to be employed. This consisted of a cooling system that, instead of water, used ethylene glycol as the cooling medium, the evaporation point of which was 140°C. A further, more important innovation was the retractable undercarriage designed by Walter Günter. Together with a high degree of surface smoothness, what was to become He 70 already represented a fast aircraft for its time. The moment of truth arrived on 1st December 1932, when the calculated data for the first prototype had to be turned into reality in test flights. During its initial trials, the He 70 already showed its superiority over other types, and during speed trials, under optimum conditions, the it attained 360km/h (224mph), and just a few months after the maiden flight, between 14th March and 28th April 1933, the two prototypes, piloted by Heinkel and Lufthansa chief test pilots Flugkapitäne Werner Junck and Robert Untucht respectively, established a series of speed records over specific closed-circuit distances.

These best performances were obtained with the He 70 V1 and V2 prototypes. In March 1933, the latter machine, Werknummer (c/n) 403, was handed over to Lufthansa, and at first sported the experimental code D-3. Later, bearing the civil registration D-2537 and re-designated the He 70B, it was made available for commercial service in the summer of 1933.

Heinkel's pioneering achievements in the field of fast aircraft were only possible with the aid of an aircraft with first-rate aerodynamics. Its method of construction was also new, and the engineers of day viewed the He 70, displayed at the Paris Aerosalon, with a critical eye. Hitherto, the fastening rivets had projected into the airstream and, because of their considerable number, they produced a noticeable amount of drag; however, the Butter brothers had developed a new, innovative countersunk smooth riveting method. All the He 70 versions, of mixed wood and metal construction, were elegantly formed aircraft with rounded tail surfaces, and elliptical wings blending into the fuselage to form a highly advanced overall appearance.

The geometry of the wooden wings came to be mirrored in a number of foreign aircraft designs. The low cantilever wing, built to modern standards, blended in a low-drag transition into the fuselage, its 'spine' consisting of a two-spar structure. The series-produced He 70G was powered by a BMW VI 7.3 Z motor, producing 750hp at take-off. The heat developed by this powerplant in operation was dispersed by the abovementioned 'hot-cooling' system, and because of its much higher evaporation point, the use of glycol led to a smaller radiator, with correspondingly lower drag.

Aircraft Operated in Parallel with the He 70 and He 111

	Period used by Lufthansa	Number registered with Lufthansa	Number in year of termination of Lufthansa
Blohm & Voss Ha 139	1937-1939	3	1
Dornier J Wal	1926-1940	9	2
Dornier Do 18	1936-1938	4	2
Dornier Do 26	1938-1939	3	3
Fokker F II	1926-1937	19	1
Fokker F III	1926-1936	16	3
Focke-Wulf A 17a	1928-1936	11	2
Focke-Wulf A 29	1929-1934	4	2
Focke-Wulf A 32 *	1934-1935	2	2
Focke-Wulf A 33	1937-1938	1	1
Focke-Wulf A 38	1931-1934	4	4
Focke-Wulf Fw 58	1938-1944	9	3
Focke-Wulf Fw 200	1938-1944	11	3
Heinkel He 70	1933-1938	15	6
Heinkel He 111	1936-1940	12+	9
Heinkel He 116	1938-1938	2	2
Junkers A 20	1926-1937	10	1
Junkers A 35	1932-?	7+	?
Junkers F 13	1926-1939	55	1
Junkers G 24	1927-1939	9	4
Junkers G 31	1928-1936	7	1
Junkers G 38	1931-1940	2	1
Junkers W 33	1928-1942	19	1
Junkers W 34	1931-1940	18	3
Junkers Ju 46	1932-1939	6	3
Junkers Ju 52/3m †	1932-1945	223	2
Junkers Ju 60	1934-1936	1	1
Junkers Ju 86	1936-1941	14+	1
Junkers Ju 90	1939-1944	11	1
Junkers Ju 160	1935-1941	20+	16
Messerschmitt M 20	1929-1943	11	2
Messerschmitt M 28‡	1932-1935	1	1
Rohrbach Romar	1929-1933	3	3

* Chartered from Deutsche Verkehrsflug; † Several Ju 52s were 'chartered' by the Luftwaffe
‡ Experimental machine, returned to the RLM

Lufthansa route service began with the V2, modified to He 70B standard, and these gradually replaced the Junkers fleet, which seemed like dinosaurs in comparison. The strength of Junkers Werke doubtless lay in the design of robust 'work-horses' suited to their intended purpose, above all in the shape of the 'Tante Ju', which was best able to fulfil its tasks. Because of its design features, the He 70 was a completely different type of aircraft. Rather small and delicate and superbly aerodynamic, its domain was clearly one of high speed, and provided Lufthansa with a means of fast transportation for four or five passengers, or alternatively 500kg (1,102 lb) of freight or mail. It made its debut in the form of He 70D D-UDAS on 15th June 1934 with the inauguration of the so-called 'Blitz Service', giving time-pressed businessmen and VIPs the possibility of winning the war against the clock! The route network stretched from the Reich capital of Berlin to Hamburg, Cologne and Frankfurt am Main, each reached within two hours; thus outward and return journeys could be accomplished on the same day. The Munich-Venice leg, a route distance of 441km (274 miles) over the Alps, could be flown in 4½ hours. The routes were mostly fully booked, and Lufthansa reacted to the success by ordering a further ten aircraft, and in addition was soon concerning itself with a larger-capacity successor. Versions of the He 70 in Lufthansa service during 1933-1938 are given below:

He 70A Designation of the prototype.

He 70B Designation of the V2 (former D-3); from June 1933 its civil registration was D-2537, later D-UHUX.

He 70D Powerplant was the BMW VI 7.3 Z. The four aircraft were D-UBAF *Sperber* (Sparrow-hawk), D-UBIN *Falke* (Falcon), D-UDAS *Habicht* (Hawk) and D-UGOR *Schwalbe* (Swallow).

He 70G Powerplant was the BMW VI 7.3 Z. Aircraft in this group were D-UBOF *Geier* (Vulture), D-UJUZ *Bussard* (Buzzard), D-UKEK

Amsel (Blackbird), D-UMIM *Albatros*, D-UNEH *Condor*, D-UPYF *Adler* (Eagle), D-UQIP *Rabe* (Raven), D-USAZ *Buntspecht* (Spotted Woodpecker), D-UVOR *Reiher* (Heron) and D-UXUV *Drossel* (Thrush).

He 70F Lufthansa operated two of these aircraft, D-UKAF and D-UVYR, in its Hansa-Luftbild air photography subsidiary, fitted with appropriate equipment.

In the course of its employment by Lufthansa, towards the end of 1934 the He 70 Blitz was also flown on the long-distance Berlin-Vienna-Budapest-Belgrade-Sofia-Salonica route, and together with the comparatively clumsy-looking Rohrbach Roland, it was used for freight carriage. At the beginning of 1934 the He 70 had to achieve a truly marathon distance when, in the course of a test flight, Lufthansa tested the possibilities of the fast Heinkel machine. It was to cover a distance of no less than 4,200km (2,610 miles) as part of the investigation of an airmail route from Berlin via Sevilla to Las Palmas. These flights were soon conducted on a regular basis and formed the airmail service for the Ju 52s, bringing the mail to Bathurst, Gambia, for onward transport in the waiting flying-boats over the South Atlantic to Natal in distant Brazil.

In the following year, 1935, Lufthansa flew a total of eleven internal and external routes with the He 70. On the most lucrative routes, however, it had subsequently to make way for the fast twin-engined, larger-capacity machines that had meanwhile become available. In its second-line role and until 1938 – the year of its withdrawal – the He 70 was being used on the Cologne-Essen-Hamburg-Karlsruhe-Mannheim-Stuttgart-Munich route. The phasing out of the He 70 had already begun in 1937 and was completed in 1938, with the last five remaining aircraft. In all, a total of 28 He 70s built for civil use left the Heinkel assembly lines.

Of more interest for Heinkel were the military contracts of much higher quantities, which significantly filled the order books. Yet even with close to 300 examples ordered, the He 70 occupied a comparatively lower position than the orders for the later He 111, which over the years ran into several thousands. Those He 70s that were flown in Luftwaffe 'uniform' undertook a wide variety of tasks. From 1934 the first He 70E bombers and He 70F reconnaissance aircraft formed part of the still secret squadrons (prior to the official announcement of the Luftwaffe's existence in May 1935). But already in 1936, the He 70, as well as the He 111, had received their 'baptism of fire' in the Spanish Civil War.

The He 70 development series also included an export version. Designated He 170, it was intended for the Hungarian Air Force. At the end of the series was the He 270, for which the He 70F served as the basis, powered by the Daimler-Benz DB 601A, a 12-cylinder in-line of 33.9 litres (2,079in³), a capacity that produced 1,175hp at take-off and a speed of 460km/h (286mph) measured at the pitot tube, which made this aircraft the fastest of the He 70 series flown under a German registration. Despite this, the He 270 V1 (D-OEHF) remained the sole prototype.

Production of the He 70 series lasted from 1933 to 1937 and came to a close with the He 170 and the He 270 V1. The total of 324 examples included 28 He 70s built for civilian use and 20 He 170s for the Hungarian Air Force. Needless to say, with this aircraft Siegfried Günter had achieved the proverbial 'big throw', as the He 70 set the trend for numerous other Heinkel designs – the He 111 and He 116 – and even certain features of the British Spitfire and the Japanese Aichi D3A (Allied codename *Val*). The He 70 Blitz was gradually replaced by Heinkel's fast He 111 commercial transport on several of Lufthansa's routes. Thus ended a career that had begun only a few years before – at least in the civilian sector.

The Specification: The Path to the He 111

Outstanding experience with the equally powerful and elegant He 70 spurred Lufthansa's decision-makers to place an order for a larger aircraft of equally high performance but capable of carrying up to ten passengers. In contrast to the He 70, this fast aircraft was to be at least twin-engined, a requirement that, because of the higher transport capacity but also in terms

Technical Data

	He 70 V1	He 70G	He 70 (G-ADZF)	He 170A	He 270 V1
Powerplant					
Manufacturer	BMW	BMW	Rolls-Royce	Gnôme-Rhône	Daimler-Benz
Type	VI 6.0 Z	VI 7.3 Z	Kestrel*	14K Mistral	DB 601A
Take-off power, hp	630	750	695	910	1,175
Dimensions					
Wingspan	14.80m (48' 2⅝")	14.80m (48' 2⅝")	14.80m (48' 2⅝")	14.80m (48' 2⅝")	14.80m (48' 2⅝")
Length	11.50m (37' 8¾")	12.00m (39' 4½")	11.55m (37' 10¾")	11.80m (38' 8¾")	11.80m (38' 8¾")
Height	3.10m (10' 2")	3.10m (10' 2")	3.10m (10' 2")	3.10m (10' 2")	3.19m (10' 5⅝")
Wing area, m² (ft²)	36.50 (392.87)	36.50 (392.87)	36.50 (392.87)	36.50 (392.87)	36.50 (392.87)
Weights					
Empty weight, kg (lb)	2,300 (5,071)	2,530 (5,578)	2,300 (5,071)	-	2,664 (5,873)
Take-off weight, kg (lb)	3,350 (7,385)	3,460 (7,628)	3,360 (7,407)	3,550 (7,826)	4,150 (9,149)
Performance					
Max speed, km/h (mph)	377 (234)	360 (224)	451 (280)	415 (258)	460 (286)
Cruising speed, km/h (mph)	310 (193)	305 (190)	380 (236)	380 (236)	428 (266)
Service ceiling, m (ft)	5,500 (18,045)	5,500 (18,045)	to 8,000 (26,250ft)	8,300 (27,230)	9,000 (29,530)
Normal range, km (miles)	800 (497)	1,000 (621)	920 (572)	917 (570)	1,000 (621)
Maximum range, km (miles)	1,400 (870) †	1,250 (777)	1,000 (621)	1,300 (808)	1,600 (994)
Payload					
Crew/passenger	2/4	1/5	1/5	3/-	2-4
Freight (only)	-	930 (2,050)	1,060 (2,337)	-	-
Armament	none	none	none	2 x 7.9mm MG	1 x MG 15 + 1 x MG 17

* With a Rolls-Royce Peregrine I of 845hp, maximum speed was 481km/h (299mph). It was scrapped in March 1945; † With extra fuel

During the period 1933-38, a total of 15 He 70s flew for Lufthansa. The He 70 V2 Blitz (D-3) is pictured here at Berlin-Tempelhof.

The He 111, seen here alongside the He 70, can hardly deny its origins.

of raising safety standards, was unavoidable. Similar development contracts were placed with Heinkel and Junkers (for the Ju 86). In view of contemporary designs such as the Douglas DC-2 and Boeing 247 on the other side of the Atlantic, the decision was taken at Heinkel to adopt a configuration with similar characteristics. The RLM Technisches Amt (Technical Office) likewise expressed an interest, but exactly when this occurred has not been recorded. Both the resulting Heinkel and Junkers design proposals were to form part of the new bomber force in the process of being established. Heinkel entrusted leadership for the development to Siegfried Günter. Contrary to the often expressed assertion in aeronautical literature, the He 111 was designed solely under Siegfried's leadership, and preliminary work included calculations made on various basic layouts. Following the final decision, work was begun on construction of a full-scale mock-up. By the day of the maiden flight, some 200,000 hours had been expended on the aircraft's design and prototype manufacture.

The Prototype: Origin and Test of the He 111 V1

After a relatively short period of development and construction, the first of several thousand examples, the He 111 V1, Werknummer 713, was rolled out of the assembly hall of the still not fully completed Heinkel Werk Marienehe in Warnemünde. Because of constructional delays, flight-testing, originally planned to commence in November 1934, first took place on 24th February 1935. To the observer the He 111 bore a truly striking external resemblance to the He 70 Blitz. The larger twin-engined aircraft also featured the elliptical planform as well as the aerodynamically proven drop-shaped fuselage, but in contrast to the He 70, the He 111 was of all-metal construction. However, this only applied to the initial prototypes: the V1 had fabric-covered wings of 25m (82ft 0¼in) span and 92.40m^2

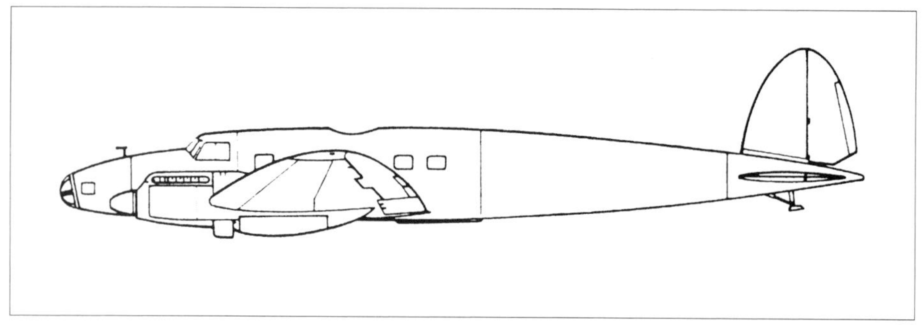

Side view drawing of the He 111 V1.

The 'great-grandfather' of all He 111s, the V1 prototype.

(994.56ft²) area. For the V2, the span was reduced to 23m (75ft 5½in) and the wing area to 88.50m² (952.58ft²). Initially, mainwheels measuring 1,000 x 375mm (39.37 x 14.76in) were fitted, replaced later by wheels of 1140 x 410mm (44.88 x 16.14in). All variants of the He 111 were fitted with a tailwheel, with the exception of the tailskid-equipped V1; those on the V2 and V3 were later replaced by a tailwheel.

In the absence of more powerful engines, the V1 was powered by two BMW VI in-lines, each of 660hp at take-off. With a take-off weight of 7,500kg (16,535 lb) the V1 achieved a maximum speed of 350km/h (217mph), a range 1,530km (951 miles) and a service ceiling of 5,500m (18,045 feet), all figures being without the payload. A significant increase in performance over the Ju 86 would, however, only become possible with the use of more powerful engines.

Heinkel's test pilot, Flugkapitän Gerhard Nitschke, gave the aircraft top marks – at least on the occasion of its first flight on 24th February 1935. Its most positive characteristics lay in the relatively high speed for the period and in the very good-natured flight and landing characteristics, which were to save the lives of many a Heinkel bomber crew during the Second World War. However, during the second test flight the V1 prototype, initially designated He 111a, revealed a weakness in an insufficient longitudinal stability during full-power flight. During the course of flight trials, other deficiencies were revealed in the tailplane area, whose dimensions and settings were not ideal.

The criticisms concentrated on the following most important points:

- Longitudinal stability was insufficient during the climb and during flight at full power.
- The relatively strong aileron forces were unsatisfactory.

On the other hand, positive evaluation was given to:

- The stable flight behaviour when cruising and during gradual descents.
- An absence of any nose-heavy tendency on extending the landing flaps.
- An absence of problems during single-engined flight.

Comparative flight trials conducted in Rechlin revealed that a significantly greater superiority over the rival Ju 86 could only be accomplished with engines of greater power.

The Competitor: The Ju 86

The development history of the Junkers Ju 86 goes back to the year 1933, when Lufthansa modernised its fleet and, in the course of doing so, required a fast twin-engined civil transport. In this case, too, the military expressed an interest. The Luftwaffe needed a modern twin-engined bomber to equip its second generation in the air force that was then being established in secret. As mentioned previously, a corresponding development order was placed with both Heinkel and Junkers. Junkers Werke was to utilise the Jumo 205 of its own manufacture, whereas Heinkel concentrated on the use of the Jumo 211 or the Daimler-Benz DB 600 powerplants.

At Junkers Dipl.-Ing. Ernst Zindel was responsible for the design of the Ju 86, and, together with his team of engineers, opted for an aircraft of all-metal, smooth-skin construction. The harmful drag caused by the corrugated skin construction was a thing of the past for the Ju 86, which became the very first Junkers aircraft to incorporate flat sheet-metal skinning. However, Zindel reverted to the proven but even then already obsolete 'double-wing' type of construction. The chief buyer for the civil variant was naturally Lufthansa, which had voiced its need for such an aircraft type as early as the beginning of 1933. The RLM likewise accepted it in 1933, but only on condition that all the aircraft delivered to Lufthansa could at any time and without considerable effort be converted to military use with the aid of Rüstsätze (field conversion sets). This, however, caused a problem that was difficult to solve, since the machines had to be considerably modified in order to meet the needs of these new tasks.

In the initial stage of the Ju 86 programme, every second airframe was to be completed as a civil version. After a period of roughly one and a half years following the placing of the construction order, the Ju 86 V1, Werknummer 4901 and registered D-AHEH, stood ready for its maiden flight on 4th November 1934. During the course of its flight-test programme, at the end of April 1935, it was transferred to Rechlin, where comparative trials with the He 111 showed no significant differences in performance, other than those attributable to the weaker BMW VI engines in the He 111. The use of more powerful engines in the He 111 altered this stalemate drastically in favour of the Heinkel design. Based on the performance figures obtained in Rechlin and the resulting conclusions drawn by the RLM, Junkers Werke and Heinkel were awarded a series-production contract. In order to turn the Ju 86 design into reality, Junkers Werke introduced construction at a breathtaking pace, which was certainly attributable to its company director Dr. Heinrich Koppenberg. The financial expenditure for the Ju 86 was also enormous. In the business year 1934/35 alone, the costs were RM 3.8 million, or 4.5% of the total annual turnover.

In all, Lufthansa definitely took 14 machines[1] consisting of the Ju 86B-1, C-1 and Z-2. Their identifications and names (all mountains) were as follows:

Ju 86B-1	D-AFAF	*Watzmann*
Ju 86B-1	D-AHYP	*Schneekoppe*
Ju 86B-1	D-ALOZ	*Zugspitze*
Ju 86B-1	D-AQER	*Inselsberg*
Ju 86B-1	D-AZAH	*Feldberg*
Ju 86C-1	D-AJUU	*Vogelsberg*
Ju 86C-1	D-AKOI	*Kaiserstuhl*
Ju 86C-1	D-AMYO	*Melikobus*
Ju 86C-1	D-AQEA	*Schauinsland*
Ju 86C-1	D-ASOE	*Hesselberg*
Ju 86C-1	D-AVOE	*Obersalzberg*
Ju 86Z-7	D-ANUV	*Wasserkuppe*
Ju 86 V4	D-AREV	*Brocken*
Ju 86 V24	D-AUME	*Annaberg*

The first six examples were added to the fleet in 1936. During airline service with Lufthansa, one Ju 86 was subsequently lost in an accident. Because of wartime needs, 12 aircraft were transferred to the RLM in 1940 and suitably modified, the last aircraft following in 1941.

Its participation in international events and the undertaking of spectacular flying demonstrations, during the course of which bridges to other continents were spanned, proved very advantageous for the image of the Ju 86, manifested by the export orders that it obtained.

Neither the competing He 111 nor the Do 17[2] was able to display such figures. However, in terms of quantities manufactured the result looked quite different. The He 111 dominated unchallenged with close to 8,000 examples being produced in Germany. In contrast to this enormous number, a mere 840 examples of the Ju 86 were built in civil and military versions. In the military sphere also, the He 111 was far superior to the Ju 86. In the category of twin-engined bombers, Junkers first made the breakthrough with the Ju 88, which was employed on all fronts. The 'stop-gap' Ju 86 was soon removed from the Luftwaffe's first-line inventory with the availability of bombers of more modern origin. Nevertheless, for a long time they served in the transport and training capacity. In the realm of German civil aviation, the brief era of the Ju 86 ended in 1941.

Technical Data

	Ju 86A	Ju 86B	Ju 86Z
Powerplant	Jumo 205C	Jumo 205C	BMW 132Dc
Take-off power	660hp at 2,200rpm	660hp at 2,200rpm	845hp at 1,690rpm
Dimensions			
Wingspan	22.50m (73ft 9⅞")	22.50m (73ft 9⅞")	22.50m (73ft 9⅞")
Length	17.41m (57ft 1½")	17.60m (57ft 8⅞")	17.60m (57ft 8⅞")
Height	4.08m (13ft 4⅝")	4.70m (15ft 5")	4.70m (15ft 5")
Wing area, m^2 (ft^2)	82.00 (882.62)	82.00 (882.62)	82.00 (882.62)
Wing loading, kg/m^2 (lb/ft^2)	97.56 (19.98)	95.73 (19.61)	100.0 (20.48)
Weights			
Equipped weight, kg (lb)	5,520 (12,169)	5,790 (12,765)	5,900 (13,007)
Take-off weight, kg (lb)	8,000 (17,637)	7,850 (17,306)	8,200 (18,078)
Performance			
Max speed, km/h (mph)	310 (193)	310 (193)	375 (233)
Cruising speed, km/h (mph)	285 (177)	280 (174)	340 (211)
Normal range, km (miles)	1,200 (746)	1,500 (932)	1,000 (621)
Max range, km (miles)	-	2,500 (1,553)	1,500 (932)
Service ceiling, m (ft)	6,100 (20,015)	5,900 (19,360)	6,900 (22,640)
Passengers/crew	10/2-3	10/2-3	10/2-3

Footnotes

1 To which were presumably added two more aircraft bearing the registrations D-ABUK and D-ADLO.

2 The Do 17 never came to be used by Lufthansa. The Do 17 V2 (also used for military trials) and V5 to V9 prototypes served as a basis for the Do 17 fast civil and comms aircraft, but did not go into series production.

The Ju 86 was a competitor to the He 111 in both the civil and military roles. This re-touched photograph, with the swastika blanked out, shows Ju 86B-1 D-AQER and Ju 86C-1 D-AKOI in front of the Lufthansa hangar at Hamburg-Fuhlsbuttel.

Chapter Two

In Commercial Service

He 111 V2 (Werknummer 715)

This prototype was the first example of the civil branch of development. It was designed to accommodate up to ten passengers, or be used alternatively as a freight carrier. The powerplants were two BMW VI 6.0 Z in-lines, replaced later by two BMW VI D engines whose cooling system consisted of ethylene glycol coolers. As in the V1 (D-ADAP) and V3 (D-ALES) prototypes, the wingspan was 23m (75ft 6½in) and the wing area 88.50m^2 (952.58ft^2), the V2 wings being likewise fabric covered.

Shortly after the first flight of the V1, the V2 (initially designated the He 111b) took to the air on 12th March 1935. Later in the year, at the conclusion of its flight trials, Lufthansa took over the aircraft and operated it as D-ALIX *Rostock* in a route-testing role. This machine was also used for an extremely secret purpose; together with two other Heinkel aircraft (He 111 V4 D-AHAO and He 111C D-AXAV, which likewise belonged to Lufthansa) it was assigned to Kommando Rowehl. This Detachment, reporting directly to Hermann Göring, was to undertake tasks of a purely military nature under its civilian cover. Its chief purpose was to carry out reconnaissance flights over French, British and Soviet territory, intended solely to provide up-to-date aerial photographs of possible targets for the Luftwaffe, which was then being built up. Despite an emergency landing made on foreign soil, this secret purpose, which would have had considerable diplomatic consequences for Germany, was able to be maintained. Similar flights were undertaken shortly before the outbreak of war in 1939 by the British pilot Sydney Cotton, who took numerous photographs of possible future targets over Germany and Italy. His well-camouflaged cameras were installed in a civil Lockheed Electra, under instructions from the British Secret Service. This method of obtaining clandestine information was therefore not an exclusively German domain. During its later use as a mail plane between Las Palmas and the African continent, the V2 was destroyed in the spring of 1937 in a landing accident at Bathurst, Gambia.

This page:

A contemporary Lufthansa advertising poster.

Opposite page:

The He 111 V2, registered D-ALIX and christened *Rostock*, entered service with Lufthansa. Flying above it is He 111C D-AXAV *Köln*.

This re-touched photograph shows the He 111 V2 parked between a Ju 86 and a Ju 160, with He 70s further along. In the background, ahead of the building, is He 111C D-AMES *Nürnberg*, and flying over the scene is He 111C D-AXAV *Köln*.

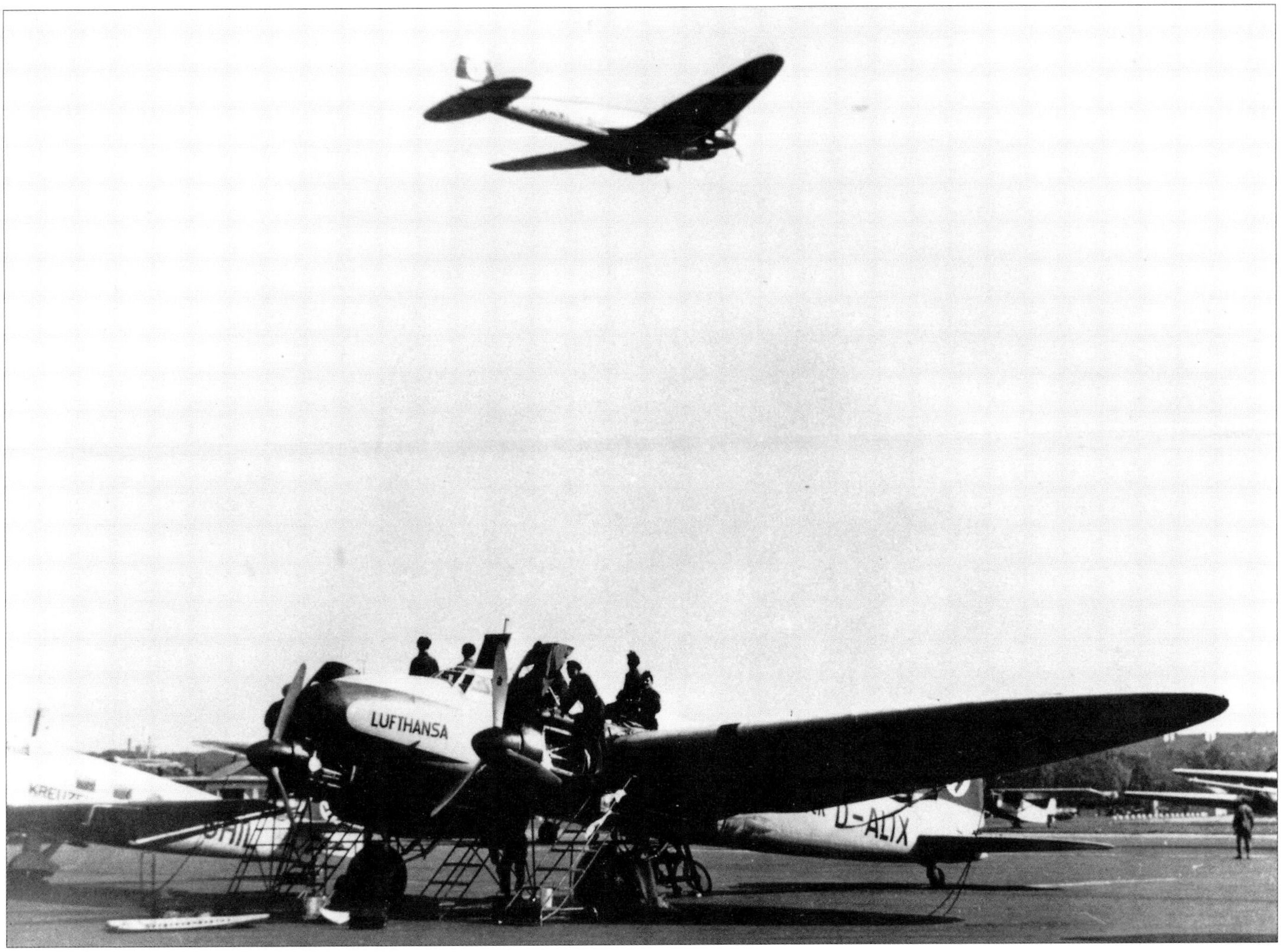
LUFTHANSA
D-ALIX

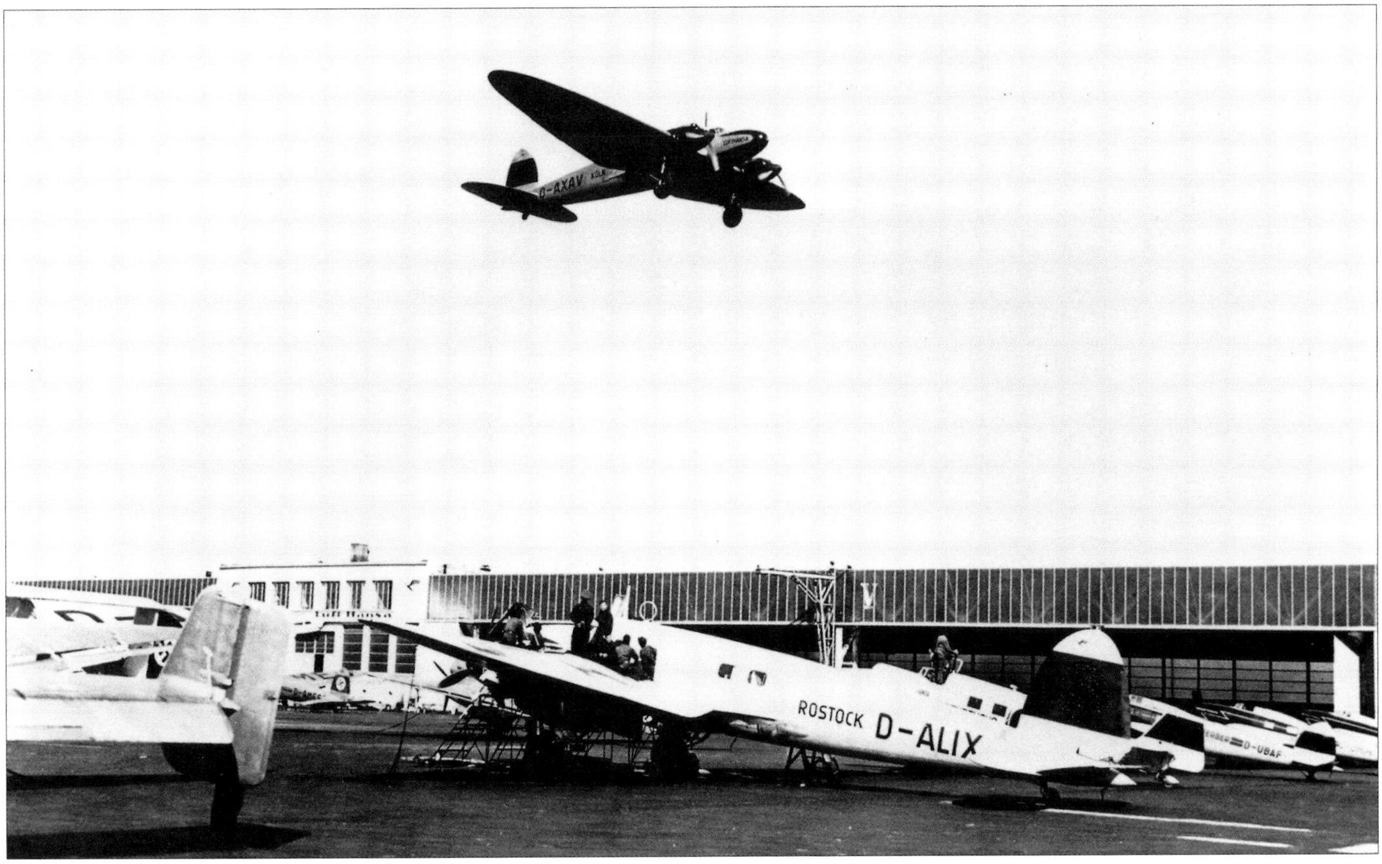
D-AXAV
ROSTOCK D-ALIX
D-UBAF

He 111 V4 (Werknummer 1968)

The He 111 V4 was the second civil machine in the development series; it left the final assembly line in November 1935 and made its first flight not long afterwards. The V4 made its public debut during a press demonstration at Berlin-Tempelhof on 10th January 1936. Nazi propaganda enhanced its performance somewhat by announcing its maximum speed as 400km/h (249mph) instead of the actual 360km/h (224mph).

The first commercial version of this design was the He 111C-0. This took the form of V4 D-AHAO, christened *Dresden* and powered by the BMW VI. Dependent upon payload and quantity of fuel carried, its range lay between 1,000km (621 miles) and 2,200km (1,367 miles). The interior of the airliner was divided into two passenger cabins, followed towards the rear by a toilet and washroom. Because of its overall design, this rear portion of the fuselage was not able to be increased in capacity, but the passenger area could easily be converted to carry freight. Furthermore, the provision of two variable-use compartments enabled a combined freight and passenger arrangement to be adopted. The V4 served as the basic model for the initial He 111C-0 series version.

He 111 V4 D-AHAO *Dresden* jacked up during undercarriage tests.

The same scene from the port side.

The jacked-up V4, this time with the undercarriage extended.

The V4 was first publicly displayed in January 1936 and aroused considerable attention from the press due to its 'maximum speed flight'.

The V4 crashed near Dortmund in April 1936.

As seen in the previous photographs, the V4 fuselage and fin bore the name Heinkel.

Above: **He 111C-0 D-AQYF *Leipzig*, Werknummer 1829, flanked by Junkers aircraft.**

Left: **An upper perspective view of *Leipzig*.**

Below: **This close-up view shows *Leipzig*'s forward area.**

Photographs on the opposite page:

This shot of He 111C D-AXAV *Köln* emphasises the wing geometry of the He 111. This aircraft was destroyed in a crash in 1937.

He 111C D-ABYE *Königsberg* had to be transferred to the RLM in 1940.

High-ranking visitors on the apron are being transported by car, with D-ABYE *Königsberg* waiting in the background.

Pictured here is He 111C-04 D-AMES *Nürnberg*, Werknummer 1828.

He 111C

The He 111C series model had wings of 22.6m (74ft 1¾in) span attached to the fuselage in the same low-wing arrangement as hitherto. The wing main spars passed through the fuselage and formed a stepped raised area in the region of the passenger cabin; this same type of hindrance, but in a more pronounced form, was also present in the American Boeing 247, a few examples of which were also flown by Lufthansa. The streamlined fuselage of oval cross-section was capable of accommodating up to ten passengers and two crew. In the case of the He 111 V1, the overall length of the fuselage was 17.1m (56ft 1¾in), increased on the He 111C to 17.5m (57ft 5in). The weights at take-off and landing were absorbed initially by forked mainwheels measuring 1100 x 375mm (43.3 x 14.76in). On later variants mainwheels of 1140 x 410mm (44.9 x 16.14in) were used, and all versions featured a tailwheel. The similarly twin-engined Ju 86 competitor had roughly the same dimensions as the Heinkel aircraft.

As mentioned earlier, Jumo 205 diesel-type powerplants were initially installed, and with these the maximum speed remained in the 220-240km/h (137-149mph) bracket, and was first able to be increased when BMW 132 radials were substituted. Setting the He 111 apart from the relatively cumbersome-looking Ju 86 was the use of smooth skin construction and a move away from the tri-motor concept that remained a feature in Italy until well into the 1940s. Multi-engined Heinkel aircraft used either two or four engines, the advantage being that the saving in weight from the central engine permitted the resulting space in the fuselage nose to be used for baggage, in addition to improving the forward view. The He 111 thus had a well-thought-out and improved airframe design.

On the powerplant side, a general problem existed in Germany during this period whereby, as a consequence of the limitations imposed by the Treaty of Versailles, the aero-engine industry had lost touch with international standards. Engines produced during this period were only partly capable of meeting the demands placed upon them. A good example of this unsatisfactory state of affairs was the fact that the Messerschmitt Me 109 V1 made its first flight powered by a Rolls-Royce Kestrel in-line engine. In the case of the He 111, maximum speed was normally 310km/h (193mph), due to the limited power available from the BMW VI. When Daimler-Benz delivered the DB 600, speed could be further increased – at least in the Heinkel machines in Luftwaffe service. This in-line unit had a performance range up to 1,050hp, which in the He 111 raised the maximum speed to 360km/h (224mph) and the cruising speed to 310km/h (193mph). The handicap in the civilian sector was that this powerplant was all too rare and was destined for military projects. For its Heinkels, Lufthansa was thus forced to fall back on the BMW VI or BMW 132.

He 111C-05 D-AQUA *Breslau* in flight, displaying its typical Heinkel elliptical wing planform.

Two BMW VI 12-cylinder in-lines provide the power on this He 111.

The cockpit area of the civil He 111. Note the auxiliary controls on the right.

Opposite page:

Internal details of the He 111C as exemplified by V4 D-AHAO *Dresden*. The inset data table includes a maximum speed (with two 660hp BMW VI) of 345km/h (214mph) and a service ceiling of 5,400m (17,720ft); with two 880hp (unnamed) motors, the corresponding figures were 410km/h (255mph) and 8,600m (28,215ft), the maximum range being 1,500km (932 miles) with either powerplant.

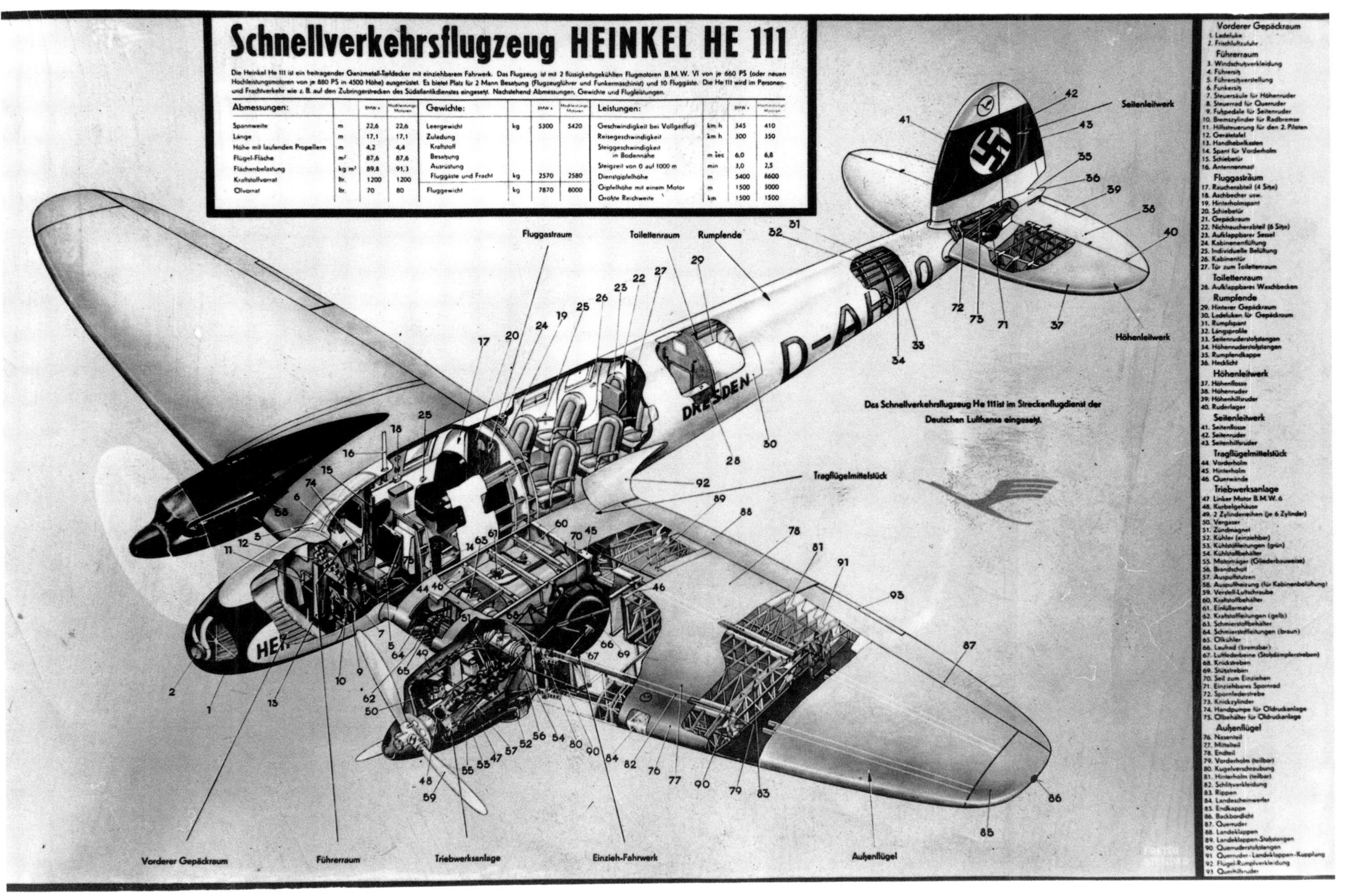

Schnellverkehrsflugzeug HEINKEL HE 111

Die Heinkel He 111 ist ein freitragender Ganzmetall-Tiefdecker mit einziehbarem Fahrwerk. Das Flugzeug ist mit 2 flüssigkeitsgekühlten Flugmotoren B.M.W. VI von je 660 PS (oder neuen Hochleistungsmotoren von je 880 PS in 4500 Höhe) ausgerüstet. Es bietet Platz für 2 Mann Besatzung (Flugzeugführer und Funkermaschinist) und 10 Fluggäste. Die He 111 wird im Personen- und Frachtverkehr wie z. B. auf den Zubringerstrecken des Südatlantikdienstes eingesetzt. Nachstehend Abmessungen, Gewichte und Flugleistungen.

Abmessungen:		BMW 6	Hochleistungs-Motoren
Spannweite	m	22,6	22,6
Länge	m	17,1	17,1
Höhe mit laufenden Propellern	m	4,2	4,4
Flügel-Fläche	m²	87,6	87,6
Flächenbelastung	kg m²	89,8	91,3
Kraftstoffvorrat	ltr.	1200	1200
Ölvorrat	ltr.	70	80

Gewichte:		BMW 6	Hochleistungs-Motoren
Leergewicht	kg	5300	5420
Zuladung			
Kraftstoff			
Besatzung			
Ausrüstung			
Fluggäste und Fracht	kg	2570	2580
Fluggewicht	kg	7870	8000

Leistungen:		BMW 6	Hochleistungs-Motoren
Geschwindigkeit bei Vollgasflug	km h	345	410
Reisegeschwindigkeit	km h	300	350
Steiggeschwindigkeit in Bodennähe	m sec	6,0	6,8
Steigzeit von 0 auf 1000 m	min	3,0	2,5
Dienstgipfelhöhe	m	5400	6600
Gipfelhöhe mit einem Motor	m	1500	5000
Größte Reichweite	km	1500	1500

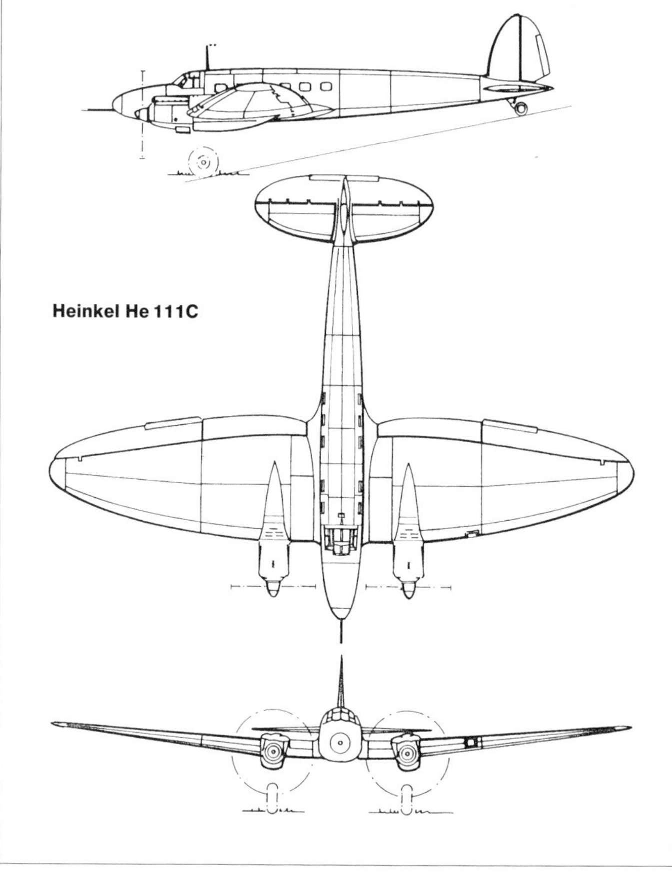

Inside the four-seat smokers' compartment directly behind the cockpit.

The six-seat non-smokers' compartment behind it, looking aft.

A more extensive view looking into the forward smokers' compartment and, beyond it, the cockpit.

He 111G

The He 111G model had a number of major differences from its predecessors. To simplify production, the outer wings now featured a straight-line outer leading edge, as did the bomber version. Various makes of powerplants were installed, such as the BMW VI and BMW 132, as well as the DB 600 and DB 601A initially used. During the period 1938/39, Lufthansa had some of its He 111C aircraft equipped with the new wings and the BMW 132H powerplant – the so-called Einheitstriebwerk (unitary or all-in-one powerplant). These radials also came to be used in other large Lufthansa aircraft such as the Junkers Ju 90 and the legendary Focke-Wulf Fw 200. They were packed as complete units together with their operating systems, and hence were conceived as quick-change engines.

The He 111G was the most powerful as well as the last commercial version. The G-0 subtype was equipped with the BMW VI 6.0 ZU, whereas the G-3 had the BMW 132. The G-4 was powered by the DB 600G in-line of 950hp at take-off, while the G-5, with the DB 601A, attained a top speed of 410km/h (255mph), and, in its role as a fast aircraft, was placed at the disposal of the Reich Government for courier and communications flights. In 1937 Lufthansa had eight examples of the He 111G in service, and in the following year had nine machines of various models in the fleet. The maximum number of He 111s was 12, and the following table lists all the Lufthansa machines, which were named after large cities.

The aircraft were operated on several routes. From 19th April 1936, the He 111 was used on the Berlin-Dortmund-Cologne and Berlin-Nuremberg-Munich routes. With the introduction of the 1936/37 Winter Flight Plan, the He 111 flew jointly with the Ju 86 on the Berlin-Posen-Warsaw, Berlin-Breslau-Gleiwitz and Berlin-Hamburg routes. From April 1937 Lufthansa additionally flew from Berlin to Halle, Leipzig, Frankfurt, Mannheim, Ludwigshafen and Heidelberg. Amsterdam was also flown to from Bremen or from Dresden, and from 1939 connections to Zürich and Vienna were added. The most distant route on which the Heinkels were flown was the transportation route to Las Palmas (Canary Islands), which was the first leg of the connection to South America. In all, the He 111 was operated on 16 routes within the Lufthansa network. Commercial development of the He 111 ended with the He 111G, whereas the military version began with the V3 prototype, which was the basis for the He 111A bomber version.

He 111G D-AEQA *Halle*, Werknummer 2534, was transferred to the RLM in 1940.

He 111G-3 D-ACBS *Augsburg* is taking aboard express packages for the RLM, destined for Warsaw.

He 111G-0 D-AYKI *Magdeburg* has also been described in published accounts as the G-1.

He 111s in Lufthansa Service

Aircraft	Werknummer	Registration	DLH name	Remarks
He 111 V2	715	D-ALIX	*Rostock*	Crashed at Bathurst, March 1937
He 111 V4 (C-0)	1968	D-AHAO	*Dresden* *	Crashed by Dortmund, April 1936
He 111C-01	1829	D-AQYF	*Leipzig*	Transferred to RLM, 1940
He 111C-02	1830	D-AXAV	*Köln*	Crashed in Cologne, 1937
He 111C-03	1831	D-ABYE	*Königsberg*	Transferred to RLM, 1940
He 111C-04	1828	D-AMES	*Nürnberg*	Transferred to RLM, 1940 [not D-AMEY]
He 111C-05	1832	D-AQUA	*Breslau*	Transferred to RLM, 1940
He 111C-06	1833	D-ATYL	*Karlsruhe*	Transferred to RLM, 1940
He 111G-0 †	2534	D-AEQA	*Halle*	Transferred to RLM, 1940
He 111G-0 †	2535	D-AKYI	*Magdeburg*	Transferred to RLM, 1940
He 111G-3	1884	D-ACBS	*Augsburg*	Transferred to RLM, 1940
He 111G-3	1885	D-ADCF	*Dresden* *	Transferred to RLM, 1940

* This name was applied twice; † Also described in published accounts as the G-1

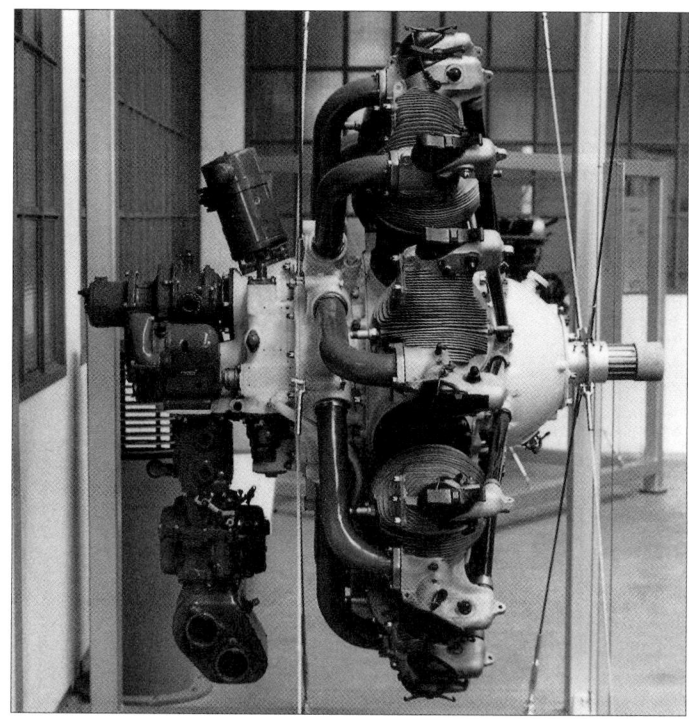

Top left: **Frontal view of a BMW 132. Two examples of the BMW 132H powered the He 111G-3.**

Top right: **Side view of the nine-cylinder BMW 132 radial of 27.74 litres capacity. Maximum power was 800hp and the continuous power 640hp.**

Opposite page: **A Heinkel collection of press reports on the He 111 V4 'high speed flight'.**

Press Reactions of the Period

To conclude this coverage of the Lufthansa He 111, some of the various press articles of the time are now quoted.

On 9th January 1936, the *Münchner Neueste Nachrichten* (*Munich Latest News*) reported euphorically on the previously mentioned He 111's 'high-speed flight' as follows:

Highest Speed 410km/h [255mph]

He 111 – The Most Modern of Lufthansa's Fast Airliners

'At Berlin-Tempelhof airport, the twin-engined He111, the most modern of German aviation's fast airliners, was presented to the public on Thursday afternoon. This aircraft is scheduled during the course of the current year to be regularly operated on routes by Deutsche Lufthansa and will thus enable a considerable increase in speed on the most important routes flown. In its maximum speed, the new He 111 exceeds the 400km/h [249mph] mark.

'Seen overall, the 11th Lufthansa year will again bring about a very significant increase in speed, for besides the He 111, as has already been reported, a new very fast twin-engined Junkers aircraft will be put into service [referring to the Ju 86 – Author] and will be in regular operation. The speed of this machine likewise exceeds 300km/h [186mph].

'With the introduction of the He 70 Blitz aircraft in the spring of 1934, Lufthansa took a decisive step in accelerating regular air traffic, for the 300km/h [186mph] mark was thus exceeded. This development will be continued in a splendid manner during the coming summer. Whereas the He 70 with four passengers attains a maximum speed of 377km/h [234mph], the new He 111 with ten passengers and baggage flies at a speed of 410km/h [255mph] and hence for the first time exceeds the 400km/h [249mph] mark for a commercial airliner. The He 111 was evolved by the Heinkel concern with the goal of achieving the best aerodynamic characteristics. As with earlier fast aircraft produced by this firm, it is likewise of low-wing configuration with a completely smooth outer skin. The internal construction, fuselage covering, wings and tail surfaces, are all of light metal. The mainwheel and tailwheel undercarriage units are all retractable. The interior offers room for ten passengers divided into smoking and non-smoking cabins, and guarantees extensive comfort. Toilets, washrooms and baggage compartments are located behind the cabins, while the two crew members – the pilot and radio operator – are housed up front ahead of the passengers.

'In flight trials, the new fast aircraft was flown with two trustworthy aero-engines consisting of the BMW VI with which a maximum speed of 345km/h [214mph] was achieved. The cruising speed lay at 300km/h [186mph]. In its final version for airline operation, the He 111 will be powered by engines of 880hp each, which will raise the maximum speed to 410km/h [255mph] and the cruising speed to 350km/h [217mph]. In two and a half minutes, this fast aircraft, which has an astounding range of 1,500km [932 miles], will be able to climb to 1,000m [3,280 feet]. In the event of loss of one of the two engines, the flight can be continued without any problem. The new aircraft enables an acceleration in air travel to be accomplished by the use of multi-engined aircraft of around 40%, a performance that speaks for itself. At a cruising speed of 350km/h, it will be possible to fly in less than one and a half hours from Berlin to Munich. In one and a quarter hours, this fast aircraft transports the Berliner to Cologne, and it will take around one and three-quarter hours to fly from Berlin to Königsberg. The not quite 1,000km (621-mile) Berlin-London stretch can, with an intermediate landing in Amsterdam, be accomplished in less than three hours.

The creation of the new He 111 fast commercial transport aircraft thus contributes to making the gap between nations ever shorter and the time distance between them ever smaller.'

The *Münchner Neueste Nachrichten – Sonderdienst* again reported on 4th February:

[A previously] *Unattained Performance*
The He 111 on the Sevilla-Berlin stretch

'A short while ago, Deutsche Lufthansa successfully introduced the new, fast twin-engined He 111 aircraft on the European leg of the South American airmail route. The He 111's smaller sister, the fast He 70, whose superb performance will still maintain its place for a long time in air travel, was previously flown between Stuttgart and Sevilla (Spain). During this period, the He 111 in scheduled mail flights achieved a cruising speed of around 350km/h [217mph]. Early on Sunday morning the aircraft took off from Sevilla and flew to Stuttgart with an intermediate landing in Marseilles. This

Technical Data for the He 111C- and G-series Airliners and their Ju 86B and Boeing 247 Competitors

	Heinkel He 111C-0	Heinkel He 111G-0	Heinkel He 111G-3	Junkers Ju 86B	Boeing 247
Powerplant	BMW VI	BMW VI	BMW 132H	Jumo 205C	Pratt & Whitney Wasp
Model	6.0 Z	6.0 ZU *	-	-	S1D1
Take-off power, hp	660	660	880	600	550
Dimensions					
Wingspan	22.60m (74' 1¾")	22.60m (74' 1¾")	22.60m (74' 1¾")	22.50m (73' 9⅞")	22.56m (74' 0")
Length	17.50m (57' 5")	17.30m (56' 9⅛") †	17.20m (56' 5⅛")	17.60m (57' 8⅞")	15.72m (56' 6⅞")
Height	4.10m (13' 5⅜")	4.10m (13' 5⅜")	4.10m (13' 5⅜")	4.70m (15' 5")	4.70m (15' 5")
Wing area, m^2 (ft^2)	87.60 (942.89)	87.60 (942.89)	87.60 (942.89)	82.00 (882.62)	77.68 (836.12)
Wing loading, kg/m^2 (lb/ft^2)	109.7 (22.45)	93.6 (19.15)	96.6 (19.77)	97.56 (19.98)	79.78 (16.34)
Weights					
Empty weight, kg (lb)	5,400 (11,905)	-	-	-	4,155 (9,160)
Take-off weight, kg (lb)	9,610 (21,186)	8,200 (18,078) ‡	8,460 (18,651)	8,000 (17,637)	6,197 (13,662)
Payload, kg (lb)	421 (928)	-	-	800 (1,764)	1,200 (2,646)
Performance					
Max speed, km/h (mph)	310 (193)	315 (196) §	345 (214)	310 (193)	293 (182)
Cruising speed, km/h (mph)	270 (168)	270 (168)	300 (186)	280 (174)	249 (155)
Range, km (miles)	2,400 (1,491)	1,000 (621)	1,500 (932)	1,500 (932)	880 (547)
Service ceiling, m (ft)	4,800 (15,750)	4,200 (13,780)	8,390 (27,525)	5,900 (19,355)	5,600 (18,375)
Landing speed, km/h (mph)	110 (68)	115 (71)	120 (75)	98 (61)	-
Passengers/crew	10/2	10/2 ¶	10/2	10/2-3	10/3

1 He 111G-4 (Staff comms aircraft for 8-10 passengers). He 111G-4 powerplants: DB 600G; He 111G-5 powerplants: DB 601A; † He 111G-4 and G-5 length: 17.1m (56ft 1¼in); ‡ He 111G-4: 8,680kg (19,136 lb); He 111G-5: 8,820kg (19,445 lb); § He 111G-4: 410km/h (255mph); He 111G-5: 415km/h (258mph); ¶ He 111G-5 (export version of the G-4).

stretch, a little over 2,000km [1,242 miles], was covered by the fast aircraft in 5 hours and 56 minutes, and for the further lap to Berlin, another 536km (333 miles), the He 111 needed exactly 1 hour and 37 minutes.

'This previously unattained performance of an aircraft in regular route service represents a progressive development better than all theoretical expectations. At the present time, there is really no commercial aircraft in Europe whose performance capabilities can even be compared with that of the fast new German aircraft.'

The *Deutsche Allgemeine Zeitung* daily newspaper commented briefly on an incident that occurred in commercial service, but which ended without problems for the passengers as follows:

Berlin, 12th April 1938

'The regular scheduled commercial aircraft on the Berlin-Mannheim route that took off from Tempelhof airport on Monday at 1750 hours, as a result of an engine malfunction was forced to make an unplanned landing in the neighbourhood of Marienfelde. After the passengers and crew had vacated the aircraft, it caught fire for reasons not yet determined. The passengers continued their journey with a substitute Lufthansa machine.'

An Offshoot: He 116, the Flying Mailroom

The history of this aircraft, certainly one of the most elegant and most closely related to the He 111, began in 1936/37. The initiator of the He 116 development was Lufthansa, which issued a specification to several firms for a long-range mail-carrying aircraft. The requirements included a layout with four engines whose power should be sufficient to be able to overcome the height restrictions imposed by high mountain ranges, as it was precisely these that presented a considerable, in some cases insurmountable, hurdle for several types of aircraft in that era of aviation. According to Lufthansa's plans, the He 116 was to replace older and less suitable aircraft on long-distance postal routes and hence take care of airmail traffic in a more efficient manner.

The requirements for this new aircraft were based on a new concept. In the past, the problems presented by such marathon flights were overcome by the use of reliable water-based aircraft that used special catapult-equipped ships as intermediate stations for refuelling and maintenance. Since the seaplane concept was dependent upon the use of floats, which thus influenced the overall design, a relatively low speed resulted. Added to that, the range in many cases was unsatisfactory. The safety factor of the floatplane or flying-boat was nevertheless greater, as in the event of engine malfunction the aircraft could descend and land largely undamaged on water and eventually be able to take off again under its own power. With a land-based aircraft, a landing on water inevitably meant the end of the journey. In accordance with the requirements drawn up by Lufthansa, the future mail carrier should be four-engined and thus possess a comfortable margin of safety. The He 116 was easily capable of three-engined flight, so the danger of 'ditching' was considerably reduced.

This future postal aircraft took shape on the drawing-boards under the leadership of Walter Günter, who was able to draw upon previous experience gained with the design and construction of the He 70 and He 111. It is therefore not surprising that the typical Heinkel elliptical wing planform was chosen, a characteristic feature that becomes immediately apparent to the observer. After the tragic accidental death of his brother in September 1937, Siegfried Günter stepped in and continued the design work as the sole project leader, all further design modifications henceforth being his responsibility.

A direct competitor to the He 116 was the Blohm & Voss BV 142. This had been developed by the firm (formerly the Hamburger Flugzeugbau) from the Ha 139 floatplane, which was operated from catapult ships. The

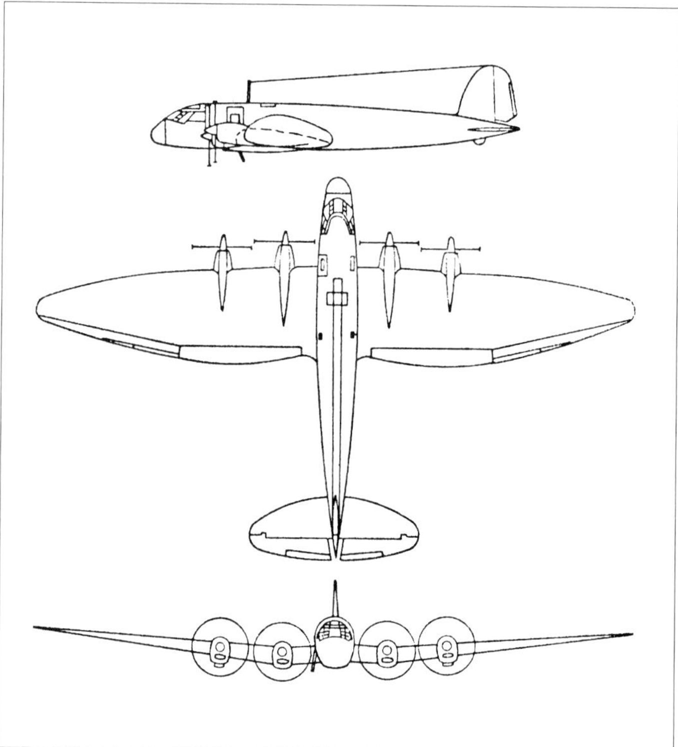

Left: **A promotional poster by Heinkel Werke documenting the line of development from the He 70 via the He 111 to the He 116.**

Above: **Three-view drawing of the He 116A.**

Opposite page: **The elegant He 116 undoubtedly counted among the most pleasing designs of the Heinkel concern. Pictured here is He 116 V2 D-AJIE *Schlesien*.**

land-based version accomplished its first flight on 11th October 1938. However, the ensuing flight trials revealed faults that indicated a limited suitability for the task. Up to the summer of the following year, a total of four BV 142s left the final assembly line.* Further trials likewise showed that the Lufthansa requirements were not being met and, in the period that followed, the aircraft were returned to Blohm & Voss and appropriately modified for military use. As it happened, the BV 142 did not go into production for either civil or military application. So much for the fate of the competitor.

* BV 142 V1 D-AHFB *Pollux* underwent structural alterations by the parent firm; BV 142 V2 D-ABUV *Kastor* bore Lufthansa livery but the airline made only a few flights with it in 1939; BV 142 V3 D-ATTA *Burgenland* was intended for Lufthansa in place of the V1, but after a few works flights it was converted for military use – Translator.

The great moment for all those involved in the project at Heinkel came in the spring of 1937. The first prototype of this elegant aircraft had already passed its initial 'crucial test' flight, following earlier flights that had also been completed satisfactorily. Its considerable capabilities had also become publicly known abroad, resulting in the visit of a Japanese delegation to Germany in 1938. The He 116 was to be suitably adapted for use in Japan, and besides two examples built for that country, a further 12 left the assembly lines for use by Lufthansa. These consisted of six commercial aircraft, plus the two sold to Japan, with the remainder built for military usage. This resulted in the RLM placing an initial order for a Fernerkunder (long-range observation or reconnaissance aircraft), which was easily filled as the He 116 had been designed for long distances and its performance in this respect had already been demonstrated.

With the He 116, Lufthansa was soon to set its sights on a long-distance record flight, for which purpose a modified version was produced. The necessary alterations were incorporated into He 116 V3 D-ARFD, which the RLM requested from Lufthansa for this record attempt. Modifications included, among others, increasing the wingspan from the original 22m (72ft 2⅛in) to 25m (82ft 0¼in) and the wing area to 75.60m² (813.73ft²). However, sources differ in detail. Whereas the Lufthansa Typesheet mentions a wingspan of 24m (78ft 8⅞in), the Heinkel Typesheet mentions 25m (82ft 0¼in). Exactly which of these is correct has not been established. As a result of these modifications, fuel capacity could be noticeably increased, but this resulted in a previously unattained take-off weight of 8,280kg (18,254 lb); thus a conventional take-off, as in previous flights, was out of the question. The solution to the problem lay in the use of rocket-assisted take-off (RATO) units, which by a hair's breadth turned out not to be the solution, but the trigger for a catastrophe for both man and machine. During the overloaded take-off, with the He 116 filled to the brim with fuel, one of the Walter rocket units became disengaged from its underwing support and resulted in heavy damage to the wing as well as to the powerplants. The shocked crew fortunately escaped uninjured.

On 30th July 1938 the V3 took off on its second attempt to complete the planned 10,000-km (6,214-mile) marathon. At exactly 0601hrs, D-ARFD *Rostock* rose ponderously into the air. The crew comprised Heinkel works pilot Rolf Jöster, co-pilot and flight mechanic Hans Lausmann from the Hirth Motoren firm, and radio operator Artur Suppa of Lufthansa. The aircraft left the runway in Peenemünde, but not in the direction of a distant destination. It had been planned instead to make several laps over the Baltic between Zinnowitz and Leba in Pomerania, thus making it possible for the crew to exceed the 10,000km non-stop goal by a further 500km (310 miles). This doubtlessly monotonous exercise was successfully completed after 49 hours and 9 minutes. With a Japanese crew, the V3 also took part in the so-called 'Saharaflug' in 1938. As was to be expected, the aircraft took up a leading position, but due to a defect in the powerplant drive system, involving the propeller pitch-change mechanism, it had to be abandoned. Continuing the flight under the power of three engines, the crew were therefore out of the running.

Despite its proven qualities, the He 116 was not able to assert itself. The reasons for its failure lay not only in its inability to fulfil military requirements, whereby, besides its use as a Fernerkunder, it was to be further developed as a bomber (!), but also in falling victim to priorities that at that time concentrated more on military rather than commercial needs.

Technical Comparison for the He 116 and BV 142

	Heinkel He 116A	Heinkel He 116B	Blohm & Voss BV 142
Powerplant	Hirth HM 508C	Hirth HM 508H	BMW 132H-1
Take-off power, hp	4 x 270	4 x 240	4 x 880
Dimensions			
Wingspan	22.00m (72' 2⅛") *	22.00m (72' 2⅛")	29.50m (96' 9⅜")
Length	13.70m (44' 11⅜")	14.30m (46' 11")	19.65m (64' 5⅝")
Height	3.30m (10' 9⅞")	3.30m (10' 9⅞")	5.05m (16' 6¾")
Wing area, m² (ft²)	62.90 (677.03)	62.90 (677.03)	130.00 (1,399.27)
Weights			
Empty weight, kg (lb)	4,050 (8,929)	4,020 (8,862)	9,200 (20,282)
Fuel capacity, litres	2,650	-	6,560
Normal take-off weight, kg (lb)	7,130 (15,719)	7,046 (15,534)	15,700 (34,612)
Performance			
Max speed, km/h (mph)	375 (233) †	325 (202) †	400 (249)
Cruising speed, km/h (mph)	300-320 (186-199)	264 (164) †	350 (217)
Normal range, km, (miles)	3,450 (2,143)	3,411 (2,120)	4,400 (2,734)
Maximum range, km, (miles)	4,100 (2,548)	-	-
Service ceiling, m (ft)	6,600 (21,655)	6,500 (21,325)	6,800 (22,310)
Crew	3-4	4	4-5

* He 116 V3: wingspan 25m (82ft 0¼in) and wing area 75.60m² (813.73ft²); † at 3,000m (9,840ft)

Chapter Three

In Uniform

Military Development of the He 111

Heinkel had commenced development of the He 111 as early as 1932. Differing accounts are found in aviation literature as to whether its foundations lay in the civilian or military sectors. The fact remains that a military background is apparent in the shape of the He 111 V1 (He 111a). It has also been recorded that Heinkel was in receipt of a top secret so-called 'duty manual' that contained precise requirements for the new bomber; the guidelines were thus outlined on which the further development of the He 111 would be based. The aircraft was actually outlined in this manual as a Mehrzweckflugzeug (multi-purpose aircraft), a designation that allowed for several options. Up until its maiden flight on 24th February 1935, no less than 200,000 development hours had been invested in it by the Heinkel concern.

By contrast, the He 111 V2 (He 111b) can be seen as a purely commercial project that served as the basis for the He 111 airliner, while the V3 represented a branch from the military development tree. Like the V2, the V3 made its maiden flight in March 1935, while the V4 served from January 1936 as a military test prototype. Flight trials in both spheres thus ran in parallel. This is confirmed by a remark made by Siegfried Günter, who stated that it was 'a compromise between a commercial aircraft for DLH powered by the BMW VI OZ and a bomber for the Luftwaffe with more modern engines.' He also added, a good 20 years after the end of the war, that the He 111 would have been an even better airliner if the military demands had not been a hindrance. At that time the Luftwaffe was forced to look around quickly for a new bomber, since the Ju 86, which had been placed almost simultaneously in civil and military service, proved to be an abysmal failure due to its weak performance. The path was thus predestined for the He 111 to become a second-generation bomber. Ernst Heinkel remarked in this connection, 'In view of this disaster, it was understandable that the Luftwaffe encouraged with particular urgency and attention conversion of the He 111 into a standard bomber. This was pursued in a similar manner to the Ju 86. Three machine-gun stands were installed that, spacewise, were more favourable, especially when the entire fuselage nose, including the cockpit, was later expanded to make provision for an all-round-vision canopy. Nobody sang praises to my fast commercial aircraft, something that eventually happened.'

For Heinkel, in terms of production quantities the He 111 was by far the most significant design within its range of aircraft types, although the future direction of the He 111 project could be no more than imagined by Heinkel at this time. In accordance with RLM planning, until the Ju 88 became available the He 111 was merely to be regarded as an interim solution, but, as history shows, it came to be quite otherwise.

Competitors to the He 111: The Ju 86 and Do 17

Parallel to the He 111, two other second-generation bomber designs were taking shape on the drawing-boards at Dornier and Junkers.

Junkers Ju 86

Similar to the He 111, this aircraft also followed two development paths. The Ju 86 V1, first flown on 4th November 1934, represented a bomber prototype, while the V2, first flown on 22nd March 1935, was a civil development. Prototypes used for military purposes were continued with the V3 and V5, the latter leaving the final assembly line in December 1935, based on the A-0 pre-production series. The V5 and V11 served as models for the Ju 86A-1 series. From the spring of 1936 the first A-1 series models left the production line, and subsequently manufacture of the Ju 86D version was begun in the late summer of that year. In late summer 1937 the first examples of the Ju 86E appeared, followed in spring 1938 by the Ju 86G. Bomber developments continued with the Ju 86H and K, and with the Ju 86P-1, P-4 and P-5 high-altitude bombers, as well as the R-3. The Ju 86P-2, P-5 and R-1 represented high-altitude reconnaissance variants. During the war the Ju 86 only served in the high-altitude reconnaissance and training roles, as well as being used operationally in the partisan war in the East. Production of this aircraft, which proved unsatisfactory in both the military and civil spheres, was ended in April 1939, and Junkers was then obliged to produce the He 111. In the course of later conversions, some Ju 86 high-altitude variants made their appearance.

Dornier Do 17

In this case, too, development followed two parallel paths. Initially designated the Do 15, corresponding plans for this mail carrier had been completed at the beginning of August 1932, and resulted in the Do 17. In May 1933 the firm received an order for the completion and thorough testing of two prototypes. Towards the end of the year it received a development order for the Do 17 in the role of a fast commercial aircraft. Simultaneously, the decision had been taken in April 1934 to build a Do 17 bomber version, for which the corresponding mock-up was completed in the following month. Approximately six months later, on 23rd November 1934, the Do 17 V1 took off on its maiden flight, followed by the V2 and V3 prototypes in May and September 1935 respectively. The ensuing test programme at Rechlin showed good results, so further orders from the RLM filled the Dornier Werke order books, involving the purchase of the V4 to V14 prototypes (30th December 1936). The order was later expanded to include the V15 to V17. The subsequent development path of the Do 17 resulted in several bomber and reconnaissance variants – the Do 17E, F and P, the Do 17Z bomber, and the Do 17Z-7 and Z-10 night fighters. While the military developments can therefore be considered to have been very successful, the commercial line ran into the proverbial sand.

He 111 V3 Prototype

The He 111 V3 (Werknummer 714), the second bomber prototype that served as the basis for the pre-production He 111A-0, stood ready for it maiden flight in mid-1935. Following works trials, and bearing the registration D-ALES, it was ferried to the E-Stelle Rechlin in January 1936, where it was put through its paces, the trials involving the variable-pitch propellers as well as the wireless equipment. The V3 was able to carry a maximum bombload of 1,000kg (2,205 lb), but when thus loaded it demonstrated that the previously unsatisfactory performance sank even lower. When the flight trials took place, the aircraft was still fitted with the extendable ventral fuselage C-Stand 'dustbin', which, in its fully extended position, caused a considerable amount of drag that further reduced its flying speed. The trials in

Rechlin were conducted with BMW VI engines; these were assumed to be satisfactory for the civil sector, but the trials proved them to be inadequate for the He 111 bomber. Subsequently the V3 was used in Rechlin as an flying engine test-bed. It was also fitted with a new wing of 22.6m (74ft 1¾in) span and 87.60m² (942.89ft²) area. In May 1936, in other words before the modification, the most important aircraft types were assembled in Rechlin and demonstrated to Hermann Göring and high-ranking officers. Junkers displayed the Ju 86 in versions powered by the BMW 132 and Jumo 205 engines, while Dornier's Do 17 and Heinkel's He 111 flew with the BMW VI. Besides these three competing types, there were also aircraft in other categories, namely the Ju 87 dive-bomber and the Me 109 and He 112 fighters.

Technical Details of the He 111 V1 to V5

Airframe dimensions of the initial prototypes differed from each another, chiefly as a result of the use of various wing planforms, which resulted in the following dimensions:

- He 111 V1 multi-purpose aircraft: span 25m (82ft 0¼in), wing area 92.40m² (994.56ft²).
- He 111 V2 airliner: span 23m (75ft 5½in), wing area 88.50m² (952.58ft²).
- He 111 V3 bomber: span 22.6m (74ft 1¾in), wing area 87.60m² (942.90ft²).
- He 111 V4 airliner: span 23m (75ft 5½in), wing area 88.50m² (952.58ft²).
- He 111 V5 bomber: span 22.6m (74ft 1¾in), wing area 87.60m² (942.90ft²).

In the case of the V1 to V4 inclusive, the fuselage length of 17.1m (56ft 1¼in) remained the same, but from the V5 onwards was increased to 17.5m (57ft 5in). Powerplants consisted of two 660hp BMW VI in-lines, which, in the military sphere, provided a totally inadequate amount of power. This resulted in the He 111 V3 having only a moderate maximum speed of 330km/h (205mph); its undercarriage main-wheels measured 1,000 x 375mm (39.37 x 14¾in) with a track of 5.23m (17ft 1⅞in), and it was fitted with a tailskid. The vertical bomb magazine in the He 111 bomb-bay was first installed upon the commencement of weapons trials with the V1 and V3 prototypes.

The Do 17 V1 accomplished its maiden flight on 23rd November 1934.

The ungainly-looking Ju 86 V1 (D-AHEH); it first flew on 4th November 1934.

The He 111 V3 (D-ALES) bomber prototype commenced flight-testing in mid-1935.

Two personalities who could each look back on a life of significant achievement: Prof. Willi Messerschmitt and Prof. Dr.-Ing. Ernst Heinkel.

Chapter Four

Progressive Development

The He 111A- to P-Series

He 111A

The original plan to begin series production with this model had to be abandoned due to the poor performance of the pre-production He 111A-0. Instead of the envisaged 15 aircraft, only seven were completed at the Heinkel Rostock plant as Werknummern 0001 to 0007, one of which was used for engine trials. On receipt of an export order, six were sold to China for RM 400,000 each. As already mentioned, the reason for the inadequate performance, and hence the failure, of this version was the use of the BMW VI powerplant. In the summer of 1936 Werknummern 1002 and 1003 were ferried to Rechlin and subjected to thorough testing. Almost entirely unsatisfactory results emerged, causing the RLM to reject the aircraft in this form. At the same time, however, it was recognised that the use of more powerful engines would certainly lead to a usable He 111 bomber, and this led to the He 111B successor.

He 111B

As early as the summer of 1936, manufacture had begun at Rostock of the pre-production He 111B-0; seven aircraft, bearing the Werknummern 1431 to 1437, were built. Daimler-Benz DB 600C engines driving variable-pitch airscrews were installed in all of them, leading to a 200hp increase per engine over the BMW VI 6.0 Z. Further differences from the He 111A version were the use of an auxiliary surface cooler in the wing nose section and the installation of an MG 15 in the fuselage nose. One of these weapons was also housed in the dorsal fuselage B-Stand, and another in the extendable ventral C-Stand position. In addition, the He 111B-0 was capable of carrying a bombload of up to 1,500kg (3,307 lb) in vertical magazines in the fuselage.

The pre-production B-0 aircraft were followed by the He 111B-1s, which were likewise built in Rostock. The B-2s, on the other hand, were built in the Oranienburg plant. In due course all the B-1s were brought up to B-2 standard.

He 111B-1

Powerplants installed in this model were two DB 600C engines. Defensive armament consisted of one 7.9mm MG 15 machine-gun in a flexible Ikaria turret in the nose A-Stand, a B-Stand with one DL 15 revolving gun-mount, and a C-Stand with one 7.9mm MG 15.

He 111B-2

This variant was powered by two 950hp DB 600CGs, which were likewise equipped with two surface coolers in combination with those installed beneath the engines. When the DB 600Ga was installed at a later date, the wing surface coolers were dispensed with.

He 111B-3

This sub-type represented the He 111B-1 modified for training purposes. With the He 111B came the large RLM production orders. The quantities required were impossible to produce in the two Heinkel plants in Rostock and Oranienburg, so the Norddeutsche Dornier Werke in Wismar was included in the He 111 manufacturing programme, and produced a total of 28 He 111B aircraft. The order had originally called for 255 aircraft, but with the increase in the production of the He 111E, only a comparatively small number left the final assembly lines. Other firms that manufactured the He 111B were Arado in Brandenburg, ATG in Leipzig and Junkers in Dessau, so that a total of six plants were producing the new standard Luftwaffe bomber in the spring of 1937. When more powerful versions of the He 111 became available later on, the He 111B was transferred largely to flying training schools.

Two He 111Bs prior to a sortie. The example on the right is coded BO+PA.

A view of an He 111B from an unidentified unit.

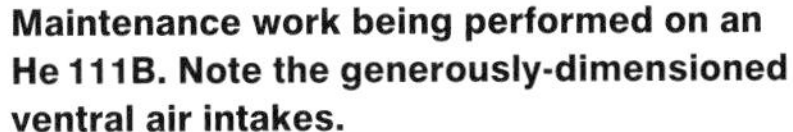

Maintenance work being performed on an He 111B. Note the generously-dimensioned ventral air intakes.

Photographs on the opposite page:

This He 111A-0 was one of the aircraft purchased by China. In the foreground is the Chinese delegation responsible for acceptance of the aircraft.

A frontal view of the He 111B (D-AHAY).

The wing-mounted surface coolers are clearly visible on this He 111B.

This He 111B-1, Werknummer 1005, was used in January 1938 for a series of supercharger tests.

An He 111B bearing the markings of the Condor Legion (2nd Staffel of K.88).

Photographs on the opposite page:

A representative of the rare He 111D-0 series.

Rear-quarter view of an He 111E (SF+GP) in the RLM 61/62/63 camouflage scheme.

He 111D

Only a few examples of the He 111D version were built. They were based on the He 111B, but had a few differences.

In order to optimise vision for the crew, efforts were being made at Heinkel as early as 1937 to completely redesign the fuselage nose. The stepped or raised cockpit was replaced by a completely glazed full-view canopy, which now gave the fuselage its characteristic drop-shaped form. Lack of availability of Daimler-Benz engines resulted in Heinkel using the Jumo 211A-1 in later variants, which replaced the DB 600 in the He 111D-0.

He 111D Pathfinder (with all-round-view canopy)

The purpose of this aircraft was to lead a bomber formation and coordinate an attack. For this task the Führungsflugzeug (pathfinder) aircraft were equipped with comprehensive radio and navigation equipment. The first prototype, the V7, initially had two DB 601As, later replaced by the DB 601C. The He 111 V10 followed as the second such prototype in summer 1939. After the results of trials became available, 30 pathfinders were produced in two configurations:

He 111D-1

The He 111D-1 was equipped with two long-wave and short-wave FuG IIIaU transmitter/receivers in the bomb-bay, but was merely regarded as an interim solution. Far more satisfactory was the FuG X (alias FuG 10), which was more suitable for operation over longer ranges. Auxiliary equipment consisted of a direction-finding Peil G V and FuBl 1 radio blind-landing aid.

He 111D-2

The He 111D-2 was similar in construction to the D-1 with the exception of its navigation equipment, the so-called Y-Gerät in its expanded version being installed in the bomb-bay.

The D-1 and D-2 had a crew of up to eight men. Besides the regular four-man crew, the aircraft had an officer responsible for navigation, two radio operators, and one other trained to perform various other tasks required. Defensive armament consisted of three MG 15s in the usual positions. This aircraft had an empty weight of 6,540kg (14,418 lb), its permissible take-off weight being a little under 11,000kg (24,250 lb).

Aircraft in this configuration were assigned to the squadrons at the beginning of 1940. A short summary of their technical equipment follows:

- FuG III (basic model): This equipment worked in the 300-600 KHz/3.0-6.0MHz frequency range. Towards the middle of 1936 the transformer-equipped FuG IIIaU came to be used in the Do 17, Ju 86 and He 111.

- Y-Gerät: this served to guide the bomber group. Its components consisted of the UKW (ultra-shortwave) audio communication and range measurement FuG 17E, the UKW FuG 28a homing beam receiver, as well as the converter and other operating equipment.

He 111E

The He 111E resulted from an RLM requirement and led to the termination of the original He 111D version. The first prototype, the V6, was powered by the Jumo 210Ga, which replaced the DB 600 originally installed, but this powerplant also proved to be in no way satisfactory. The more powerful Jumo 211A-1 was eventually installed, but was not yet completely reliable and hence insufficiently developed to enter production.

He 111E-1

Salient details of this model were as follows:

- The powerplant was the Jumo 211A-1.
- The lubricant cooler was now integrated into the engine cowling.
- Unlike the basic model, the coolers beneath the powerplant cowling were retractable.
- Armament corresponded to that of the He 111B-2.
- As a result of these modifications, the maximum take-off weight was now 10,900kg (24,030 lb).

Initial production machines were rolled out in February 1938, and in the following month the first examples arrived in Spain, where they were used by the Condor Legion in raids against the Republican forces. After their use by bomber squadrons, numerous He 111E-1s were later flown by training units.

He 111E-2

This variant was distinguished by improvements to its radio equipment. Normally powered by the Jumo 211A-1, the Jumo 211A-3 also came to be experimentally installed.

He 111E-3

This variant corresponded to the He 111E-2 with the exception of the powerplants, which were now the series-built 1,100hp Jumo 211A-3.

He 111E-4

Besides the four vertical magazines in the bomb-bay, this variant was capable of carrying an external load of 1,000kg (2,205 lb). Powerplants were again the Jumo 211A-3.

He 111E-5

This variant had an increased range capability through the installation of an additional 835-litre fuel tank on the left side of the bomb-bay for its Jumo 211A-3 powerplants.

It is almost certain that only a few examples of the last two variants were built.

He 111F

The most important difference here lay in the wing planform. In order to simplify production, Heinkel had developed a wing with a straight outboard leading-edge and sheet-metal covering, the wing having a span of 22.6m (74ft 1¾in) and an area of 87.60m² (942.90ft²). In the summer of 1936 the He 111 V7 prototype, fitted with this wing, underwent an extensive series of trials. During the course of flight trials from July 1937 the V11 also became involved, serving as

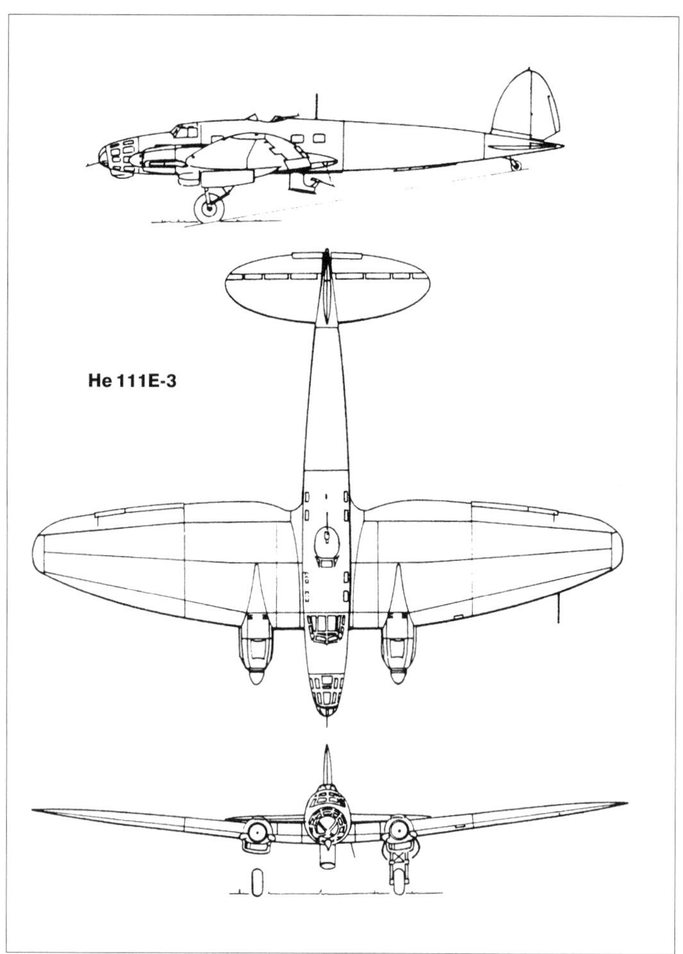

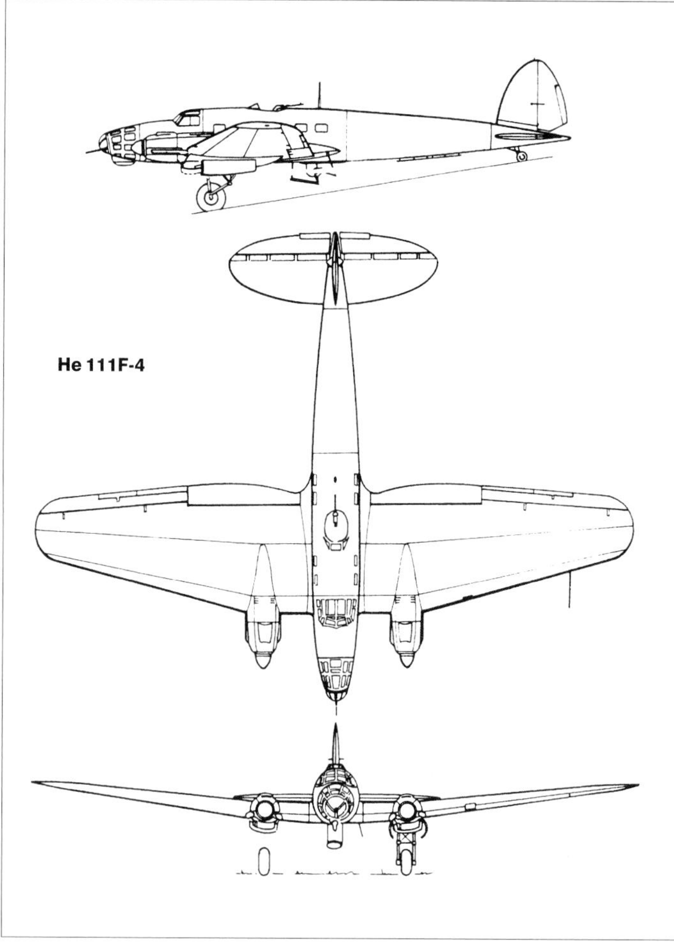

the basis for the He 111F-1 powered by the Jumo 211A-3. A few examples were also equipped with the Jumo 211A-1. However, series production of the aircraft was initially delayed by a lack of sufficient manufacturing capacity.

He 111F-1

This initial series variant left the final assembly lines up to the end of 1937. In addition to its production for the Luftwaffe, the He 111F-1 was also produced for export, Turkey receiving 24 examples.

He 111F-2

A total of 20 examples of this variant were built by Heinkel. The most important difference from the F-1 lay in the installation of optimised technical wireless equipment.

He 111F-3

This consisted of a planned reconnaissance variant in which the bomb release equipment was replaced by RB cameras. Powerplants were to have been two Jumo 211A-3 engines.

He 111F-4

A small number of Staff communications aircraft were manufactured under this designation. Its equipment was very similar to that of the He 111G-5, and in the powerplant area the exhaust gas system was modified.

He 111F-5

This was conceived as a bomber. In terms of the powerplant and bomb jettison equipment, it corresponded to the He 111E-5, but was not put into production as the already available data on the He 111P-1 was shown to be superior.

He 111J (with raised cockpit)

The He 111J version developed in 1936 was powered by two DB 600G engines whose radiators were not yet made retractable. This version was to be a torpedo-bomber variant and, instead of the normal level-bombing equipment, was fitted with two suspension racks for torpedoes. Maximum payload in this case was limited to 2,000kg (4,409 lb). The few pre-production He 111J-0 machines were powered by the DB 600G, but since the performance of the DB 600 left much to be desired, their use as a torpedo-bomber did not materialise. This experience resulted in Heinkel producing 60 examples (author Heinz Nowarra mentions 90) under the designation He 111J-1, presumably in the 1937/38 period. The aircraft were completed with the vertical bomb magazines and thus to normal bomber standard. Except for the Daimler-Benz engines, the He 111J-1 largely corresponded to the He 111F series, and up to 1944 was mainly used by flying training schools.

The Turkish Air Force took 24 He 111F-1 aircraft. According to Ernst Heinkel it was very difficult to keep this continually complaining client satisfied.

Right: **An He 111 pictured with a line-up of bombs in the foreground, in operational use in Spain.**

Below left: **The bomb-aimer's compartment in the fuselage nose (raised cockpit version).**

Below right: **A view inside the stepped cockpit in the fuselage.**

Bottom: **Only between 60 and 90 He 111J-1s left the final assembly lines. In the line-up here are aircraft belonging to KGr. 806.**

Translator's Note:
As a continuation of the alphabetical sub-types, in his book *Sturmisches Leben (A Stormy Life)* Ernst Heinkel refers no fewer than four times to his *Kampfflugzeug* as the He 111K, the nomenclature under which the He 111 (Series H) was known in the UK during the Second World War until corrected in October 1943. In 1942 the 'He 111K' was also believed to be in service with the Japanese Army Air Force, but powered by two radial engines. In the expectation that German aircraft purchased or ordered by Japan would be encountered in combat, each was assigned an Allied codename: He 111 *Bess*, He 112 *Jerry*, Fw 190 *Fred*, Fw 200 *Trudy*, Ju 52/3m *Trixie*, Ju 87 *Irene*, Ju 88 *Janice*, Bf 109 *Mike* and Bf 110 *Doc*. In some published accounts the BMW 132-powered civil He 111 has been described as the He 111L.

He 111P
As already mentioned during development of the He 111, instead of the raised cockpit the He 111P series featured a fully glazed fuselage nose that offered better visibility for the crew. Development work on this series began in 1936 and subsequently led to further sub-types. The He 111 V8 (D-AQUO) served as the prototype for this version, consisting of a suitably modified He 111B-0 powered by the DB 600G that was initially also installed in the pre-production He 111P-0. Conversion to the DB 601Aa took place in 1938. The He 111P-0 wing had the same planform, span and wing area as mentioned above for the He 111F, the fuselage length being 16.4m (53ft 9⅝in). Its take-off weight of 11,660kg (25,706 lb) was noticeably less than that of the He 111P-1.

He 111P-1
As with the P-0, the He 111P-1 also featured numerous differences over its predecessors, as follows:

- Two DB 601Aa powerplants each of 1,150hp.
- Retractable oil coolers.
- Self-sealing tanks for added protection from enemy fire.
- The production-simplified wing planform as used on the He 111F.
- An asymmetrical fully glazed nose. (with Ikaria A-Stand gun-mount for the MG 15)
- Introduction of a sliding hood for the dorsal fuselage B-Stand (one MG 15).
- Installation of a ventral blister or gondola as a C-Stand (one MG 15).
- Bomb jettison equipment consisting of two 4 ESAC-250/III vertical magazines.
- Installation of the Siemens K4ü automatic gyro compass and the FuG III.
- A semi-retractable tailwheel.
- An increase in take-off weight to 13,300kg (29,321 lb).

The He 111P-1 was introduced into squadron service from the spring of 1939, and besides its use by bomber units it was also employed for transport duties. A few machines were additionally used by Erprobungsstellen (Flight Test Centres) or as experimental weapons carriers tested by manufacturers.

He 111P-2
The second in this production series had the following differences:
- Installation of the FuG X, replacing the FuG IIIaU.
- Replacement of the initially installed DB 601Aa by the DB 601A-1.
- Use of the Lotfe 7 periscopic bombsight.
- The previously weak defensive armament strengthened with the aid of a Rüstsatz (field equipment set) comprising four or five MG 15 machine-guns.
- Bombing capacity raised by the installation of two 4 ESAC-250/IX vertical magazines.
- An empty weight of 6,020kg (13,272 lb), a loaded weight increased to 12,570kg (27,712 lb), and a maximum range of 2,100km (1,305 miles).

Like the preceding variant, besides its use as a bomber the He 111P-2 was also used for test programmes carried out by various E-Stellen and by industry. Its operational spectrum was expanded by its use not only as an airborne ambulance and for transport duties, but also (quantity unknown) by training units.

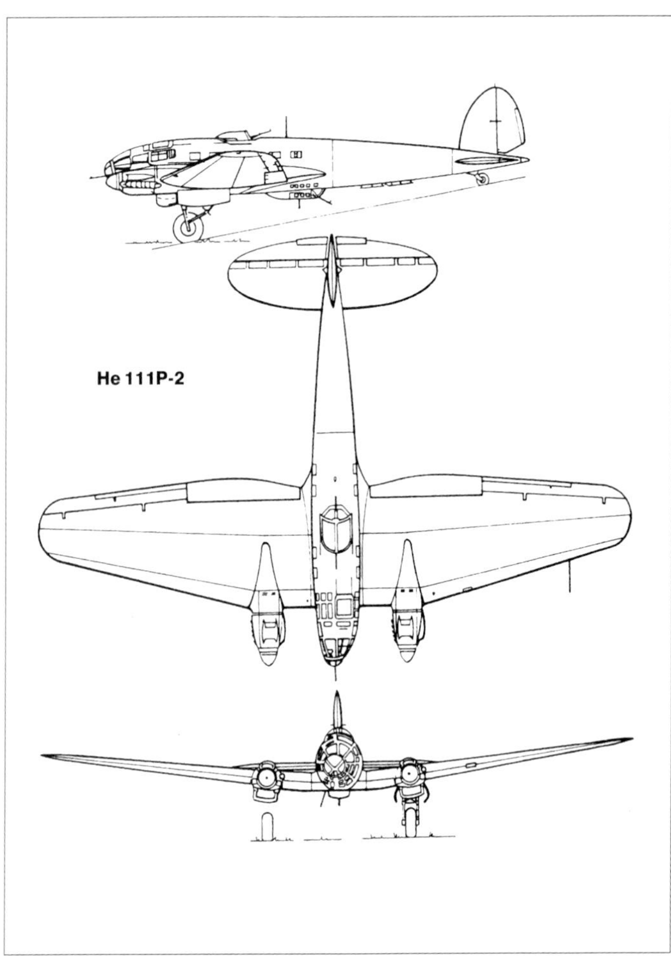
He 111P-2

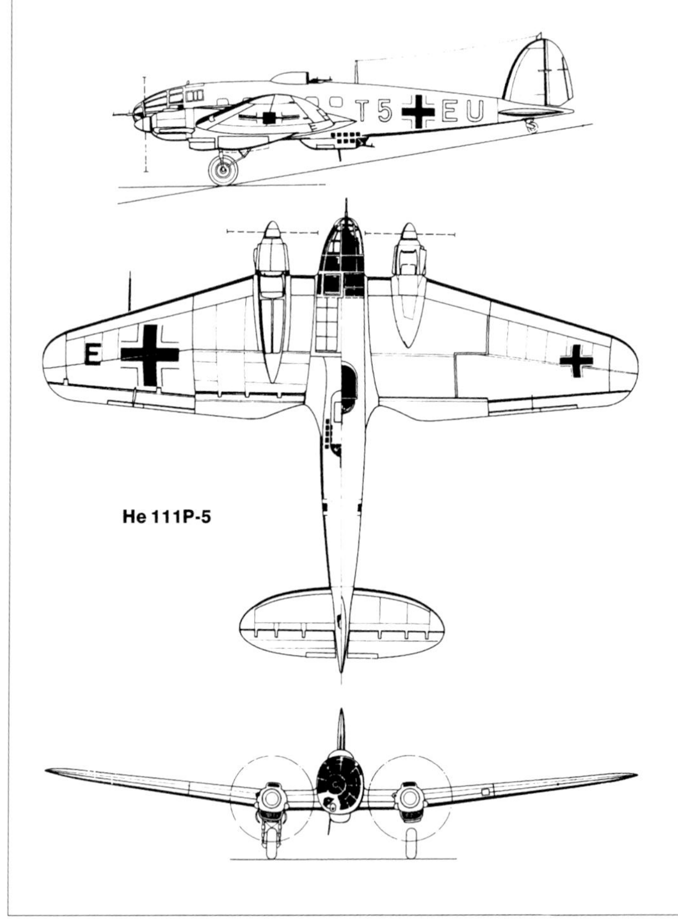

He 111P-5

He 111P-3

With a mere eight examples completed, the He 111P-3 appears to be almost insignificant in respect of the total number of aircraft produced. It consisted of a training variant equipped with dual controls, the aircraft corresponding to the He 111P-2 and equipped with the 1,150hp DB 601A-1. The possibility also existed of this aircraft being able to take off with the assistance of the KL-12 land catapult, for which purpose a towing hook was mounted beneath the fuselage in the cockpit region for attachment to a towing cable. Besides the originally produced He 111P-3, which was delivered without bomb jettison equipment, an unknown quantity derived from the appropriately modified He 111P-1 and P-2 were also produced.

He 111P-4

This variant was intended from the outset as a level-bomber, and gradually replaced the He 111P-2. The most noticeable changes in the He 111P-4 were:

- Powerplant was the DB 601A-1.
- Jettisonable loads were capable of considerable variation, for example: two SC 1800 external bombs; two LMA air-dropped mines; one SC 1800 plus four SC 250 bombs; or one SC 2500 external bomb on an ETC Rüstsatz. Depending on the make-up of the load, in place of the vertical bomb magazine an 835-litre fuel tank and a 120-litre oil tank could be carried.
- Defensive armament had previously consisted of only three MG 15s. As this was in no way compatible with front-line needs, armament was therefore increased to six MG 15s and one MG 17.
- W/T equipment consisted of the FuG 10, Peil G V and FuBl 1.
- Because of the considerably increased defensive armament, it became necessary to raise the crew total from four to five.
- The P-4 corresponded dimensionally to the P-1 to P-3. Empty weight increased to 6,775kg (14,936 lb) and, as a result of the above-mentioned alterations, take-off weight rose to 13,500kg (29,762 lb).

He 111P-5

The He 111P-5 served for pilot training, and for this purpose at least 24 examples were built, with varying items of equipment. When used by training units, the aircraft was often flown unarmed, and in this connection the bomb jettison gear was removed in several instances. Not confirmed is a suggestion that the He 111P-5 was also flown equipped with PVC bomb racks. Various aircraft of the P-5 series were fitted with meteorological equipment and used by weather service squadrons. The He 111P-5 was again powered by the DB 601A.

Top: **He 111P-4, Werknummer 3107, coded NO+GP.**

Centre: **He 111P-4, Werknummer 3106, coded NO+GO.**

Above: **An He 111P-5, coded T5+AU, of the Aufklärungsgruppe des ObdL (Reconnaissance Wing of the Oberkommando der Luftwaffe) shortly before take-off.**

Technical Data Comparison

	He 111A-0	He 111B-2	He 111D-0	He 111E-1	He 111F1	He 111J-1
Powerplant	BMW	Daimler-Benz	Daimler-Benz	Junkers	Junkers	Daimler-Benz
Type	VI 6.0 Z	DB 600CG	DB 600Ga	Jumo 211A-1	Jumo 211A-3	DB 601Aa
Take-off power, hp	660	850	1,050	1,000	1,100	1,150
Dimensions						
Wingspan	22.60m (74' 1¾")	22.60m (74' 1¾")	22.60m (74' 1¾")	22.60m (74' 1¾")	22.60m (74' 1¾")	22.60m (74' 1¾")
Length	17.50m (57' 5")	17.50m (57' 5")	17.50m (57' 5")	17.50m (57' 5")	17.50m (57' 5")	16.40m (53' 9⅝")
Height	4.10m (13' 5⅛")	4.00m (13' 5⅛")	4.00m (13' 5⅛")	4.20m (13' 9⅜")	4.20m (13' 9⅜")	4.20m (13' 9⅜")
Wing area, m^2 (ft^2)	87.60 (942.90)	87.60 (942.90)	87.60 (942.90)	87.60 (942.90)	87.60 (942.90)	87.60 (942.90)
Weights						
Empty weight, kg (lb)	5,400 (11,905)	5,860 (12,919)	6,000 (13,228)	6,135 (13,525)	6,200 (13,669)	6,200 (13,669)
Take-off weight, kg (lb)	8,220 (18,122)	8,600 (18,960)	8,800 (19,400)	10,600 (23,369)	10,600 (23,369)	10,600 (23,369)
Performance						
Max speed, km/h (mph)	310 (193)	370 (230)	410 (255)	430 (267)	440 (273)	440 (273)
Cruising speed, km/h (mph)	270 (168)	310 (193)	340 (211)	380 (236)	385 (239)	360 (224)
Range	1,100 (684)	1,050 (652)	1,050 (652)	1,820 (1,131)	1,820 (1,131)	1,800 (1,118)
Service ceiling	4,800 (15,750)	4,800 (15,750)	5,000 (16,405)	5,800 (19,030)	6,000 (19,685)	5,200 (17,060)
Military Load						
Armament	3 x MG 15	3 x MG 15	3 x MG 15	3 x MG 15	3 x MG 15	3 x MG 15
Bombload	500 (1,102)*	1,500 (3,307)	1,200 (2,646)	2,000 (4,409)	2,000 (4,409) †	2 x LTs
Crew	4	4	4	4	4	4

* Maximum bombload 1,000kg (2,205 lb); † planned.

	He 111P-1	He 111P-2	He 111P-4	He 111P-5	He 111P-6
Powerplant	Daimler-Benz	Daimler-Benz	Daimler-Benz	Daimler-Benz	Daimler-Benz
Type	DB 601Aa	DB 601Aa *	DB 601A-1	DB 601A-1	DB 601N †
Take-off power, hp	1,150	1,150	1,100	1,100	1,200
Dimensions					
Wingspan	22.60m (74' 1¾")	22.60m (74' 1¾")	22.60m (74' 1¾")	22.60m (74' 1¾")	22.60m (74' 1¾")
Length	16.40m (53' 9⅝")	16.40m (53' 9⅝")	16.40m (53' 9⅝")	16.40m (53' 9⅝")	16.40m (53' 9⅝")
Height	4.00m (13' 5⅛")	4.00m (13' 5⅛")	4.00m (13' 5⅛")	4.00m (13' 5⅛")	4.00m (13' 5⅛")
Wing area, m^2 (ft^2)	87.60 (942.90)	87.60 (942.90)	87.60 (942.90)	87.60 (942.90)	87.60 (942.90)
Weights					
Empty weight, kg (lb)	-	6,020 (13,272)	6,775 (14,936)	-	-
Take-off weight, kg (lb)	13,300 (29,321)	12,570 (27,712)	13,500 (29,762)	13,820 (30,468)	14,000 (30,864)
Performance					
Max speed, km/h (mph)	-	390 (242)	398 (247)	380 (236)	425 (264)
Cruising speed, km/h (mph)	-	310 (193)	373 (232)	-	-
Range, km (miles)	-	2,100 (1,305)	2,400 (1,491)	-	-
Service ceiling, m (ft)	-	7,800 (25,590)	8,000 (26,250)	-	-
Military Load					
Armament	3 x MG 15	4-5 x MG 15	6 MG 15/1 MG 17	Mostly removed	3 x MG 15
Bombload, kg (lb)	2,000 (4,409)	1,500 (3,307)	2,500 (5,512) ‡	gear removed or 1 x 4 ESAC	2 x 4 ESAC + 1 PVC
Crew	4	4	5	-	-

* DB 601A installed at a later date; † Jumo 211A-1 also used; ‡ Maximum bombload.

He 111P-6

This variant, deliveries of which were completed by the summer of 1940, corresponded largely to the P-5. The most notable difference lay in the use of DB 601N engines. Delivering 1,175hp at take-off, these powerplants were also used in the Bf 109E, which had absolute priority; thus only a few of the He 111P-6 machines were able to be equipped with these rare units, which, after a fly-off, were replaced by the Jumo 211A-1. With these latter engines, the aircraft were known as the He 111H-1. The normal operational role of the P-6 could be expanded by the installation of a tow-coupling for cargo gliders, this variant being known as the P-6/R2. A total of ten P-6 machines were delivered to Hungary.

He 111P-7

This designation would normally apply to the next sub-type in the series. Unfortunately, neither in the archives of the Deutsches Museum in Munich nor in aviation literature is any reliable information to be found concerning the details or use of this variant.

He 111P-8

In this case, too, it is questionable whether this model was actually built. It is said to have been derived from a modified He 111H-5 fitted with dual controls. In none of the sources consulted could its existence be definitely established.

He 111P-9

This was an export variant intended for Hungary, but was never delivered; instead it was put to other use. The project foundered due to continual lack of DB 601E engines. Only a small number left the Heinkel assembly lines and were used by the Luftwaffe as towcraft.

The He 111P-9 was the last of the P series, production of which was terminated by the RLM in summer 1940. In all, 388 examples of all the variants described were produced, by Heinkel in Rostock, Dornier in Wismar and Arado in Brandenburg. Generally they were powered by Daimler-Benz engines, but the Jumo 211 was installed in the succeeding He 111H models.

To conclude the subject of the He 111 variants covered thus far, the data tables on the opposite page provide salient details of the aircraft and includes several of the He 111P sub-types.

The HV Report: Technical and Efficiency Evaluation

The following is an evaluation of the He 111 in the Junkers Hauptverwaltung (HV – Central Administration) Technische und Wirtschaftliche Berichterstattung (Technical and Efficiency Report) dated 8th October 1938. Classified as confidential, in parts it is less than flattering in its remarks on the He 111.

Only the most important passages are reproduced below:

The HV Technical & Efficiency Report

Dessau, 8th October 1938

Document Remarks

Ref: He 111

'Two aircraft were able to be inspected on 6th October in Bernburg.* Apparent are the externally poor, less carefully designed components at various locations, especially at the junction between the empennage and the rear fuselage. All parts give an impression of being very weak; especially when one is used to taking a long look at Junkers designs, one cannot dispel a feeling of uncertainty. The visible flexing of the wings in flight must also be extraordinarily high.

'The left and right [Jumo 211] powerplants are interchangeable. Each motor has an exhaust-gas heater on one side, but is not connected to the fuselage since it is probable that as a result of incorrect air feed, the warm air in the fuselage is not free of CO [carbon monoxide].

'The fuselage is not subdivided into individual segments, but is attached over its entire length, after completion, to the wing centre section. Outboard of the powerplants, the wings are attached by universal joints. The latter can in no way be satisfactory and have been the cause of several failures...'

* The Junkers Bernburg plant produced 40 He 111s in 1938 – Translator.

He 111R and Other Projects

Besides the He 111H and Z described in subsequent pages, the variety of sub-types was enriched by the He 111R, which was to have been a so-called Gleitbomber (glide-bomber). For this type of operational use, strengthening of the airframe was necessary. The proposal was submitted to the RLM in three variants, powered by the DB 603. As a result of the higher weight due to the strengthening, larger wheels became necessary, the empennage surfaces and ailerons being modified accordingly. The three variants, which did not go into production, were as follows:

- He 111R-1:Based on the He 111H-5 and H-6; the prototype was derived from a modified He 111H-3 (D-APZL).
- He 111R-2: The basic model for this was the He 111H-11, but no construction was started.
- He 111R-3: The He 111H-20 served as the basic model, equipped with the Hirth-DVL TK-9 turbo-supercharger. Carrying an external bombload of two 1,000kg (2,205 lb) and an armament of five MG 131s plus an MG 131 in a rotatable turret, it remained only a project.

The following developments are also worthy of mention. In 1944 Heinkel sought to convince the RLM of the advantages of yet another He 111 variant in order to prevent a total halt in production of the aircraft. His design office now proposed a version powered by the Jumo 213, using the Jumo 213A and E models, the installation of which required a considerable number of modifications. Because of the limited availability of the Jumo 213, for which the Focke-Wulf Fw 190D-9 was accorded top priority, the He 111 powered by that unit could not be realised.

As a result, a number of other types of powerplant came to be proposed. The range, including those from the very beginning, was BMW VI, BMW 132, Daimler-Benz DB 600, DB 601, Jumo 210 and Jumo 211, up to the proposed use of the DB 603, Jumo 213 and Jumo 223.

Flying view of an He 111P in RLM 70/71/65 camouflage.

Chapter Five

The Technical Details of the He 111H

Parallel to production of the He 111P series between 1938 and 1940, Heinkel developed the He 111H, which in the summer of 1940 took shape as the sole version on the production lines. Except for matters of detail, the design features of the He 111H had already been decided in the autumn of 1938, so test prototypes were able to be completed and subjected to thorough trials. This was most probably accomplished by using the He 111P-1 series airframes, as the He 111 V17, V18 and V19 prototypes, which formed the pre-production He 111H-0 series, commenced flight trials in July of the following year. Aerodynamic refinements, together with airframe weight-saving measures, were initially coupled with weaker powerplants in the He 111H-1. The difference between the 1,000hp Jumo 211A-1 and the 1,100hp DB 601A-1 was thus 100hp per engine. In succeeding He 111H production variants, the Jumo 211s used delivered 1,200-1,340hp. Subsequent production of the He 111H-series aircraft consisted of numerous, some extremely specialised, variants that ranged from the H-1 to the H-23, the He 111H-16 forming the focal point of the following description. This portrayal is based largely on original documents, allowing authenticity to be preserved and hence presenting a realistic picture of the technical details of the He 111H, the text being expanded by self-explanatory photographs and works illustrations from original Handbooks. Partly because of the unsatisfactory quality of the original documents, and partly for space reasons, the text has been reduced to essentials in this narrative.

The Fuselage

The following general details are reproduced from the relevant text from the He 111H-16 Handbook, Part 1 (August 1943 edition):

The fuselage consists of the structure itself, the cockpit, and the installations in both. The fuselage has an oval cross-section and, measured from the central datum line, is symmetrical, while because of the A-Stand, the fuselage nose is offset to starboard. The fuselage supporting framework consists of 27 transverse frames and numerous stringers, of which four are the main load-bearers. The stiffened smooth covering panels are attached to the framework by flush rivets.

The fuselage is of monocoque construction, the material consisting mainly of dural sheet with fittings of dural and steel, the skin of aluminium and Elektron sheet. The transparencies are of Plexiglas, special clear-vision panels being made of polished Sigla anti-splitter glass panels.

The fuselage space is divided into the cockpit, bomb-bay, radio operator/gunner's compartment, rear fuselage, and tail end with detachable tailcone. The compartments are separated from each other by full bulkheads, each having an opening enabling passage through them along the fuselage. In the first bulkhead there is a sliding door, and in the third a hinged door.

The pilot and bomb-aimer are housed in the cockpit, and in the forward spar box an emergency seat is provided for the Staffelführer [squadron commander]. The radio operator/gunner's compartment further serves to accommodate three crew members.

Entry and exit is by way of a hatch in the floor of the radio operator/gunner's compartment. From here, the cockpit can be reached via a gangway passing through the bomb-bay. Exit in an emergency is through the sliding panels in the cockpit roof and the emergency exit window at the right, and, for the radio operator, the entrance hatch. Depending upon the aircraft's role, the fuselage tailcone serves as a cover for catapult or towing gear. The fuselage installations can be converted for tropical operations.

For attachment of the wing to the fuselage, the transverse frames 4 and 8 each consist of a double bulkhead, between which the wing spars are anchored. At the transition from the fuselage to the wing, there is a wingroot fillet on both sides. The fin and tailplane are attached at frames 25 and 27, which are likewise double frames.

For crew protection there is armour-plating, which is also secured against rupture in hard landings. In the event of single-engined flight, the armour-plating is jettisonable…

Exact measurements are visible on the drawings, the fuselage construction being documented in the fuselage framework sectional drawing.

Nose Section (Cockpit)

This description is limited solely to the relevant parts of the framework. Cockpit details are described separately later.

The cockpit consists of a self-contained constructional element and is attached to the foremost fuselage bulkhead at frame 4a, where this separation point is made watertight by a rubber lining. The cockpit consists of the front welded tubular framework together with the panelling forming the fuselage nose. The front end of the cockpit consists of a glass cone through which the armament housing projects. The Plexiglas panels provide the pilot with good visibility on all sides. Individual panels are exchangeable, curved according to the shape of the canopy, and by means of sealing are attached in a watertight manner to the supporting framework.

The sheet-covered cockpit portion consists in the main of two lower stringers and the four vertical transverse frames to which they are attached. The individual frames are riveted to longitudinal profiles. This framework, covered with smooth dural sheet, has two hatches on the underside. The upper framework is covered by transparencies for the pilot and observer, and for access to the ventral cockpit installations there are two access hatches in the cockpit floor at the right.

Centre Fuselage Framework

This part of the Handbook concentrates on the framework of the centre fuselage, the bomb-bay and the radio compartment.

The fuselage is manufactured as a complete assembly and consists primarily of longitudinal stringers, the transverse frames or formers and the sheet skin covering. The stringers are largely of 'U' profile, serving as stiffeners for the skin panelling ,while a few, due to their thicker special profiles, provide the requisite stiffness to the fuselage framework and include the four main fuselage longerons. For manufacturing purposes, the fuselage is sub-divided into smaller elements that are riveted and connected together to support the skin. The interior

Opposite page:

Three-view drawing of the He 111H. The highlighted fuselage items are on the He 111H-11 and He 111H-16 only.

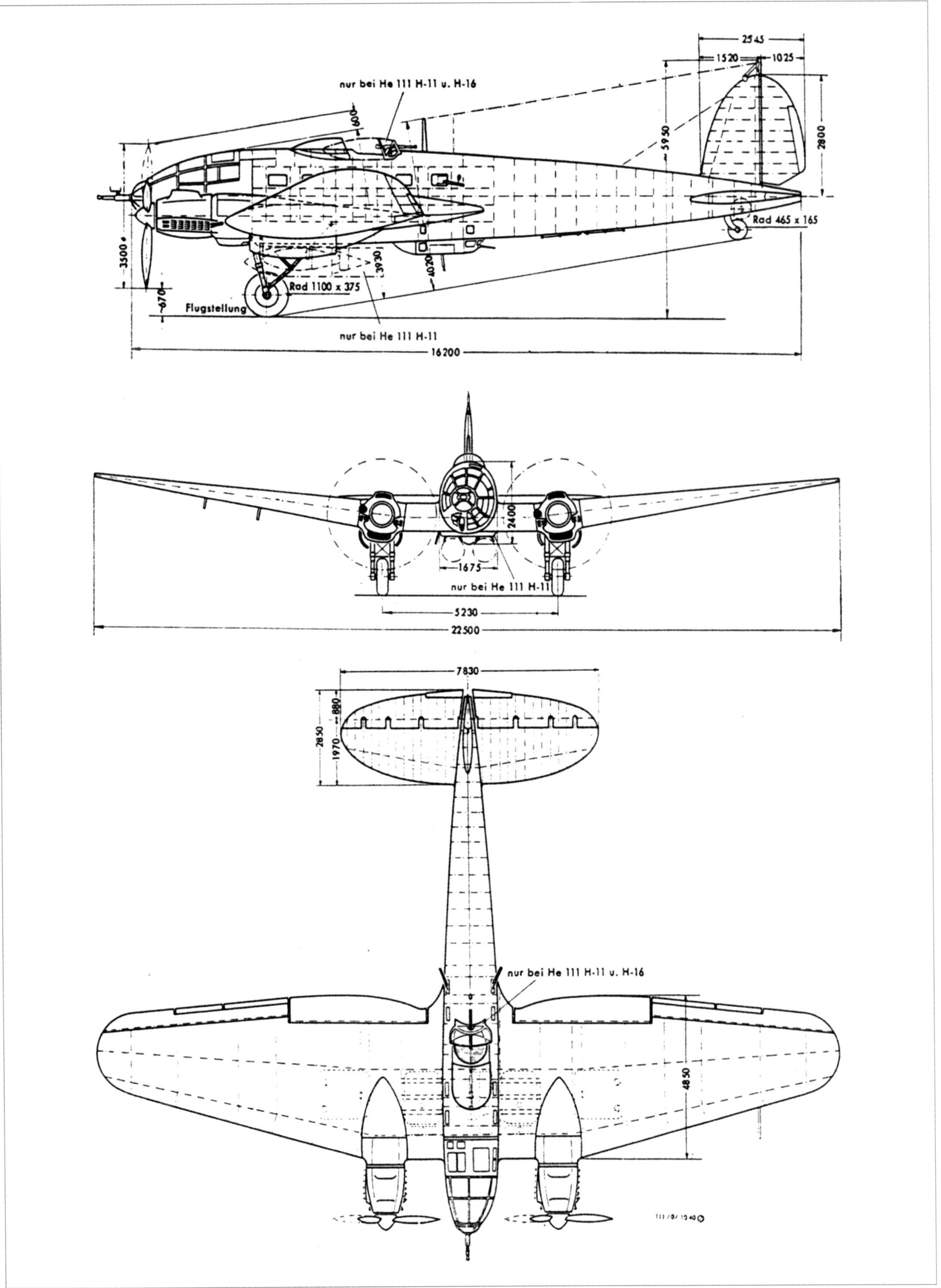
2545
1520
1025
nur bei He 111 H-11 u. H-16
600
5950
2800
Rad 465 x 165
3500
3930
4020
Rad 1100 x 375
670
Flugstellung
nur bei He 111 H-11
16200
2400
1675
nur bei He 111 H-11
5230
22500
7830
880
2850
1970
nur bei He 111 H-11 u. H-16
4850

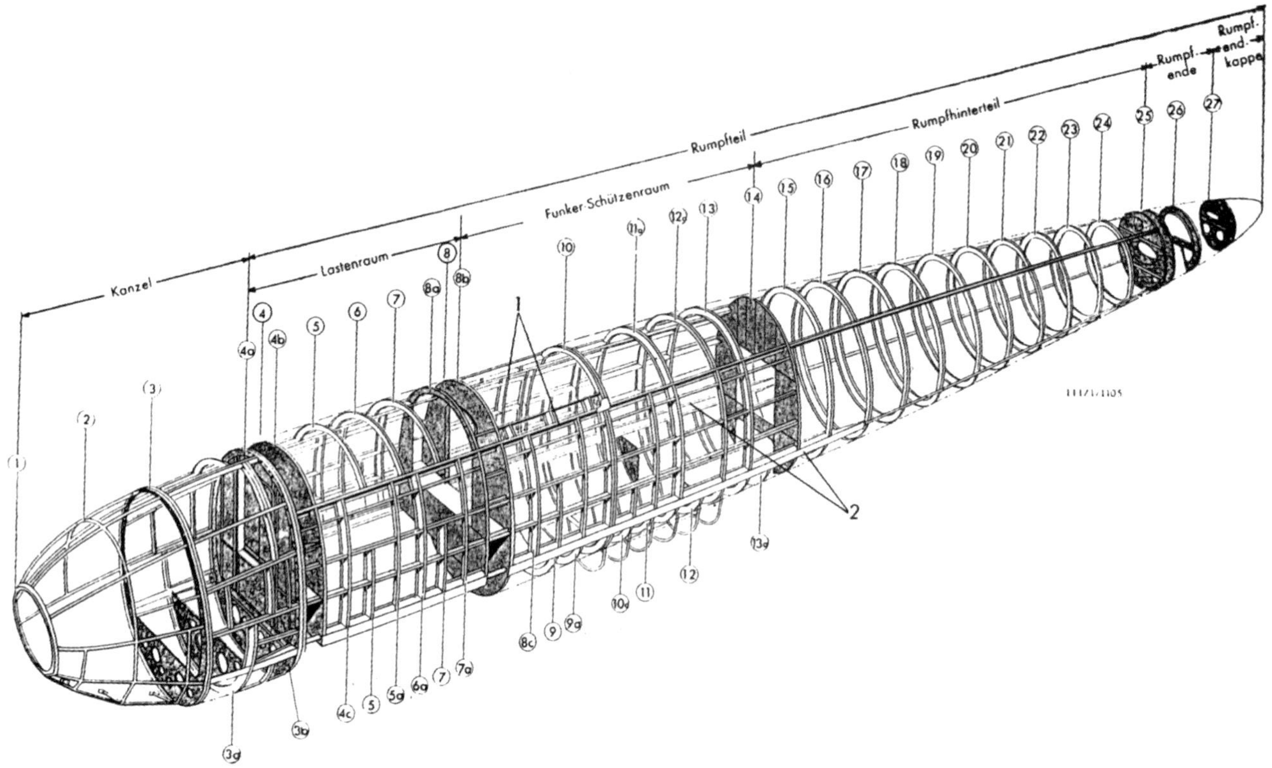

Kanzel
Lastenraum
Funker-Schützenraum
Rumpfteil
Rumpfhinterteil
Rumpf-ende
Rumpf-end-kappe

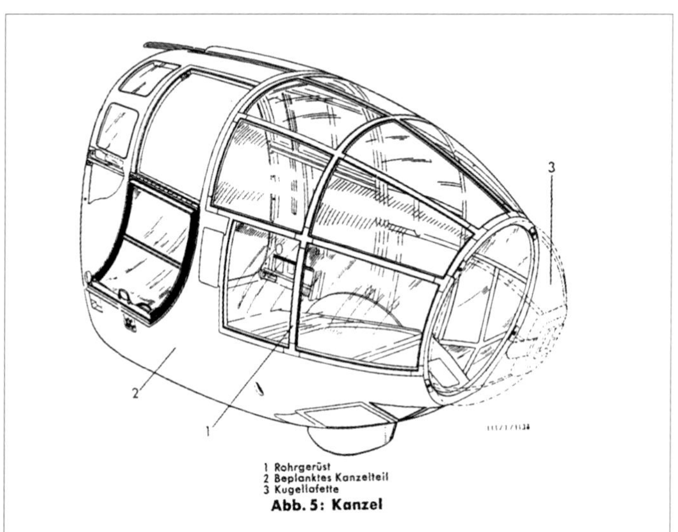

1 Rohrgerüst
2 Beplanktes Kanzelteil
3 Kugellafette
Abb. 5: Kanzel

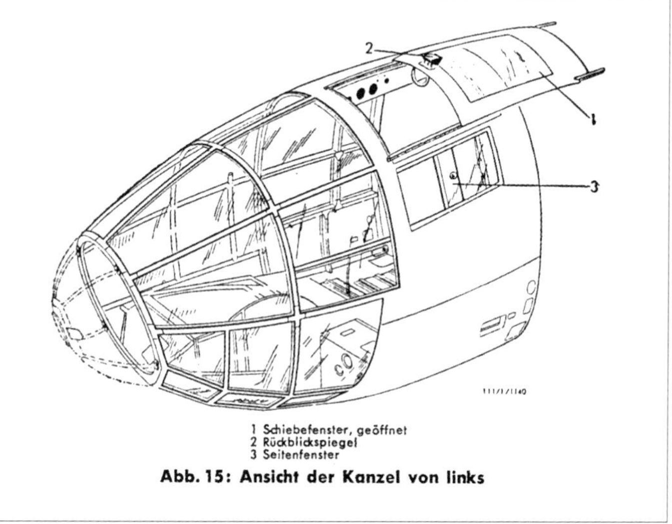

1 Schiebefenster, geöffnet
2 Rückblickspiegel
3 Seitenfenster
Abb. 15: Ansicht der Kanzel von links

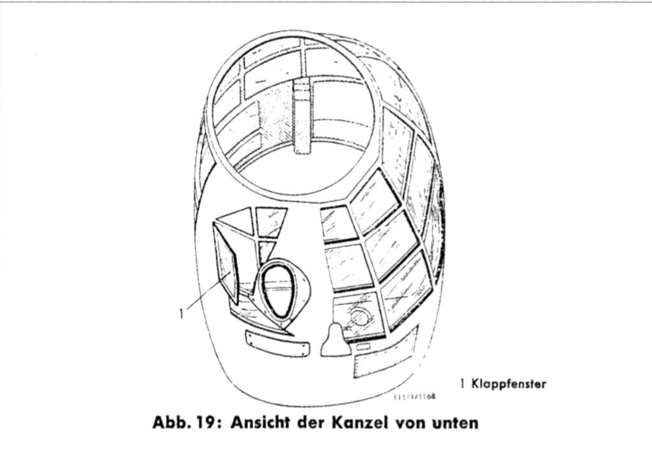

1 Klappfenster
Abb. 19: Ansicht der Kanzel von unten

Top: **The fuselage frames and bulkheads (He 111H-16, Part 1).**
Key: Upper row (from left to right): cockpit (1-4a), fuselage (4a to end)
Lower row: bomb-bay (4a-8a), radio operator/gunner's compartment (8b-14), rear fuselage (14-25), fuselage tail (25-27) and tailcone (27 to end).

Above left: **The cockpit.**
Key: 1 Cockpit framework; 2 Sheet-covered portion; 3 Nose gun-mount.

Above right: **Port side view of the cockpit.**
Key: 1 Sliding window; 2 Rear-view mirror; 3 Side window, opened.

Left: **Cockpit view from beneath. Key: 1 Hinged window.**

Opposite page, top: **The bomb-bay (He 111H-16, Part 1). Key:**
1 Load-bearing frames (beams); 2 Sliding doors; 3 ESAC bomb containers
4 Lubricant pump installation; 5 Storage batteries.

Opposite page, bottom: **Centre fuselage structure (He 111H-16, Part 1). Key:**
1 Upper fuselage longeron; 2 Lower fuselage longeron; 3 Floor longeron
4 Side windows. Circled numbers are fuselage transverse frames.

of the fuselage is brightened by the insertion of several windows. On either side in the radio operator/gunner's compartment there are two windows, while in the bomb-bay there are two blind window flaps positioned at the same level. Furthermore, in the central compartment, visibility in vertical directions is provided by vision panels in the ventral blister and in the opening to the dorsal B-Stand armament cupola. This fuselage segment comprises the bomb-bay vertical bulkheads (frames 4-8), the radio operator/gunner's compartment (frames 8-14), the rear fuselage (frames 14-25) and the fuselage tail (frames 25-27), the external attachments comprising the tailcone and the fuselage/wingroot fillets.

Bomb-Bay (He 111H-16)

The bomb-bay, extending from the fuselage vertical frames 4-8, is restricted on its lower side by the load-bearing girders of the wing centre section. It is separated from the cockpit rear wall by a two-part sliding door. In each of the door halves is a peephole that can be covered over by a sliding panel. In the bomb-bay, on both the left and right sides, there are four vertically positioned ESAC bomb magazines and, in the centre gangway, the lubricant pump installation.

1 Lastenträger (Tragwerk)
2 Schiebetür
3 Bombenschächte (ESAC)
4 Schmierstoffumpumpanlage
5 Akku

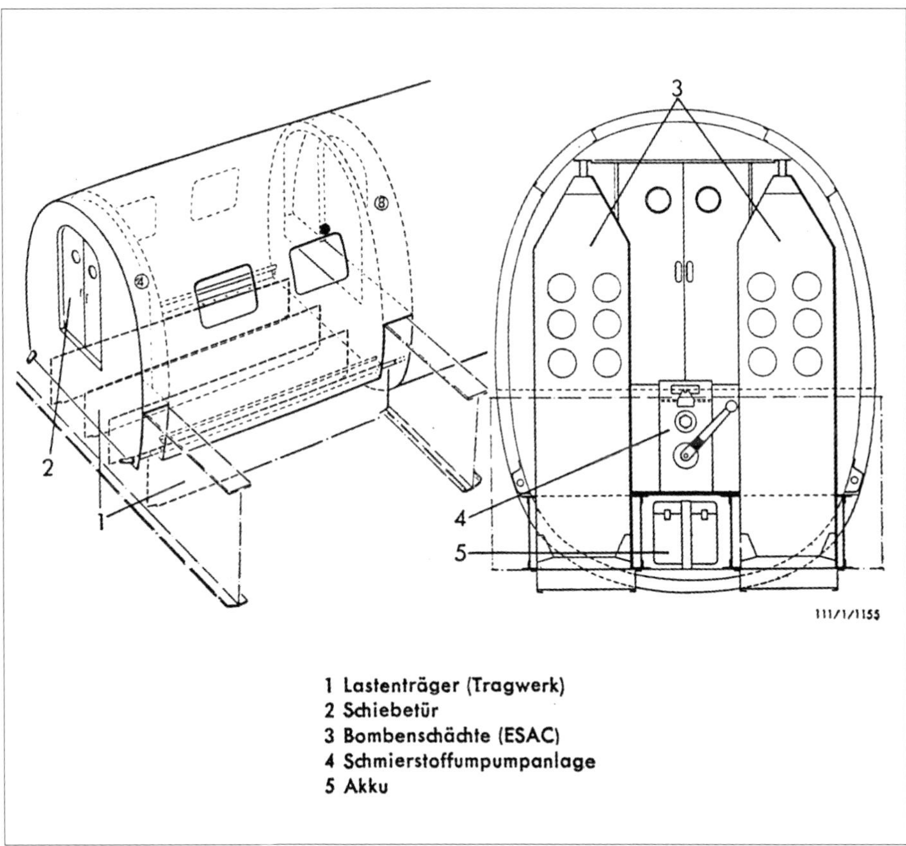

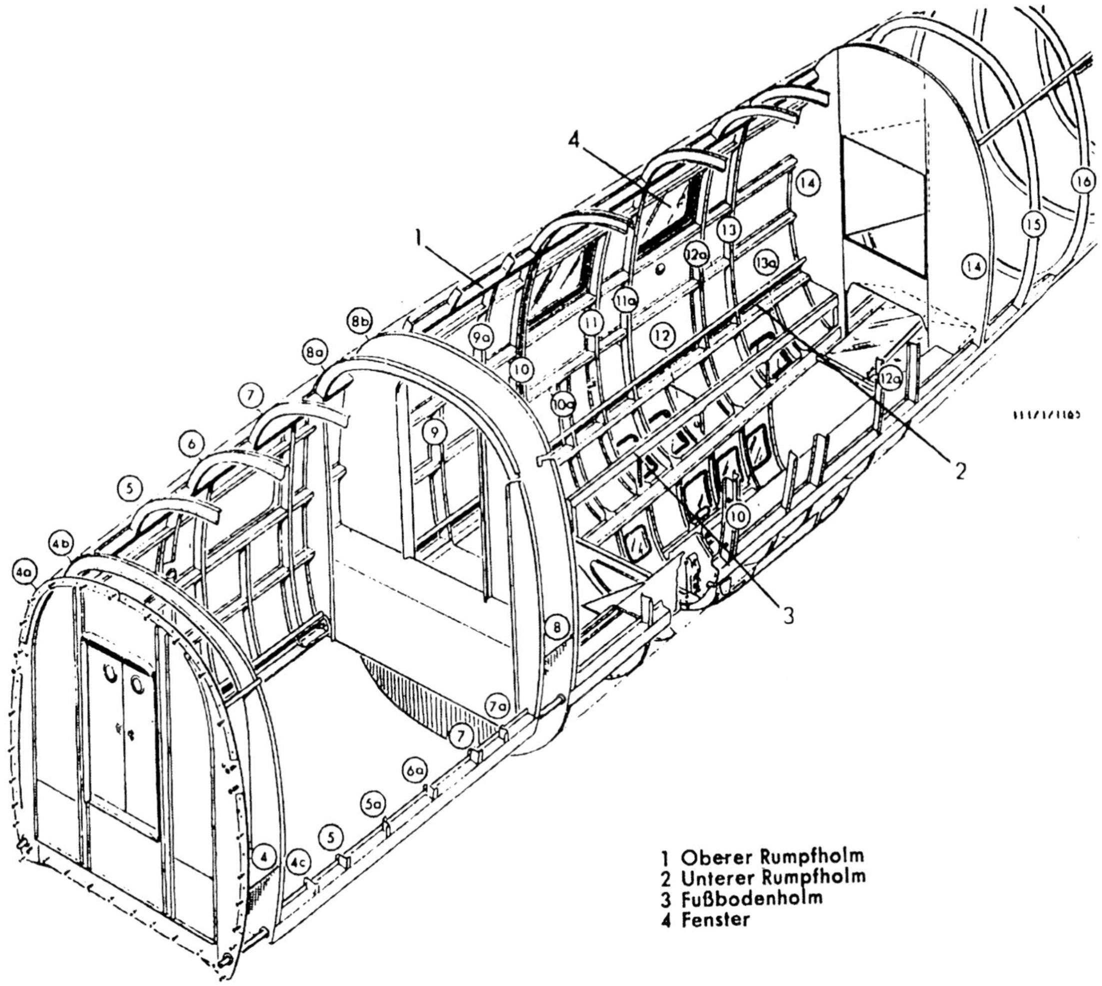

1 Oberer Rumpfholm
2 Unterer Rumpfholm
3 Fußbodenholm
4 Fenster

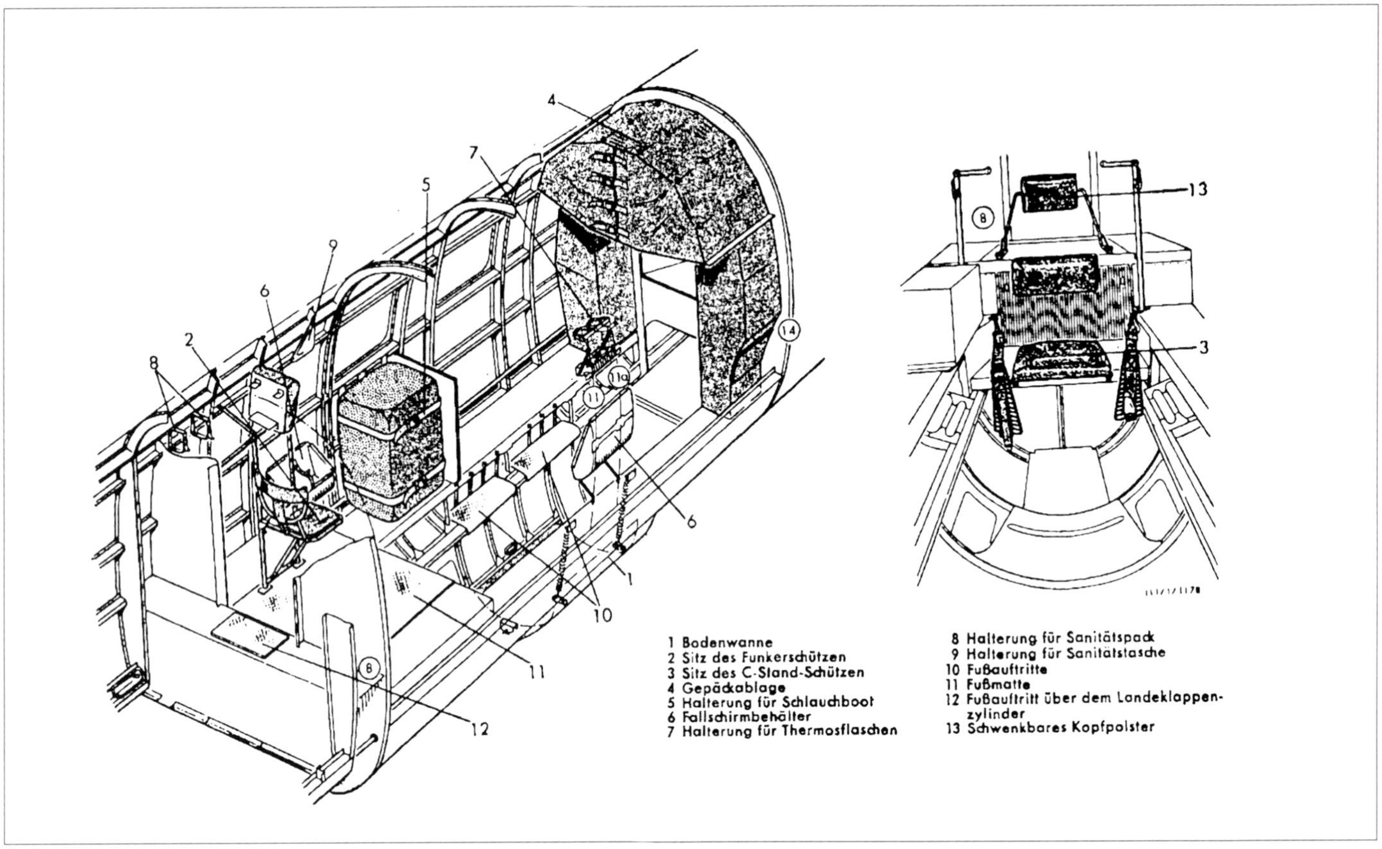

1 Bodenwanne
2 Sitz des Funkerschützen
3 Sitz des C-Stand-Schützen
4 Gepäckablage
5 Halterung für Schlauchboot
6 Fallschirmbehälter
7 Halterung für Thermosflaschen
8 Halterung für Sanitätspack
9 Halterung für Sanitätstasche
10 Fußauftritte
11 Fußmatte
12 Fußauftritt über dem Landeklappen-zylinder
13 Schwenkbares Kopfpolster

Space division in the radio operator/gunner's compartment (He 111H-16, Part 1). Key:

1 Ventral gondola
2 Radio operator/gunner's seat
3 C-Stand gunner's seat
4 Luggage enclosure
5 Dinghy fastening straps
6 Parachute container
7 Thermos flask holders
8 First-aid pack supports
9 Sanitary/first-aid bag
10 Foot rests
11 Foot mat
12 Foot step above landing flap cylinder
13 Adjustable upholstered head pad

(Circled numbers not listed).

1 Rückenschutzpanzerung f. d. B-Stand (abwerfbar)
2 Seitenschutzpanzerung (abwerfbar)
3 Kopfschutzpanzerung f. d. C-Stand (abwerfbar)
4 Untere Panzerung für den C-Stand
5 Panzerschutz für Schlauchboot (abwerfbar)
6 Kopfschutzpanzerung für den B-Stand

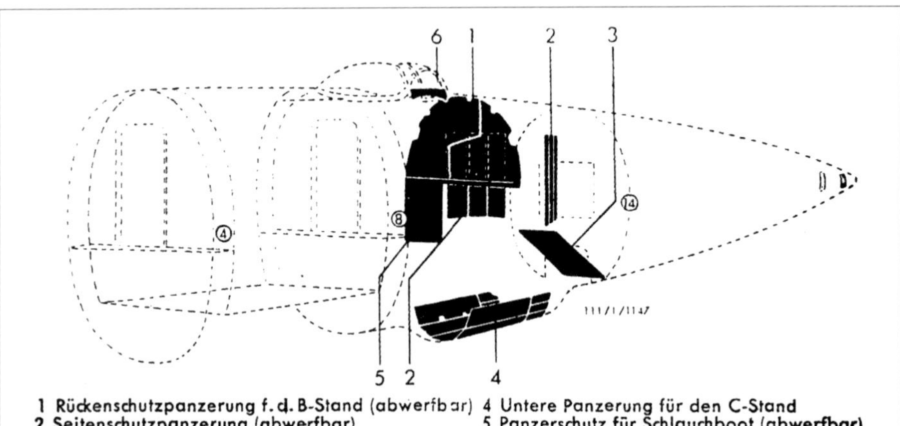

Armour-plating in the radio operator/gunner's compartment (He 111H-16, Part 1). Key:

1 B-Stand rear armour-plating (jettisonable)
2 Side armour-plating (jettisonable)
3 C-Stand head armour-plating (jettisonable)
4 C-Stand ventral armour-plating
5 Dinghy armour-plating (jettisonable)
6 B-Stand head armour-plating.

1 Anschlußbolzen für Leitwerk
2 Anschlußbolzen für Sporntraverse
3 Klappe
4 Anschlußbolzen für Sporngabel
5 Blindstopfen für das Heißen

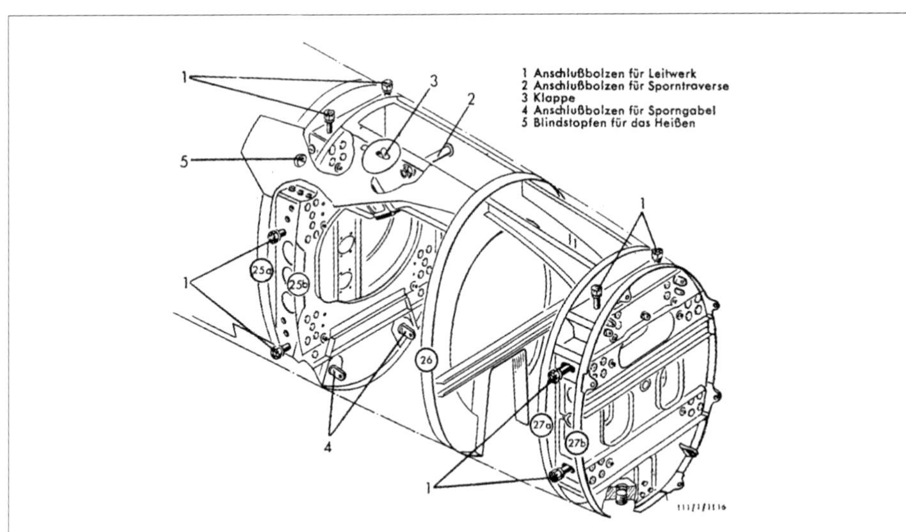

The tail section (He 111H-16, Part 1). Key:

1 Fin and tailplane connecting bolts
2 Tailwheel traverse connecting bolts
3 Hatch cover
4 Wheel-fork connecting bolts
5 Plugs for the hoist

(Circled numbers are fuselage transverse frames).

For the 'B' Rüstzustand [equipment condition] there are two hatches in the fuselage roof for filling the fuel and lubricant tanks. [These were installed in place of the vertical ESAC bomb containers – Author.] Beneath the floor compartment is housed the battery compartment and the geballte Ladung [self-destruction explosive charge – Author]. Above the door at frame 4 is an attachment for the cable to the explosive charge…

The lowermost main spars are joined to the spar boxes in frames 4 and 8 by fittings for the wing centre section attachment bolts. The wing spars are inserted into these spar boxes. The wing skin consists of four shaped Elektron sheets provided with metal strips to provide stiffening at the supporting points. The skin panels are attached to the fuselage and wing centre section by flush screws.

Radio Operator/Gunner's Compartment

Installations in this compartment, which extends from transverse frames 8 to 14, include:

- The Plexiglas sliding hood above the B-Stand, the folding seat in the B-Stand, and the armour-plated as well as Plexiglas-equipped ventral cupola built as a C-Stand with combined entrance/emergency escape hatch.
- The upholstered seat for the C-Stand gunner and footrests to the left and right in the flooring.
- A baggage storage compartment, a protective housing for the towing antenna, two parachute containers, and stowage for the dinghy, supports for the first-aid pack, Thermos flasks, brake cable, first-aid pouch, and so on.
- Additionally, the radio operator/gunner's compartment installations include the windows, the padding for the ventral gondola and armour protection.

To protect the radio operator/gunner from the external airflow, there is a forward-sliding hood made of Plexiglas above the B-Stand. This connects at its rear end with the turret substructure, which is also of Plexiglas. To open the sliding hood, the anchoring lever is pushed forward, whereupon the holding pin is withdrawn from its countersunk cylinder. On moving the sliding hood forwards, the pin glides along the groove and is locked by spring pressure into the front cylindrical opening. In its closed state the sliding roof is secured against the external airflow by a sealing strip.

The ventral gondola is located between frames 9 and 12a and forms a trough-shaped enclosure for the C-Stand in the region of the radio operator/gunner's compartment. It has a Plexiglas frame that forms a gun position at the rear. Behind the external skin of the front portion of the gondola there are two windows, one each on the left and right side. The gun- position side walls likewise have two lateral windows and a further two rear window panels. Entry and emergency exit is via an armoured hatch beneath the left side of the gondola, the hatch being hinged on the left side. To protect the C-Stand gunner, the side walls and the ventral gondola hatch are armour-plated.

Rear Fuselage

The rear fuselage consists of a conically tapered structure that supports the empennage and houses the tailwheel. For this section, the Handbook has this to say:

The fuselage rear section lies between frames 14 and 25, in which is housed the fuel quick-release conduit, the oil-pressure conduit for tailwheel operation, the rods and trim cables of the rudder and elevator controls, and the electrical distributor box and control runs. The compartment for the master compass is located between frames 19 and 20. Installations in the rear fuselage comprise the door in frame 14, the emergency provisions container, and the jacks for guidance of the control leads. The latter are positioned on the left side of the rear fuselage, fastened to the frames and supported by two struts. On the lower portion of frame 25 are two lugs for attachment of the tailwheel fork. In the double frame 25 are two hoists, and in double frame 27 is the lifting jack for the rear fuselage.

The tailwheel is housed in a three-layered closed compartment when retracted, and is bolted to the lower skin and frames 25 and 26. In front of the tailwheel compartment is an airflow deflector and a sprung flap, which closes when the wheel is retracted and opens downward when it is lowered. Between frames 25 and 26 there is a double-walled longitudinal connection in which the shock-absorber leg is housed. Two hand-hole hatches in the outer covering enable access to the tailwheel position bolts.

At frame 27 is a sheet-rubber covering affixed and made dust-tight by means of adhesive tape, which encases the control runs passing through the bulkhead. The tailcone rounds off the rear fuselage and covers the built-in catapult and towing mechanism. This cap is made of Elektron sheet and has quick-release hatch openings above and below to allow access to the interior fittings.

The Empennage

The typical Heinkel empennage area gave the He 111 an extremely elegant appearance. The following technical description in the words of the Handbook Part 3 of July 1943 provides an insight into this area.

Tailplane

Each of the tailplane halves consists of the forward spar, the rear spar, the curved leading and trailing edge surfaces, the sheet skin, fittings, and the detachable fuselage fillet. The ribs consist largely of lattice or truss ribs and are divided by the front spar into nose and rear ribs. The spars consist of upper and lower U-shaped sheet profiles stiffened by intermediate web ribs. At the root ends of the front and rear spar are dural connecting clasps, which serve as attachment points for the tailplane to the fuselage by means of four bolts.

Because of its adjustability, in the forward clasp there are three pairs of holes that enable incidence angles settings of -1.5°, -3° and -4.5°. The uppermost pair are normally used for the -1.5° setting. The rear tailplane clasp has a centrally arranged bolt that enables the tailplane to be adjusted in the rear fuselage fitting.

In aircraft without armour-plating and without rear armament, or alternatively without a catapult take-off hook, the tailplane is set at -4.5°. The attachment points for the elevator on each side are at four outriggers on the rear spar.

Elevators

The elevators consist of a spar, the ribs, the curved trailing-edge bow, trim tab, surface covering and fittings, and are attached to the tailplane at four locations…

The nose of the rudder serves as an internal mass-balance. Within it, at the Lager II attachment point, there is a removable compensating weight with which the elevator is balanced up to 20%. The brackets consist of U-shaped fittings on to which they are attached. Lager II is axially fixed, while the others are axially movable. Elevator trim tab deflection is limited by rubber stop settings. These are screwed into Lager II and are moved with the outrigger to the stop. The elevator trim tab serves as a load relief as well as for trimming.

Fin

The fin structure consists of the forward spar, the rear spar, the ribs, the curved leading-edge bow, the surface covering, the fittings and the detachable fuselage fillet. Construction is the same as for the tailplane. The fin is likewise attached to the fuselage by two bolts at each of the front and rear spars. The attachments for the rudder are located behind the rear spar, into which the connecting bolts pass. In the upper portion of the fin are three lugs for antenna attachment. The curved fillet at the base serves as an intermediate join between the fuselage and the fin, and has small hatches to enable access to the handgrip covers over the fittings inside the fuselage.

Rudder

The rudder consists essentially of the rudder nose spar, the rear auxiliary spar, the ribs, the skin and the fittings. The rudder is open at the nose (!) and is attached at three points to the fin. The brackets consist of U-shaped channels in which the rudder is fixed. Lager I, on which the weight of the rudder is supported, is axially fixed, the others being arranged to be

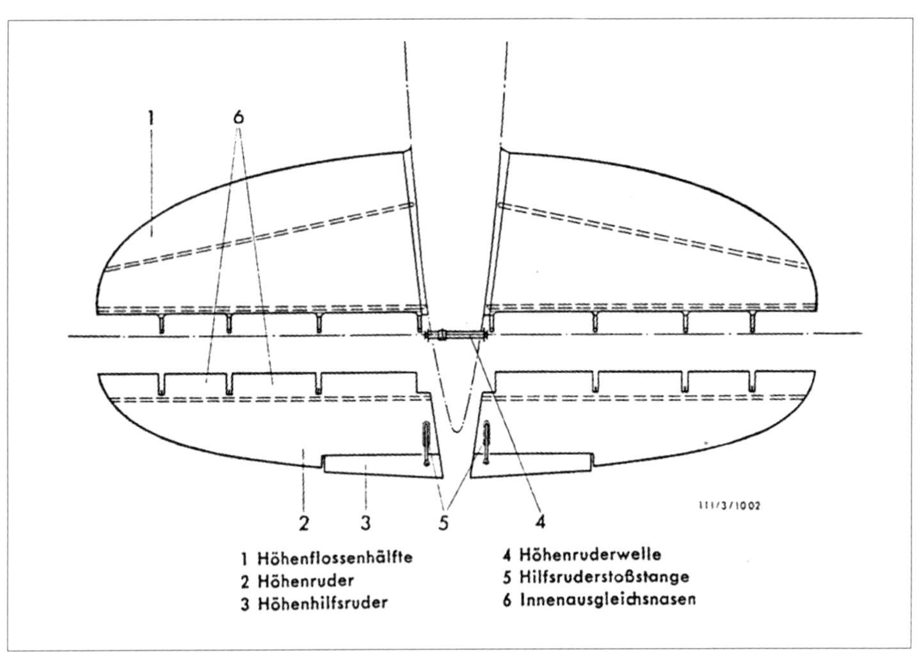

axially movable. At Lager I are the rubber stops for limiting rudder deflection. Further stop fixtures are located on the control runs inside the fuselage. Assisted by two forward-directed struts at Lager II is a horizontal mass-balance bow made of cast steel with which the rudder is 100% compensated. This bow has free movement within the cut-out provided for it in the fin. The rudder actuating mechanism is located in the fuselage and attached to the rudder by flanges at Lager I. At its lower end is the power lever, which is connected to the control rods…

The rudder trim tab is attached to the rudder at three points on the auxiliary spar and is actuated by a leather-covered strut, which is attached by a shackle to the trim-tab actuator.

The description of the structural groups in the fuselage area ends at this point. The rudder control mechanism is treated separately under the 'Controls' section on page 49.

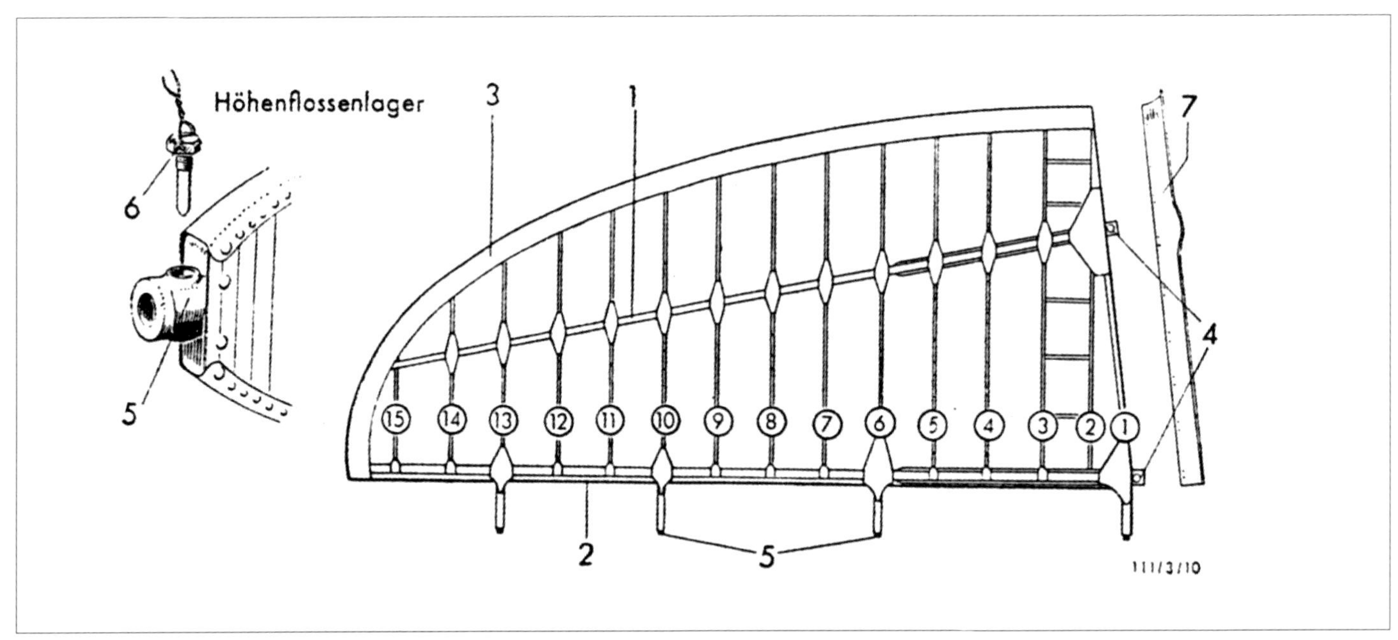

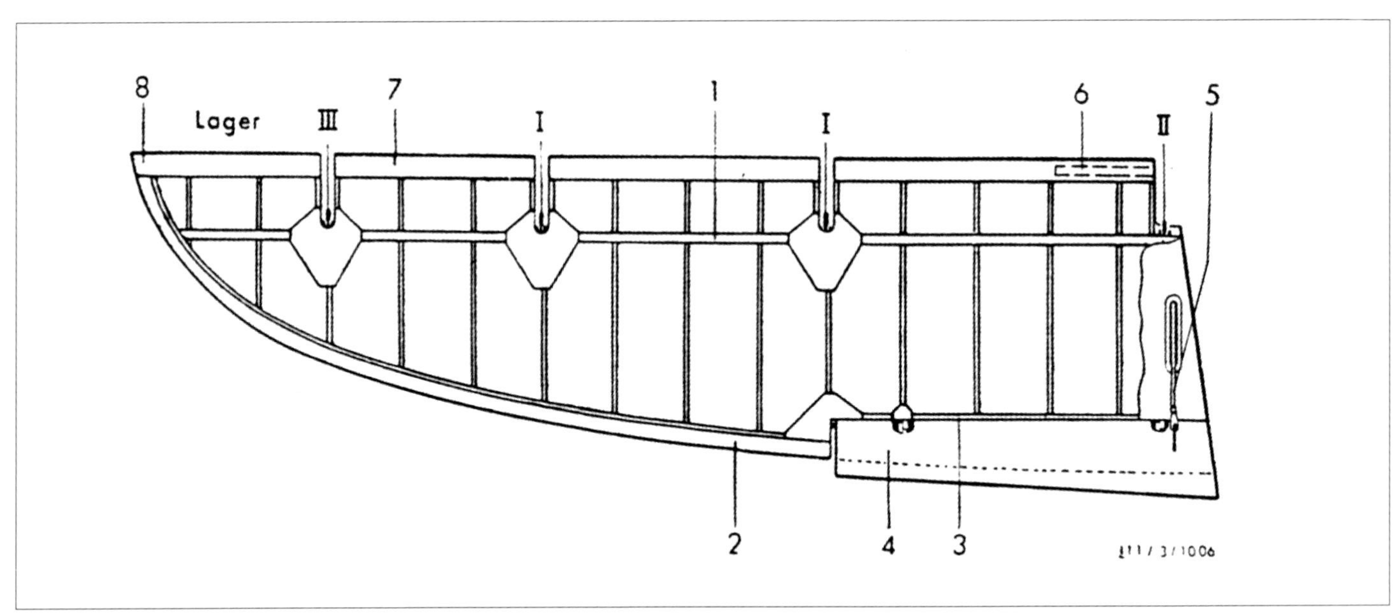

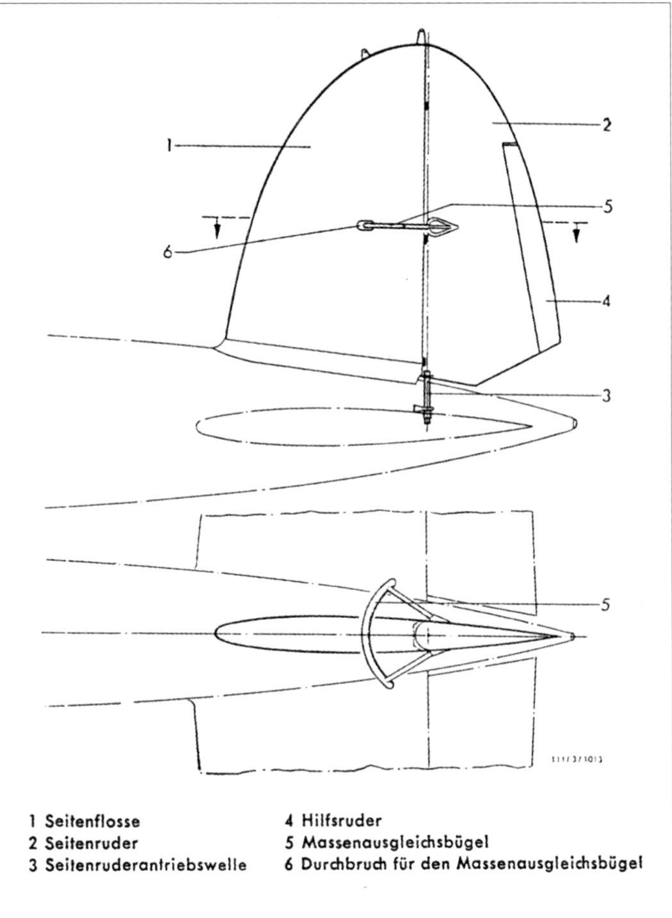

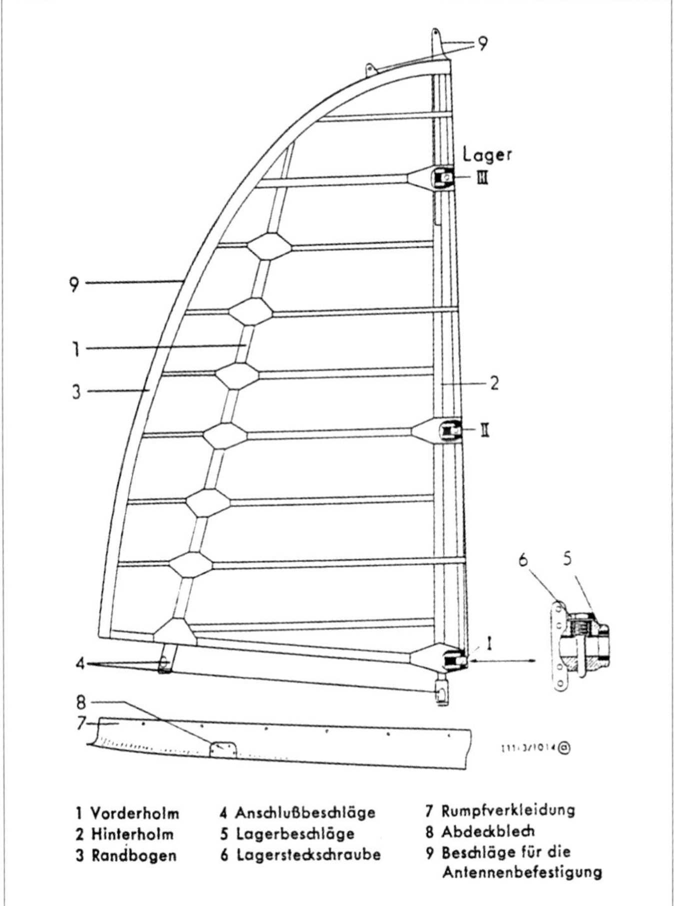

Above left: **Fin and rudder construction (He 111H-16, Part 3). Key:**

1 Vertical fin; 2 Rudder; 3 Rudder actuator; 4 Trim tab
5 Mass-balance bow; 6 Opening for the mass-balance.

Above right: **The fin structure (He 111H-16, Part 3). Key:**

1 Front spar; 2 Rear spar; 3 Leading-edge bow; 4 Spar attachments
5 Rudder attachments; 6 Lager insert plugs; 7 Fuselage fillet
8 Access cover; 9 Antenna attachment lugs

Lager I/II/III – attachment points.

Right: **The rudder, with attachment points Lager I to III and the mass-balance. Key: beweglich = movable; fest = fixed.**

1 Rudder nose spar; 2 Auxiliary spar; 3 Trailing-edge bow; 4 Trim tab
5 Trim tab actuator; 6 Rudder mass-balance bow; 7 Supporting arms
8 Support covering; 9 Attachment holder; 10 Resitex disc
11 Electrical bridge/jumper.

Illustrations on the opposite page:

Top: **The connecting points for the elevators (He 111H-16, Part 3). Key:**

1 Tailplane half; 2 Elevator; 3 Elevator trim tab; 4 Elevator shaft
5 Trim tab actuator; 6 Internal nose balances.

Centre: **The tailplane internal structure (He 111H-16, Part 3). Key:**

1 Front spar; 2 Rear spar; 3 Leading-edge bow; 4 Attachment lugs
5 Lager insert plugs; 6 Attachment bolts; 7 Fuselage fairing.

Bottom: **Elevator details (He 111H-16, Part 3). Key:**

1 Elevator spar; 2 Trailing-edge bow; 3 Auxiliary spar; 4 Trim tab
5 Trim tab actuator; 6 Balance weight; 7 Inner nose balance
8 Solid end-piece

Lager I /II/ III – attachment points.

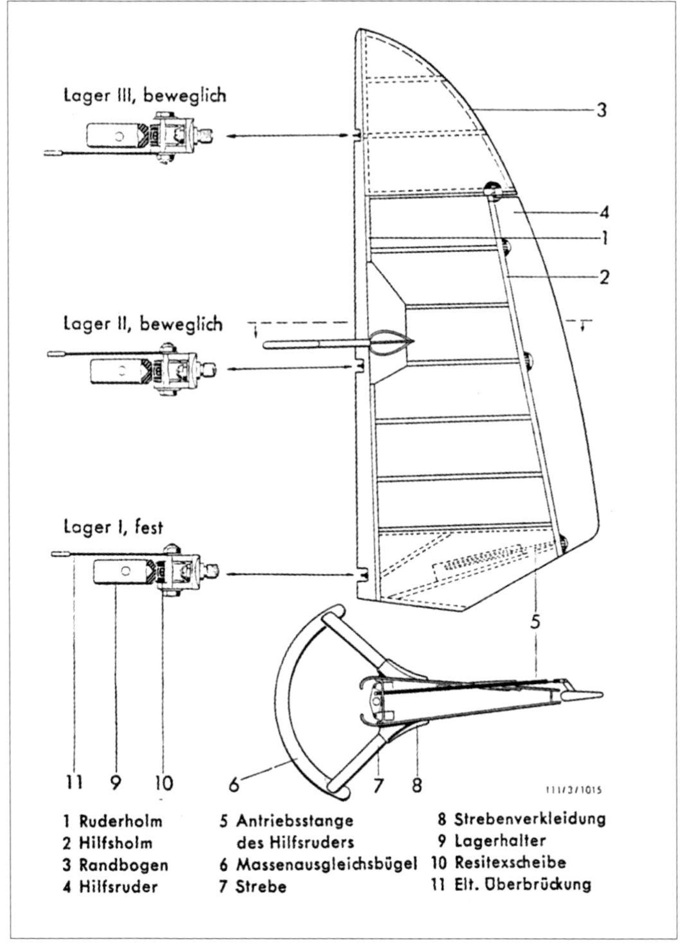

The Wing

This lifting element had the typical Heinkel elliptical form that was used in several designs by this aircraft manufacturer and which became its 'trademark'. A number of Japanese aircraft, as well as the British Spitfire, also used this prominent design feature. In the course of He 111 development, various wing planforms were employed and, although differing in structural detail, the elliptical shape was largely retained in the simplified production version. The elliptical planform with a straight leading-edge, simplified for production reasons, was first applied to the He 111F. The description, illustrations and textual extracts relating to the wing are taken from the He 111H-16 Handbook, Part 5.

General Description

The two-spar cantilever wing consists of the centre section attached to the fuselage, and the two outer wing sections. The deep centre section is horizontal and is integral with the fuselage. The upward-canted outer ends of the centre section and the outboard portions have a 7° dihedral and have full-span trailing-edge ailerons and flaps. The rectangular centre section trailing-edge tapers inwards in the wing root region. The trapezoidal outer sections end in elliptically rounded wingtips.

The wing profile has conventional curvature and incidence. The wing chord of the centre section is constant in thickness and reduces proportionally towards the wingtips. Furthermore, the wing incidence is also reduced towards the tips and results in a certain amount of twist.

The load-bearing components consist of two spars, the ribs and the stressed-skin covering. The structure is largely of dural or dural sheeting, the highly stressed parts such as fittings, bolts, etc, being fabricated mainly of steel or Elektron. The smooth sheet skin is attached with countersunk rivets.

The entire wing leading-edge serves as a 'Kuto-Nase' for the purpose of cutting balloon cables. (In future this Kuto-Nase will be dispensed with on the He 111H-16.)

The wing centre section is attached to the fuselage by two bolts at each of the front and rear spars, and additionally by two rearward-directed bracing stays to the fuselage. The outer wings are attached to the centre section at two connecting points at the front and main spars. Wing torque is taken up by the ribs and skin panels stiffened by curved formers, and at the joins between the centre and outer wing sections, at four attachment points, and led into the fuselage.

Wing Centre Section

The periphery of the wing centre section is rectangular. The leading-edge features cut-outs for the powerplants and the trailing-edge cut-outs for the landing flaps. The centre section is horizontal, each outer end having a 7° dihedral. The riveted framework consists principally of:

- The one-piece front and rear spars.
- The nose, centre, and end ribs.
- The chord-wise walls I, II and III built as ribs.
- The girders supporting the fuel tanks.
- The four load-bearers in the fuselage region.
- The wing skin.

To this component, to the left and right on each side, are attached the following large detachable assemblies:

- Attachment fittings for the wing, undercarriage, powerplants and undercarriage doors.
- The upper and lower engine cowling profiles.
- A cover and strut for the fuel tank compartment.
- The nose covering.
- The front spar firewall and two fireproof nose ribs at the powerplant cut-out.
- Two end compartments at the landing flap cut-out.
- A supporting frame for jettisonable weapons.
- The five-part transverse frames covering.
- The wing/fuselage bracing struts.

The spars are built as double-T load-bearers. They consist of the upper and lower spar girders, the spar webbing and the Z-profiled stiffeners riveted to them fore and aft. Besides the cut-out for the powerplants is the nose portion of the wing ahead of the front spar, consisting of the nose ribs, the divided nose spar, and the nose skinning stiffened by profiles. The cables, fittings, tubing and installations in this nose section are accessible from above by a large hatch, attached by three quick-release locks.

The front spar, on its powerplant side, has above and below it arched fire protection bows on to which the fireproof bulkhead is screwed, the firewall fitting covering the aileron control rods located there. To provide protection for the lubricant cooler, an armoured plate is screwed a short distance away on to the ventral portion of the firewall.

Close to the fuselage, the front and rear spars are connected by four load-bearing beams. These are connected to the spars' Z-profiles and supported laterally by stays attached to the neighbouring ribs. These consist of an upper and lower spar beam and a wall plate strengthened by vertical profiles. Beneath the two left-hand load-bearers in the He 111H-14 and H-16 there is a load-bearing frame for the carriage of jettisonable weapons, while on the H-11 there is a larger load-bearing frame beneath all four load-carriers, which itself belongs to the jettisonable weapon load. This load-bearing frame is bridged by three rubber-covered diagonal struts, which serve to support the fuselage fuel tanks.

The centre wing ribs between the front and rear spars – centre ribs 1, 7 and 11 – serve as transverse partition walls I, II and III. These consist of full metal ribs with upper and lower beams. In the space between I and II are the centre ribs with supports for powerplant container suspension. These load-bearers consist of U-shaped profiles of dural sheet. The powerplant container compartment is supported in its lower area by a removable strut and covered on its underside by a large access panel.

A console type of load support is attached to the transverse wall in the connecting undercarriage compartment, serving as the attachment for a retraction jack for undercarriage operation. Among other items, the leg lock with signal switch is positioned on this support. Behind the firewall are located the two detachable undercarriage doors, each attached at two positions to the undersides of partition walls II and III.

The rear engine cowling profiles on the wing upper side behind the firewall, and on the wing lower side behind the undercarriage doors, are detachable. The upper profile rests on the wing surface covering, while the lower profile is formed to shape and replaces the wing covering.

Behind the end rib space are two detachable end plates that cover the nose of the landing flaps located there. Between the two end coverings is the similarly detachable end piece of the landing flap ribs (end rib 7), to which the adjustable support fitting is attached. The upper and lower gap coverings of this space are each formed as two-part smooth sheets, which cover the gap between the wing centre and outer sections, these being fixed by angle brackets and fastenings.

The wing centre section is attached to the fuselage by four connecting bolts at the forward and rear spars, at the fuselage double frames 4 and 8. The connecting fittings consist of dural butts, each having eight screw bolts and attached to the Z-profile spars. Above these

**Wing centre section (He 111H-16, Part 5). Key:
1 Forward spar; 2 Rear spar;
3 Load-supporting structure; 4. Rib wall I;
5 Wing nose section; 6. Inner rib firewall;
7 Outer rib firewall;
8 Engine cowling upper rear profile;
9 Engine cowling lower rear profile;
10 Undercarriage doors;
11 End covering plates;
12 Wing-joint covering strip;
13 Wing connection fitting;
14 Spar connection fitting;
15 Powerplant connection fittings;
16 Undercarriage support joint;
17 Wing hoist position; 18. Detachable strut;
19 Balloon cable cutter profile.**

**Wing outer section rib and spar locations (He 111H-16, Part 5). Key:
1 Forward spar; 2 Rear spar; 3 End spar
4 Nose rib; 5 Centre rib; 6 Rear rib
7 Access hatch; 8 Landing light; 9 Pitot tube
10 Recognition light; 11 Fuel tank compartment
12 Balloon cable cutter
Schnitt = cross-section (A-B)
Querruderlager = aileron attachment points
Landeklappenlager = landing flap attachment points; verstellbar = adjustable.**

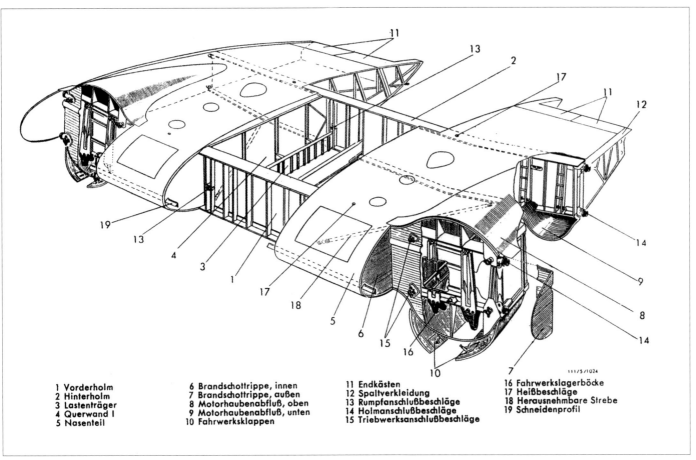

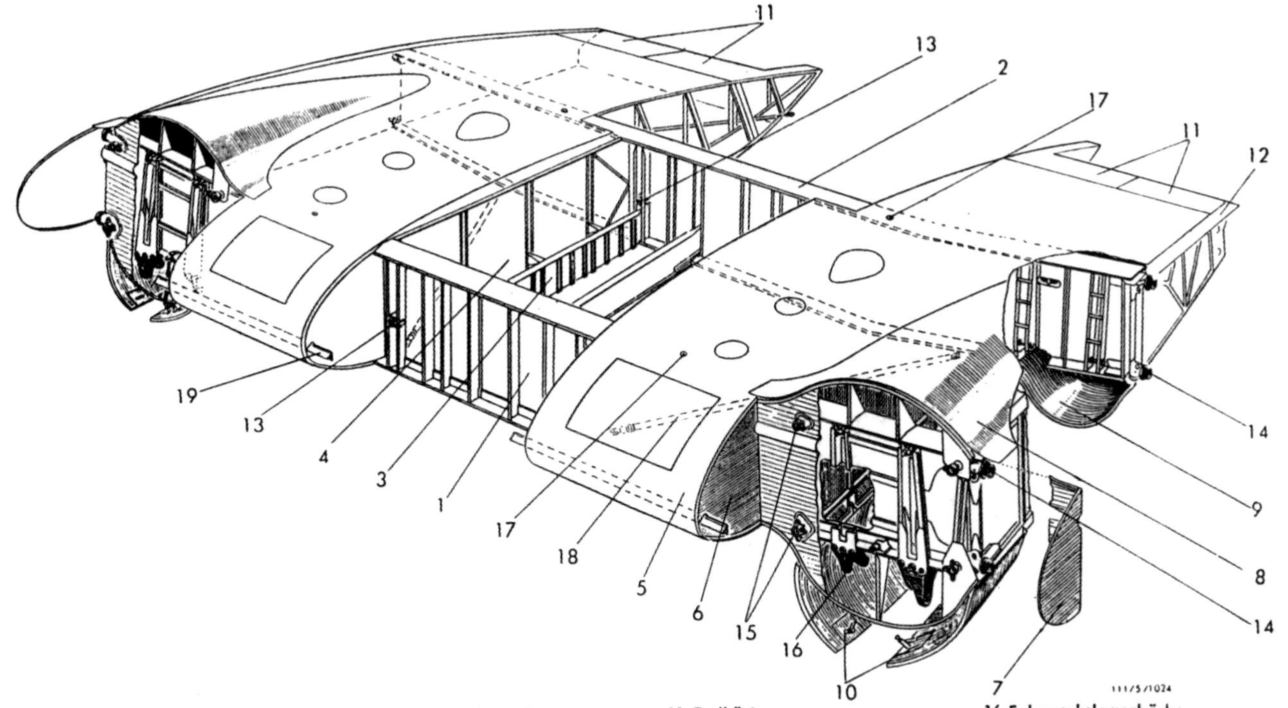

111/5/1024

1 Vorderholm
2 Hinterholm
3 Lastenträger
4 Querwand I
5 Nasenteil
6 Brandschottrippe, innen
7 Brandschottrippe, außen
8 Motorhaubenabfluß, oben
9 Motorhaubenabfluß, unten
10 Fahrwerksklappen
11 Endkästen
12 Spaltverkleidung
13 Rumpfanschlußbeschläge
14 Holmanschlußbeschläge
15 Triebwerksanschlußbeschläge
16 Fahrwerkslagerböcke
17 Heißbeschläge
18 Herausnehmbare Strebe
19 Schneidenprofil

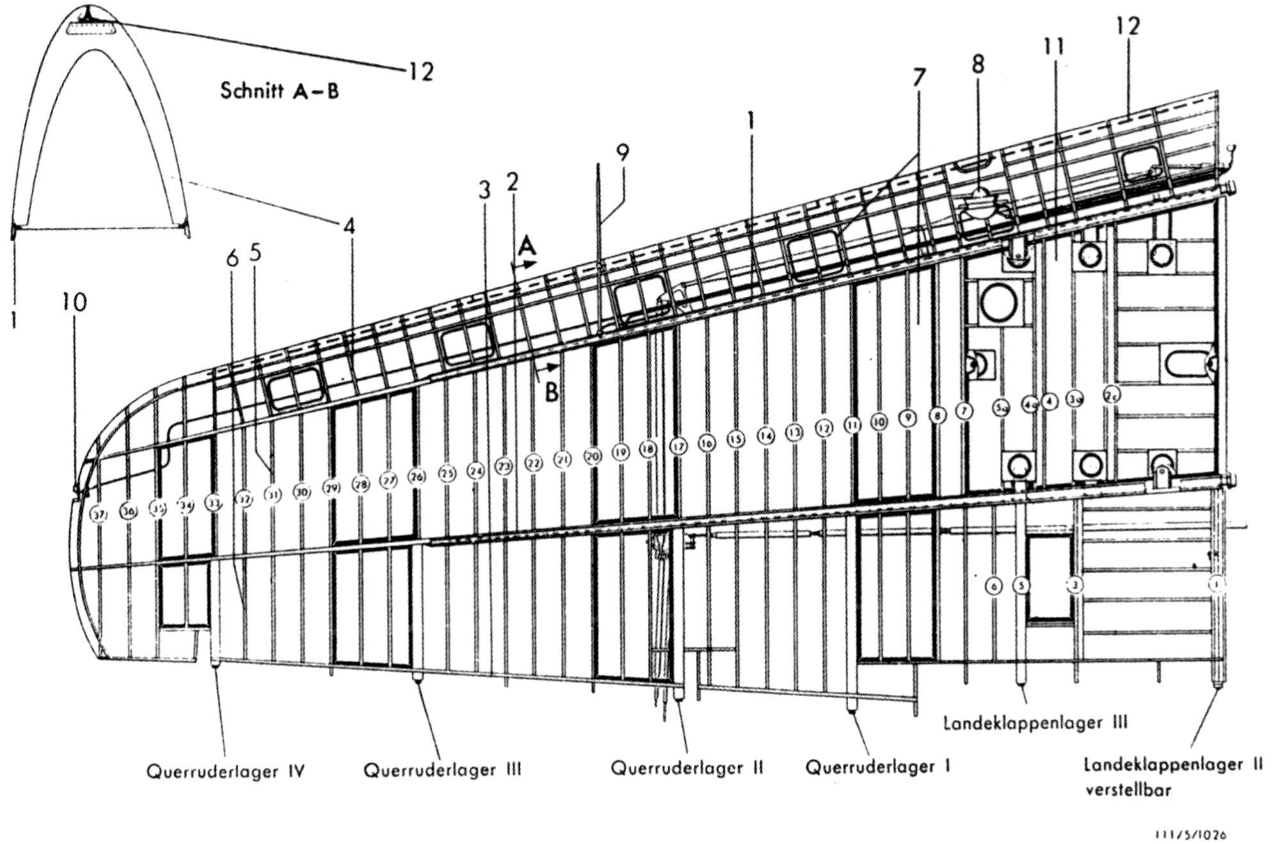

Schnitt A–B

Querruderlager IV
Querruderlager III
Querruderlager II
Querruderlager I
Landeklappenlager III
Landeklappenlager II verstellbar

111/5/1026

1 Vorderholm
2 Hinterholm
3 Endholm
4 Nasenrippe
5 Mittelrippe
6 Endrippe
7 Deckel
8 Scheinwerfer
9 Staurohr
10 Kennlicht
11 Kraftstoffbehälterraum
12 Schneidenprofil

connecting fittings are projections that serve as guides for wing attachment to the fuselage.

The wing is further joined to the fuselage via the outer load-bearers, each connected to both fuselage walls by ten screw bolts. In addition, the wing centre section rear spar is attached to the fuselage by tension cables, which attach it to the fuselage at the fuselage/wing bracing. The connecting cables are protected against vibration by support fittings located at end rib 4. For attaching the outer wings to the inner wing section, there are four connecting fittings at left and right located at the ends of the two wing spars. These fork-shaped fittings are of cast steel, which grip both ends over the spar web. They are secured partly by countersunk screw bolts and partly by hollow bolts and washers that can be detached from the spar and on to which the outer wings are attached with round-head bolts and nuts.

Wing Centre Section Space Utilisation

In the powerplant section of the wing centre section is the intermediate engine supporting frame. The undercarriage compartment behind it, between transverse walls II and III, serves to house the mainwheel undercarriage. In the nose portion beside the fuselage are located the fittings, the fuel pumps and conduits. In the space behind the nose girder, between transverse walls I and II, is a fuel tank and a lubricant tank, each fastened by belts to the beams supporting the upper wing skinning. In the end rib space are the landing flap operating rods, a warm-air conduit (left) and the main cylinder for undercarriage operation (right).

Wing Outer Sections

In its planform, the outer wing tapers towards the tips, reducing in profile thickness. It consists principally of the forward spar, rear spar, nose, centre and rear ribs, wingtip end caps and wing covering. The double-T spars are made up of upper and lower girders and spar webs strengthened by vertical profiles. At its outer extremity, the spars are fitted with an end-profiled sheet to which the wingtip caps are riveted. The nose ribs are of formed sheet and at their forward extremity is a built-in triple cutting profile for cutting balloon cables, which will no longer be installed in the newer He 111H-16 aircraft.

The wing covering is attached to the spars and ribs by flush rivets, the upper sheeting on the wing trailing-edge projecting at the rear so as to cover the nose portion of the ailerons and landing flaps. At connecting rib I, the wing sheet covering is strengthened by crosswise profiles.

On the underside of the outer wing there are large removable panels for inspection and repair purposes, as well as for access to the internal fittings. The landing flaps and ailerons are attached at projections on ribs 1, 5, 11, 17, 26 and 33. These consist of the landing flap attachment points Lager II and III and the aileron positions Lager I to IV, which have holes for accommodating the landing flap and aileron holding bolts.

Between the full-walled fireproof ribs 1 and 7 is a fuel tank compartment, accessible from above by a number of rubber-lined hand-hole access covers and from beneath by a panel that extends over the entire fuel tank compartment. This panel is stiffened by profiles riveted on to it, and at its deepest point has a water run-off drain. On the spars and ribs in the fuel tank compartment are eight profiles to which the fuel tanks are attached, on supporting frames, to the wing.

The outer wing is joined to the wing centre section at four connecting points located at the ends of the front and rear spars. These consist of welded fittings riveted to the spar at top and

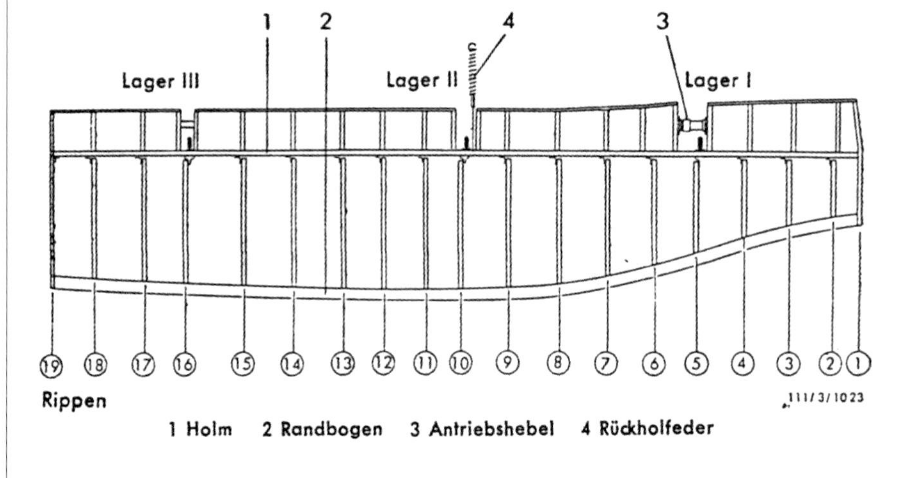

Starboard landing flap features (He 111H-16, Part 3). Key: 1 Flap spar; 2 Trailing-edge bow; 3 Actuator lever; Retraction spring. Rippen = ribs, circled.

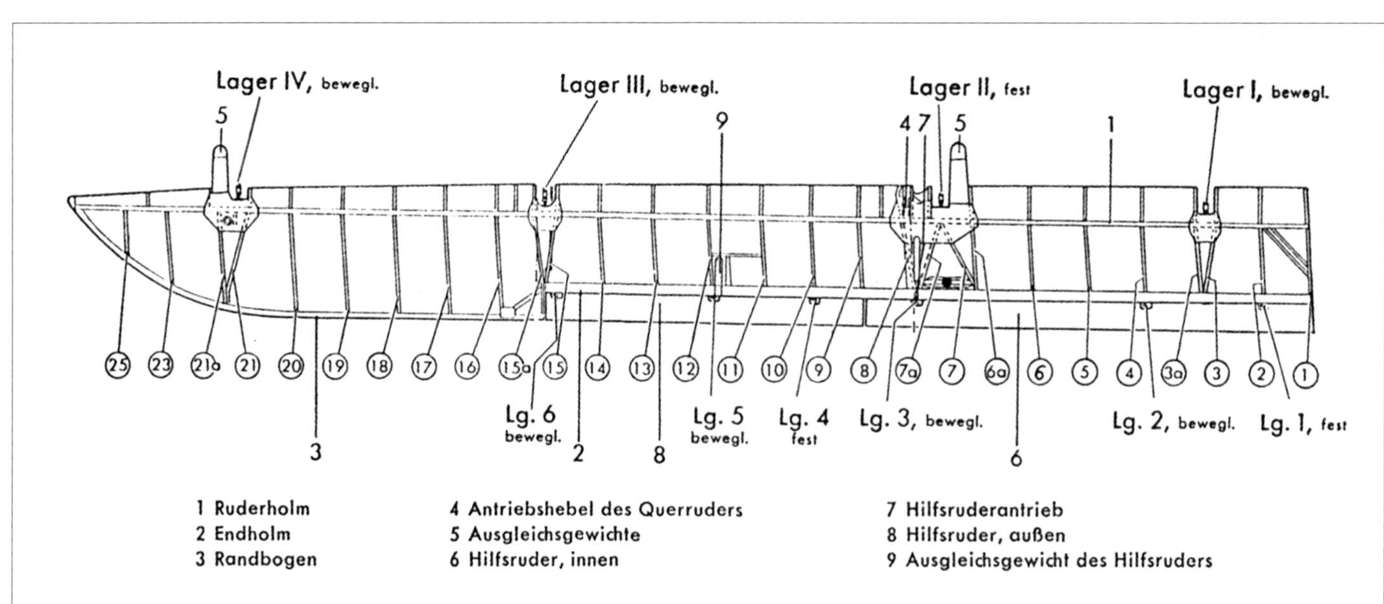

Aileron structure and fittings (He 111H-16, Part 5). Key: 1 Aileron spar; 2 Rear spar; 3 Trailing-edge bow; 4 Aileron actuator lever; 5 Balance weights; 6 Inner trim tab; 7 Trim tab actuator; 8 Outer trim tab; 9 Trim tab balance weight. beweg(ich) = movable, fest = fixed.

bottom with Whitworth wormscrew-anchored spherical nuts and bolts. The nuts and bolts of the other three attachments have a horizontally movable bearing, which compensates for workshop inaccuracies.

Outer Wing Space Utilisation

In the space between ribs 1 and 7 is a fuel tank. In the wing nose section ahead of the front spar are the aileron control runs from the wing centre section. Between ribs 6 and 7 is a landing light, and at rib 17 a pitot tube, both of the latter only on the port side. In the wingtips on both sides are the side recognition lights.

Ailerons

The aileron is attached at four positions to the rear auxiliary spar and completes the wing planform. Left and right ailerons are identical, and consist of the aileron spar, ribs, rear spar, trailing-edge runner, fittings, and fabric covering. The nose portion of the aileron is sheet covered, and because of its low-lying axis of rotation, its profile is that of a quarter circle. The ailerons consist of U-shaped profiles within which the attachment points are contained. Lager II is axially fixed, the others being axially movable. Actuation is at Lager II by means of two levers riveted into the aileron nose, which project forward from its profile. Upon operation of the landing flap, the ailerons coupled to the control system are also moved, the ailerons being further able to be operated unhindered. Aileron movement both up and down is limited in its anchoring by rubber-lined shock-absorbing stops. Balance weights are located beside Lager II and IV and are fixed in position and, upon angular deflection, similarly move within the corresponding wing cut-outs. With these balance weights, the aileron weight is 100% compensated.

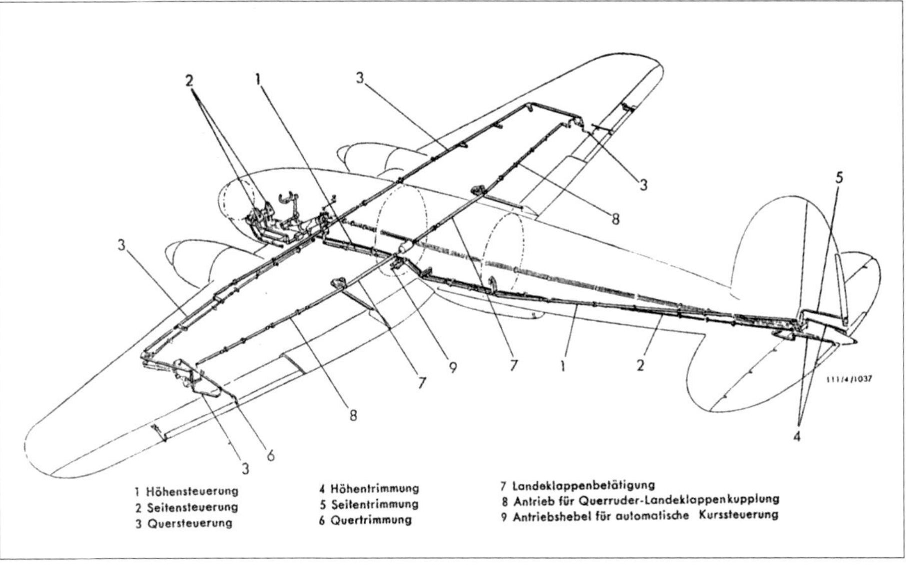

Overall layout of the control runs (He 111H-16, Part 4). Key:
1 Elevator control circuit
2 Rudder control circuit
3 Aileron control circuit
4 Elevator trim
5 Rudder trim
6 Aileron trim
7 Landing-flap activation
8 Drive for aileron/landing-flap coupling
9 Drive lever for automatic course control.

Landing Flaps

The landing flaps are attached at three positions to the rear edge of the wing, located at Lager I on the wing centre section and Lager II and III on the outer wing section, their profile, like the ailerons, completing the wing planform. The flaps serve to increase lift at take-off and landing, and for this purpose can be partially or completely depressed in a downward direction.

The landing flaps consist primarily of the spar, the ribs, the trailing-edge bow, fittings and sheet covering. The majority of the ribs consist of rib frames, their construction being similar to that of the ailerons. Lager II is axially fixed, while Lager I and III are movable. Activation is by an oil-pressure-filled cylinder, which works through the lever at Lager I. To the left and right of the screwed-on actuation lever are handhole covers for installation and inspection. Their return from the angle of depression to the normal retracted position is effected by the external airflow and by a retraction spring at Lager II and wing end rib I.

The Controls

The accompanying illustrations provide a good insight into the layout of the controls.

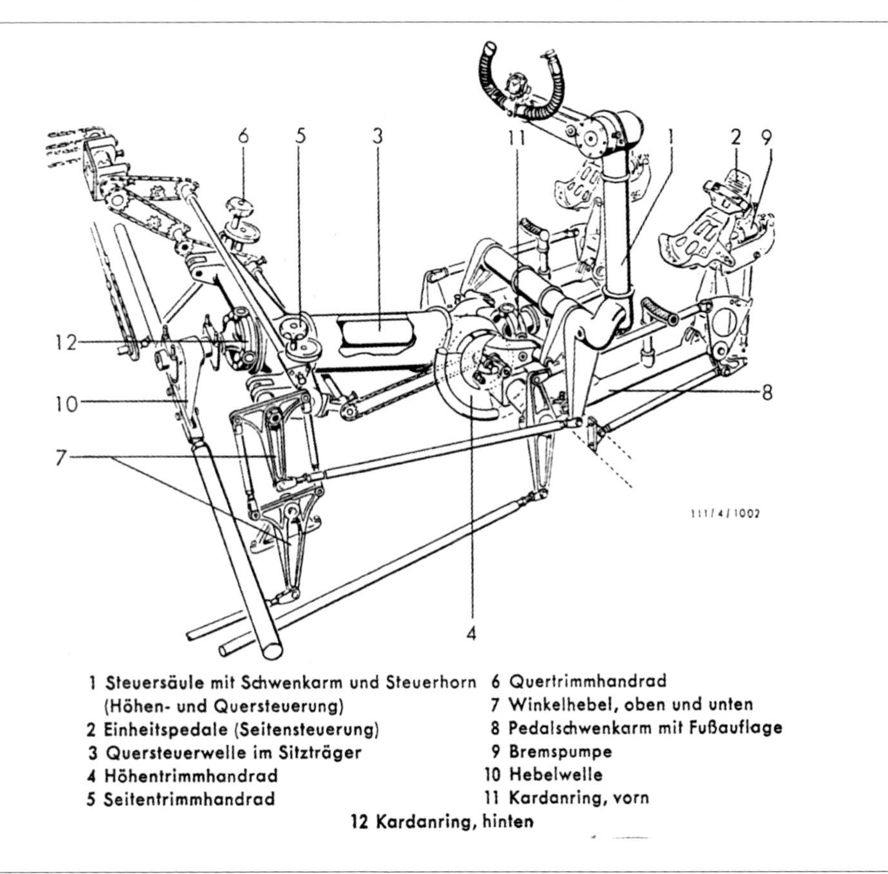

Control mechanisms in the cockpit region (He 111H-16, Part 4). Key:
1 Control column with swivel arm
2 Rudder pedals
3 Control shaft beneath seat
4 Elevator trim handwheel
5 Rudder trim handwheel
6 Aileron trim handwheel
7 Upper and lower levers
8 Foot-pedal swivel arm
9 Brake pump
10 Lever shaft
11 Shaft-drive, front
12 Shaft-drive, rear.

The Undercarriage

The aircraft's rolling components are shown here from the He 111H-16 Handbook Part 2. In this section also, the design details are provided exclusively from illustrations rather than text.

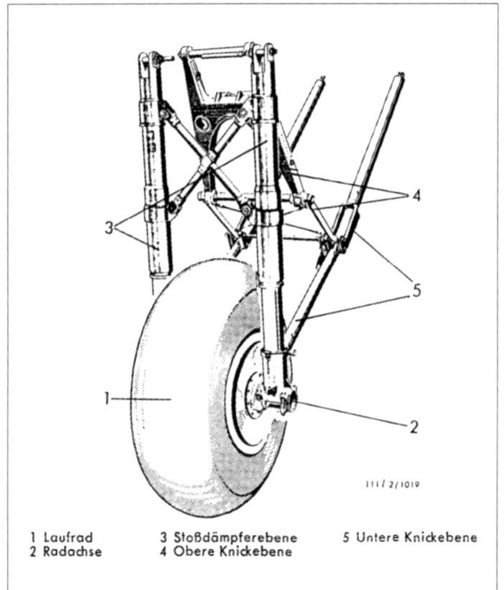

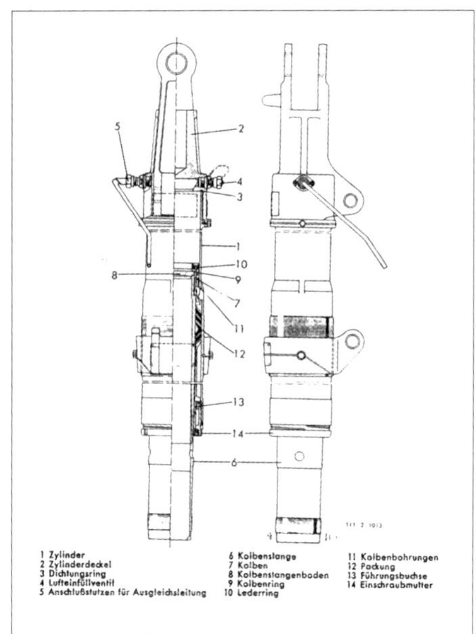

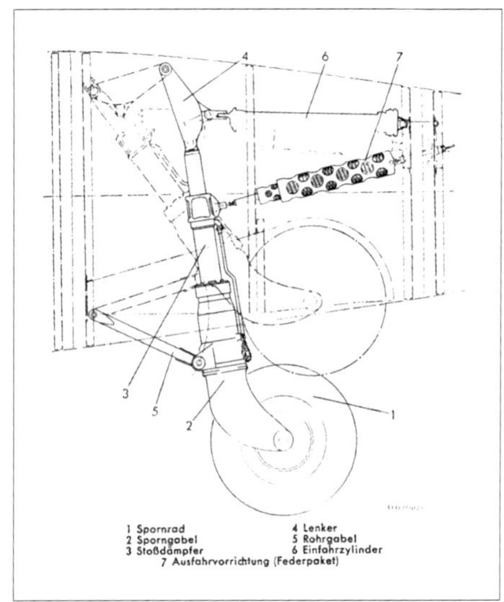

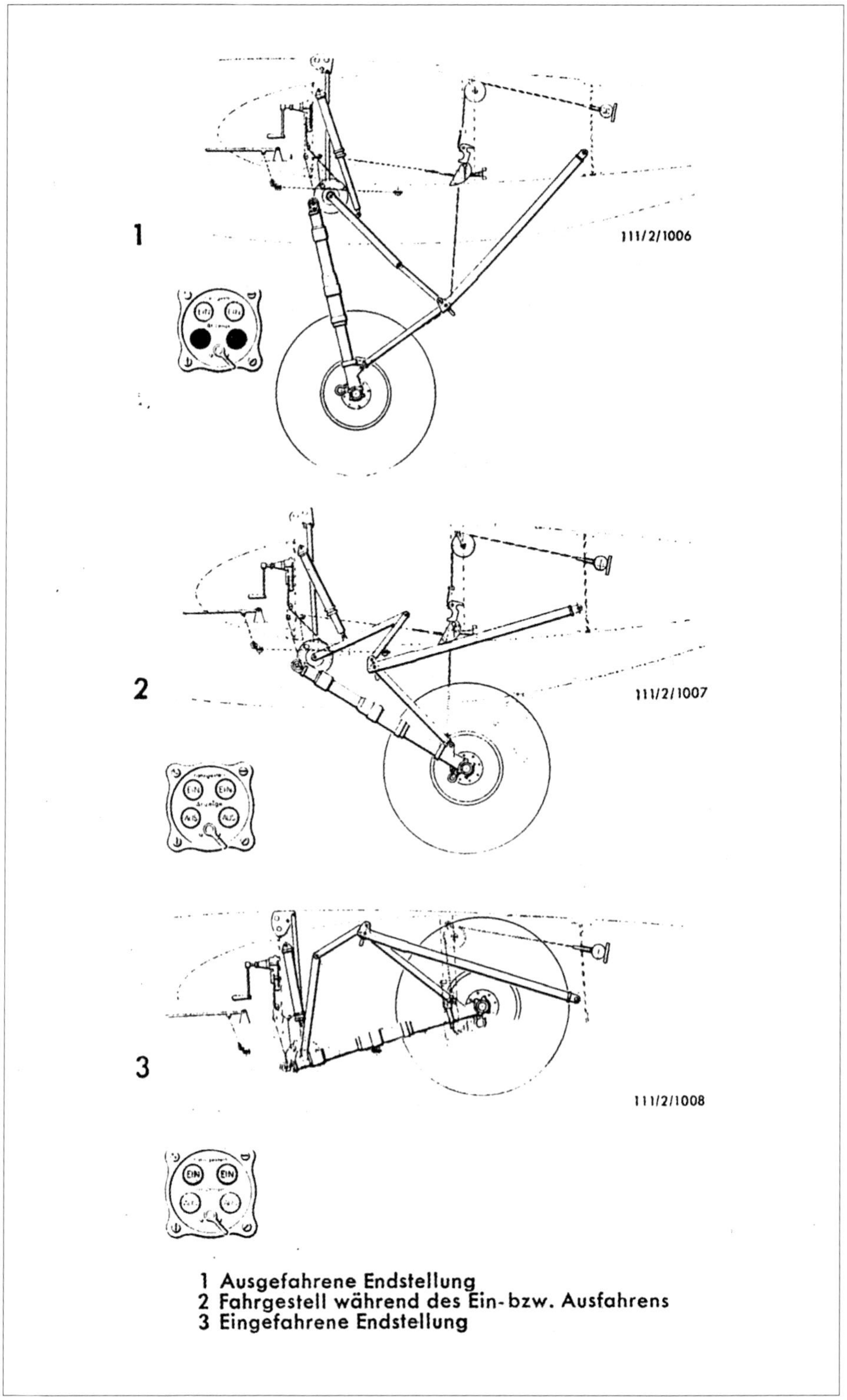

1

111/2/1006

2

111/2/1007

3

111/2/1008

1 Ausgefahrene Endstellung
2 Fahrgestell während des Ein- bzw. Ausfahrens
3 Eingefahrene Endstellung

Top left: **Mainwheel undercarriage detail (He 111H-16, Part 2). Key: 1 Wheel; 2 Axle; 3 Shock-absorber region 4 Upper folding region; 5 Lower folding region.**

Centre left: **Cross-section of a VDM-Faudi compressed air shock-absorber leg. Key: 1 Cylinder; 2 Cylinder cap 3 Sealing ring; 4 Air filling valve 5 Connection for compensating circuit 6 Piston cylinder; 7 Piston 8 Piston cylinder base; 9 Piston ring 10 Leather gasket; 11 Piston borings 12 Packing; 13 Guide canister 14 Adjustment screw.**

Bottom left: **Tailwheel in extended and retracted positions (He 111H-16, Part 2). Key: 1 Tailwheel; 2 Tailwheel fork 3 Shock-absorber leg; 4 Steering arm 5 Tubular fork; 6 Retraction cylinder 7 Spring extension mechanism.**

Above: **Mainwheel in extended and retracted positions (He 111H-16, Part 2). Key: 1 Mainwheel in fully extended position 2 Mainwheel during retraction/extension phase 3 Mainwheel fully retracted.**

The Powerplants

As has previously been indicated, individual series-produced He 111 aircraft were equipped with diverse powerplants. These ranged from the BMW VI, the Daimler-Benz DB600 and DB601 versions to the Junkers Jumo 211, the latter being installed in the He 111E and F variants. We shall now deal with the history as well as the technicalities of these proven powerplants.

The accompanying photographs show one of the total of 68,248 examples of the Jumo 211 that left the assembly lines during 1938-40 in the Jumo plants in Magdeburg, Leipzig and Köthen, and in the licence-manufacturing plants in Muldenstein and Stettin. The Jumo 211, turned out in eleven series variants, was the most widely built German aero-engine. Its good performance was in contrast to its poor robustness, which was attributable not to its design, but to the lack of high-grade materials during the progress of the war. As a result of these circumstances and the rigorous operational requirements, these units had an operating life of less than 200 hours.

The example illustrated is the Jumo 211F-2, Werknummer 1081330259, which was left abandoned for half a century. The restoration team at the Schleißheim Werftverein (workshop association) transformed this 'scrapheap' in the course of 5,000 hours of unpaid work into a fully refurbished pristine exhibit, and it has formed a part of the Schleißheim collection since 1994.

The Jumo 211 is a double-bank 12-cylinder inverted-V in-line engine with a total cylinder volume of 34.97 litres (2,134in³), delivering 1,340hp in its F-2 version, corresponding to a figure of 38.3hp/litre (0.63hp/in³) of cylinder volume. To improve its altitude performance, it incorporated a mechanically driven two-speed supercharger. The most important difference between the F-1 and F-2 versions was that the latter used a crankshaft with eight counterweights instead of the F-1's six, and had strengthened connecting rods, more resistant ball-bearings and an optimised cooling system. Junkers Jumo 211 powerplants were installed in the following aircraft:

- Heinkel He 111E, F and H.
- Junkers Ju 87B and D.
- Junkers Ju 88A, C, D and P.
- Focke-Wulf Ta 154A.
- AVIA 199 (the Czech-built Me 109G-14; CS-199 = Me 109G-12).
- CASA 2.111 (the Spanish licence-built He 111P, later powered by the Rolls-Royce Merlin).

Restoration of this Jumo 211F was carried out by the members of the Schleißheim Werftverein.

The restored Jumo 211F, seen next to the Rolls-Royce Merlin-powered CASA 2.111, is now part of the Schleißheim Flugwerft collection.

Technical Data for the Junkers Jumo 211F

No of cylinders	12, inverted-V
Cylinder volume, total	34.97 litres (2,134in^3)
Cylinder volume, each	2.914 litres (177.8in^3)
Bore	150mm (5.90in)
Stroke	165mm (6.50in)
Compression ratio	6.5
Performance	
at low level:	
Take-off power	1,340hp at 2,600rpm
Combat power	1,120hp at 2,400rpm
Continuous power	910hp at 2,250rpm
Boost pressure	1.40 atmospheres
with low-level supercharger:	
Combat power	1,210hp at 2,400rpm
Continuous power	1,040hp at 2,250rpm
Boost pressure	1.25 atmospheres
Fuel consumption	226gm (0.50 lb)/hp·h
with high-level supercharger:	
Combat power	1,060hp at 2,400rpm
Continuous power	900hp at 2,250rpm
Boost pressure	1.25 atmospheres
Fuel consumption	243 gm (0.54 lb)/hp·h
Rated altitude	5,300m (17,390ft)
Supercharger type	two-speed
Engine data	
Length	2,173mm (85.55in)
Width	804mm (31.65in)
Height	1,053mm (41.46in)
Dry weight	720kg (1,587 lb)
Coolant	water/glycol

To accompany the above data table, a description of the Jumo 211F is now given, from the He 111H-16 Handbook, Part 7.

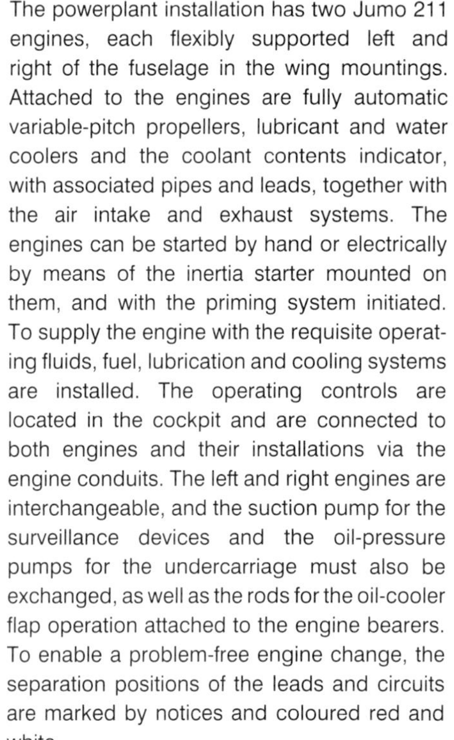

The powerplant installation has two Jumo 211 engines, each flexibly supported left and right of the fuselage in the wing mountings. Attached to the engines are fully automatic variable-pitch propellers, lubricant and water coolers and the coolant contents indicator, with associated pipes and leads, together with the air intake and exhaust systems. The engines can be started by hand or electrically by means of the inertia starter mounted on them, and with the priming system initiated. To supply the engine with the requisite operating fluids, fuel, lubrication and cooling systems are installed. The operating controls are located in the cockpit and are connected to both engines and their installations via the engine conduits. The left and right engines are interchangeable, and the suction pump for the surveillance devices and the oil-pressure pumps for the undercarriage must also be exchanged, as well as the rods for the oil-cooler flap operation attached to the engine bearers. To enable a problem-free engine change, the separation positions of the leads and circuits are marked by notices and coloured red and white.

The engine is a liquid-cooled 12-cylinder inverted-V with a fuel injection high-pressure blower, automatic pressure regulation and automatic two-speed gear-shift transmission for automatic switching from low-level to high-level and vice versa, as well as for economic cruise operation.

The cowling is ventilated by two tubular ducts situated forward on both sides of the engine. To the left of the engine there is a ventilation duct for the generator, whose opening lies in the ram pressure intake.

The Propellers

Power from the engines was transmitted to three-bladed Junkers VS 11 propellers, which are now described as follows from the He 111H-16 Handbook, Part 7:

The fully automatic hydraulically operated three-bladed variable-pitch propellers rotate to the right. The blades are delivered by the Schwarz or Heine firms in metal-cased light wood or in a quality wood version. An oil-motor provides the power for the drive, which is largely a geared oil pump acting as the drive motor. On the oil-motor housing are the connecting pipes for the pressurised oil from the governor. The oil-motor is located inside the propeller boss, which also houses the gearing, and is attached by a rubber sealing ring to the spinner mounting flange. The rpm regulator, located on the equipment side of the engine, serves as the control device for the variable-pitch energy delivered by the pump. The oil-motor connection is via a duplex pipe located in the engine cannon shaft.

By operating the rpm selector lever, the desired engine rpm is effected via the governor. When the flight condition and the boost pressure regulator are altered, the rpm is kept at a constant value by the governor. On the lower portion of the governor housing is a feathering mechanism for the propellers. In the event of an engine shut-down, this mechanism sets the propeller blades to the feathered position. It is operated from the cockpit via a key switch, and can likewise be called upon to retrieve the propellers from the feathered position.

By coupling the gearing with the oil-motor, in the event of a gear rupture, blockage, or oil circulation failure, the propeller is self-arresting and remains in operation as a fixed-pitch propeller. It is connected to the self-operating oil-filled engine circuit, so lubrication and maintenance of the propeller is unnecessary. By means of the hot pressurised oil from the engine circulatory system, the propeller is kept so warm that even at very low ambient temperatures it is fully reliable in operation.

The Fuel, Lubricant, Cooling and Hydraulic Systems

The accompanying illustrations show the layout and method of functioning of these complex operating systems.

Engine change – a typical scenario for the diorama modeller.

Sicherheitsventil
Sieb
Reglerpumpe
Fliehgew.
Reglerfeder
Druckminderventil
Ölmotor
Steuerschieber
Einstellscheibe für Regeldrehzahl
Druckrückschlagventil
oberer Steuerkolben
Segelstellungs-pumpe
unterer Steuerkolben
Rückschlagventil
Umkehrmotor für Segelstellungspumpe
Druckleitung
Sicherheitsventil
Saugleitung

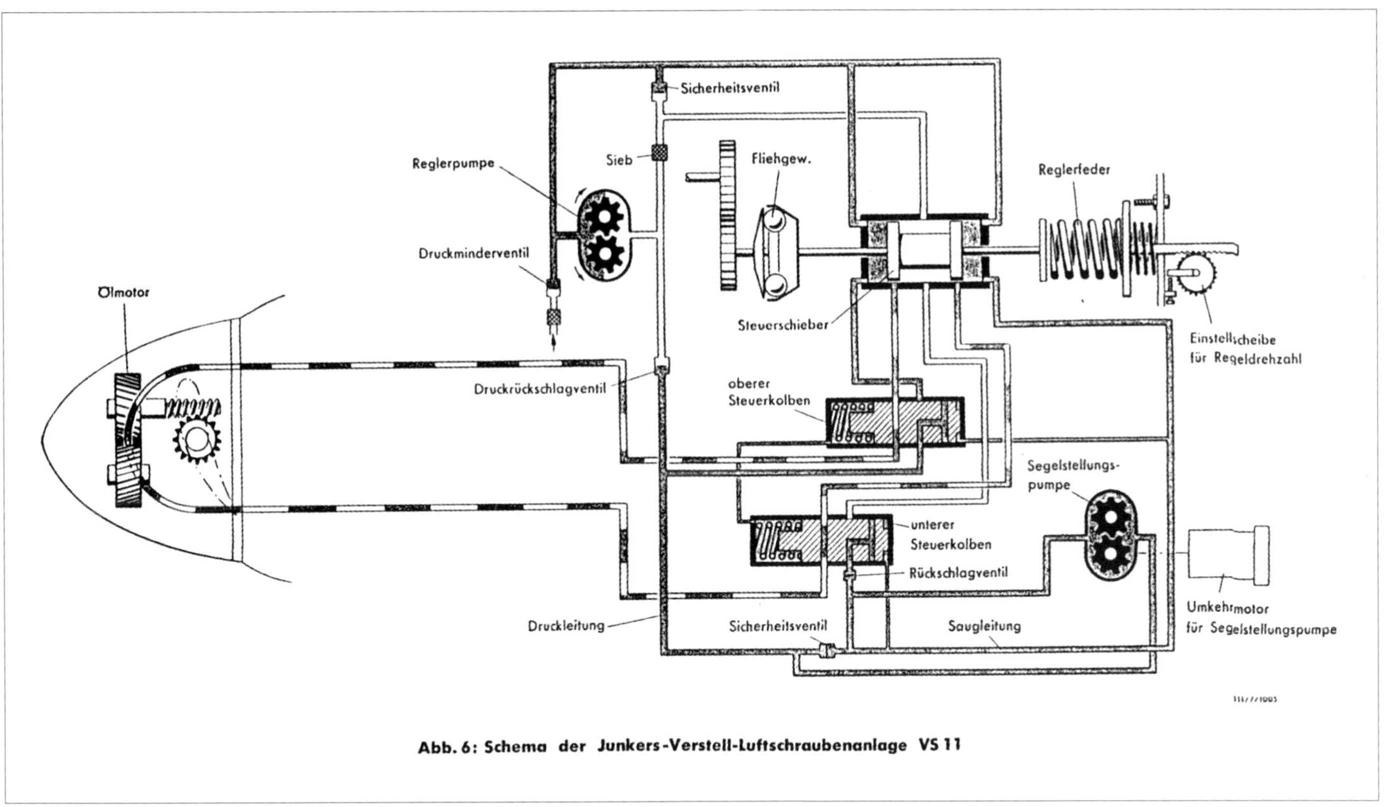

Abb. 6: Schema der Junkers-Verstell-Luftschraubenanlage VS 11

Functional diagram of the Junkers VS 11 propellers.

Fuel tank locations in the wing (He 111H-16, Part 8). Key:
1 Fuel withdrawal tank, left; 2 Fuel withdrawal tank, right
3 Fuel supply tank, left; 4 Fuel supply tank, right
5 Lubricant withdrawal tank, left
6 Lubricant withdrawal tank, right
7 Coolant tanks (for more details, see Part 7).

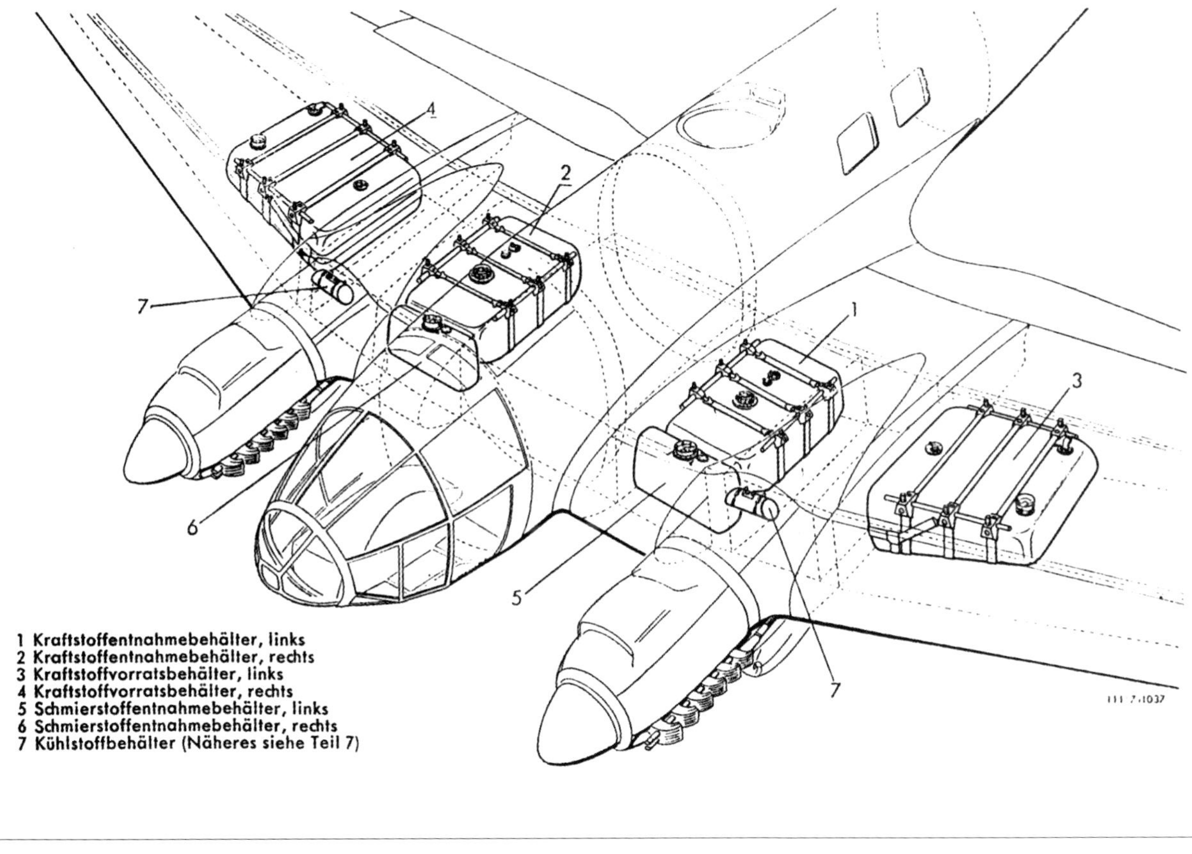

1
2
3
4
5
6
7
7
1 Kraftstoffentnahmebehälter, links
2 Kraftstoffentnahmebehälter, rechts
3 Kraftstoffvorratsbehälter, links
4 Kraftstoffvorratsbehälter, rechts
5 Schmierstoffentnahmebehälter, links
6 Schmierstoffentnahmebehälter, rechts
7 Kühlstoffbehälter (Näheres siehe Teil 7)

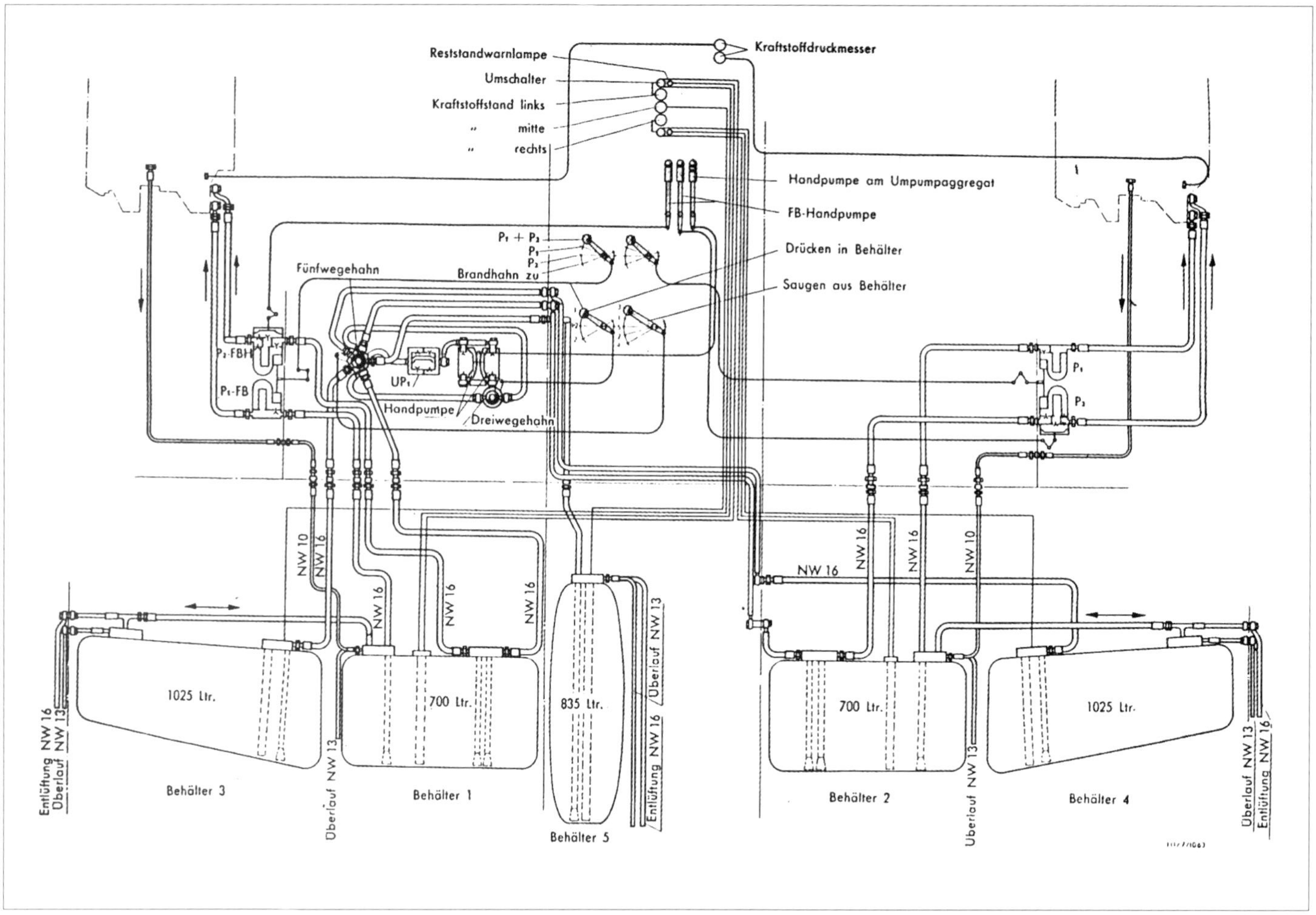
Reststandwarnlampe
Umschalter
Kraftstoffstand links
" mitte
" rechts
Kraftstoffdruckmesser
Handpumpe am Umpumpaggregat
FB-Handpumpe
Drücken in Behälter
Saugen aus Behälter
Fünfwegehahn
Brandhahn zu
Handpumpe
Dreiwegehahn
NW 10
NW 16
NW 13
1025 Ltr.
700 Ltr.
835 Ltr.
Behälter 3
Behälter 1
Behälter 5
Behälter 2
Behälter 4
Entlüftung NW 16
Überlauf NW 13
Überlauf NW 13
Entlüftung NW 16

Schematic diagram of the fuel flow system for the five fuel tanks (He 111H-16, Part 7).

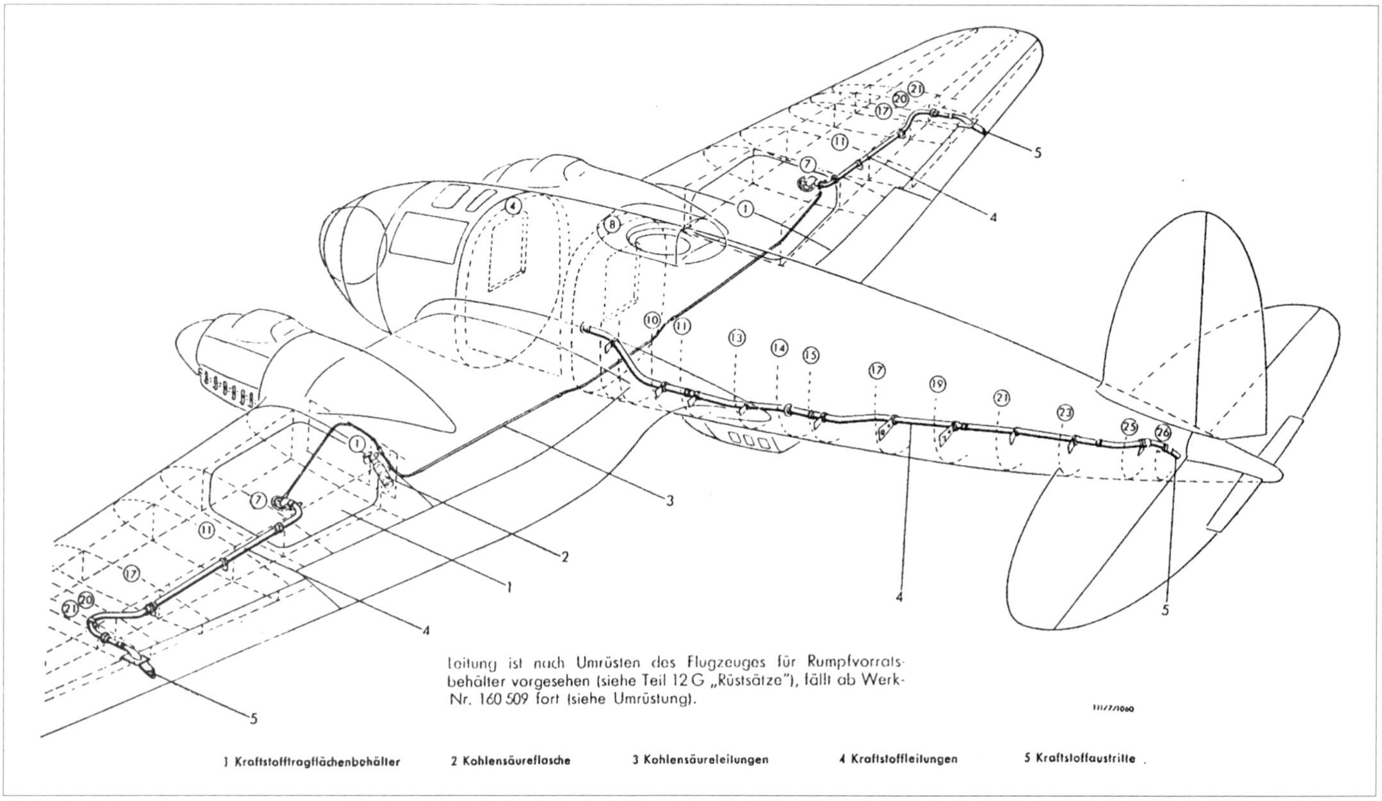
Leitung ist nach Umrüsten des Flugzeuges für Rumpfvorratsbehälter vorgesehen (siehe Teil 12 G „Rüstsätze"), fällt ab Werk-Nr. 160 509 fort (siehe Umrüstung).
1 Kraftstofftragflächenbehälter
2 Kohlensäureflasche
3 Kohlensäureleitungen
4 Kraftstoffleitungen
5 Kraftstoffaustritte

Layout of the fuel quick-release system (He 111H-16, Part 7). Key: 1 Wing fuel tank; 2 Carbon dioxide bottle; 3 Carbon dioxide pipes 4 Fuel pipes; 5 Fuel outlet nozzles. (Circled numbers are wing ribs and fuselage formers).

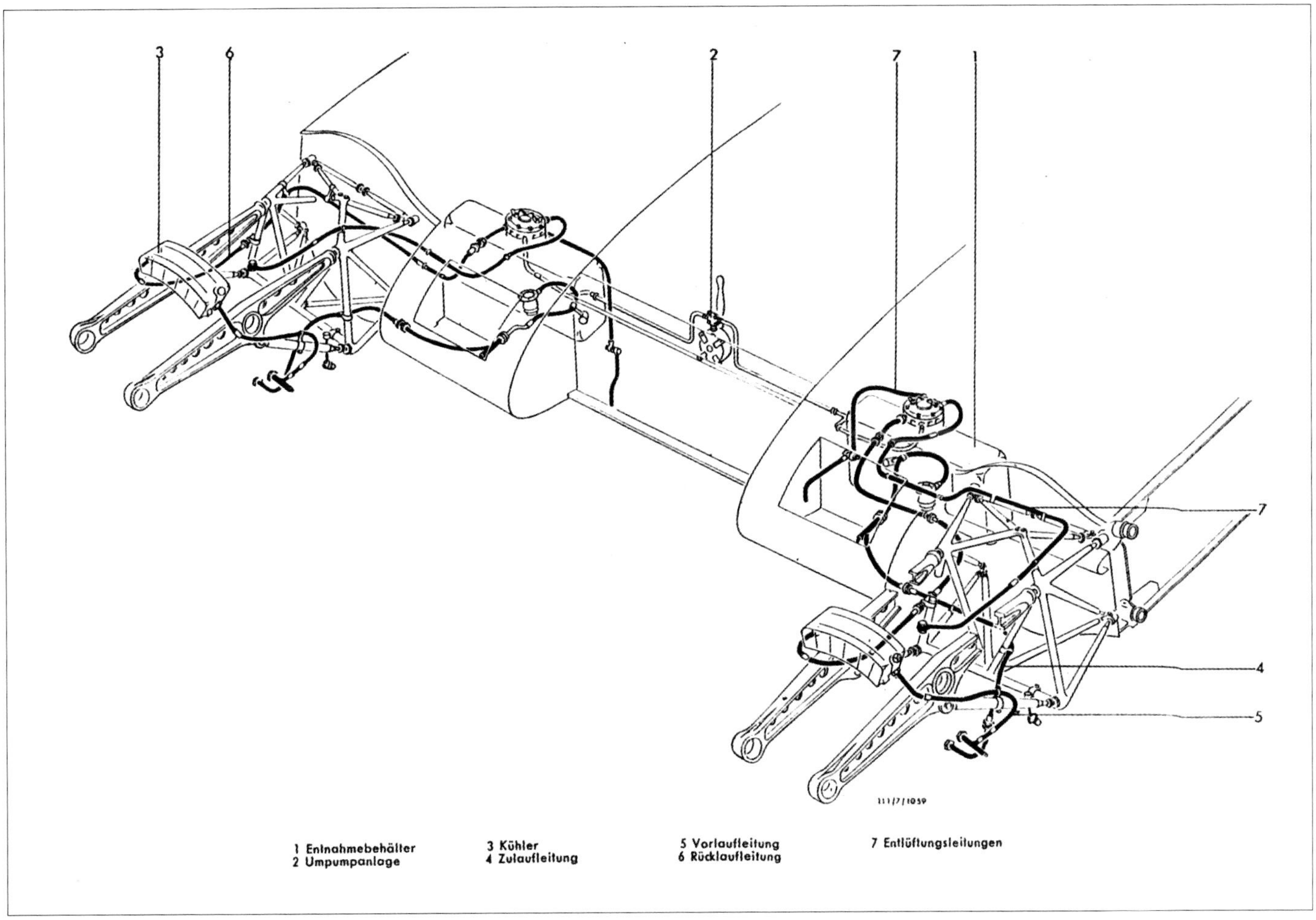

1 Enlnahmebehälter
2 Umpumpanlage
3 Kühler
4 Zulaufleitung
5 Vorlaufleitung
6 Rücklaufleitung
7 Entlüftungsleitungen

The lubricant system and engine bearers (He 111H-16, Part 7). Key:
1 Withdrawal tank; 2 Transfer pump; 3 Cooler; 4 Feed pipes
5 Feed pipes to cooler; 6 Return pipes from cooler
7 Ventilation pipe.

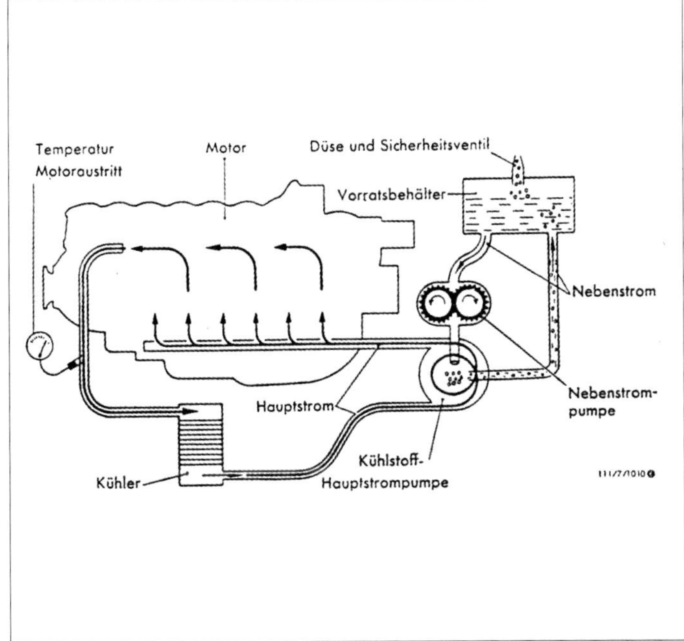

The cooler circulation system (He 111H-16, Part 7).
Key: (clockwise from top left):
Temperature/motor outlet; motor; safety valve and nozzle
Supply tank; Secondary feed lines; Secondary feed pump
Coolant fluid main feed pump; main feed lines; cooler.

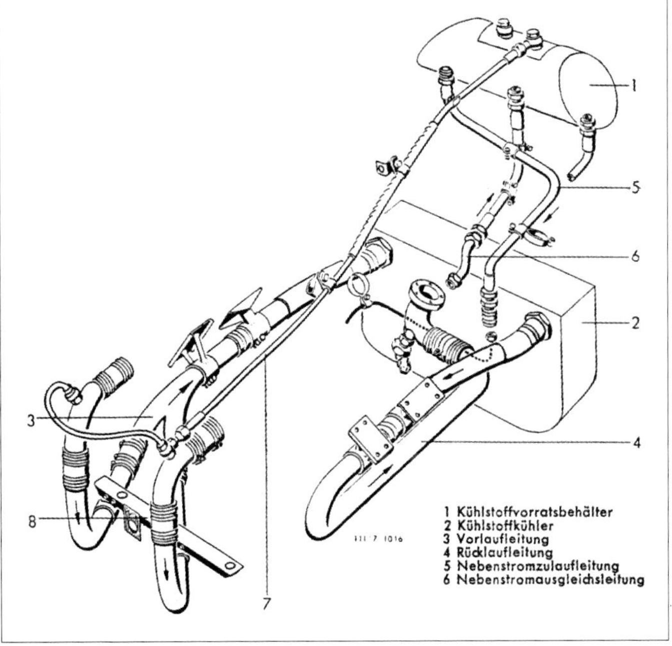

The coolant circuit (He 111H-16, Part 7). Key:
1 Coolant supply tank; 2 Coolant cooler/radiator
3 Feed pipe to cooler; 4 Return pipe from cooler
5 Secondary feed circuit; 6 Secondary feed compensating circuit
7, 8 – not defined on the drawing.

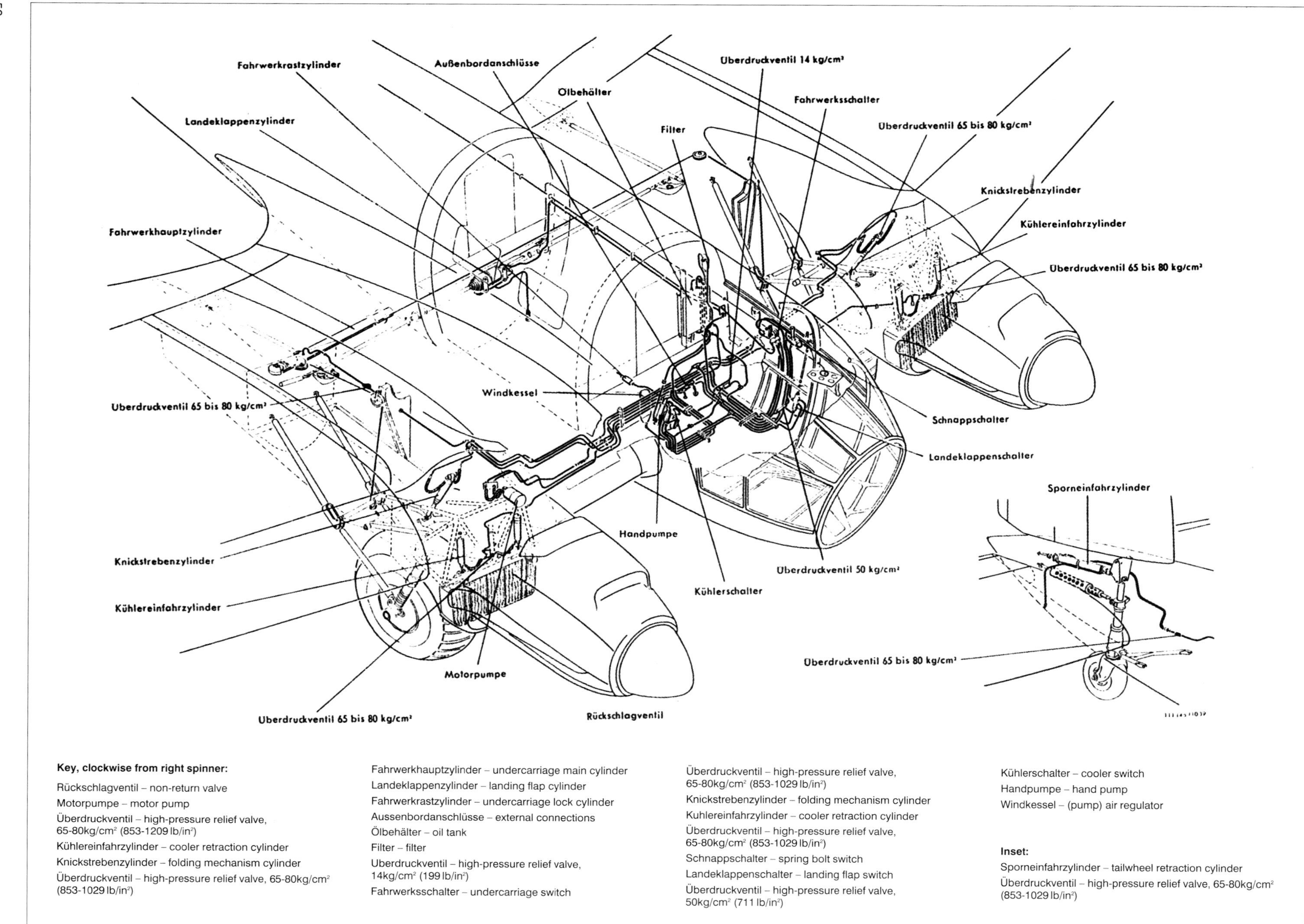

Key, clockwise from right spinner:

Rückschlagventil – non-return valve
Motorpumpe – motor pump
Überdruckventil – high-pressure relief valve, 65-80kg/cm² (853-1209 lb/in²)
Kühlereinfahrzylinder – cooler retraction cylinder
Knickstrebenzylinder – folding mechanism cylinder
Überdruckventil – high-pressure relief valve, 65-80kg/cm² (853-1029 lb/in²)
Fahrwerkhauptzylinder – undercarriage main cylinder
Landeklappenzylinder – landing flap cylinder
Fahrwerkrastzylinder – undercarriage lock cylinder
Aussenbordanschlüsse – external connections
Ölbehälter – oil tank
Filter – filter
Uberdruckventil – high-pressure relief valve, 14kg/cm² (199 lb/in²)
Fahrwerksschalter – undercarriage switch
Überdruckventil – high-pressure relief valve, 65-80kg/cm² (853-1029 lb/in²)
Knickstrebenzylinder – folding mechanism cylinder
Kuhlereinfahrzylinder – cooler retraction cylinder
Überdruckventil – high-pressure relief valve, 65-80kg/cm² (853-1029 lb/in²)
Schnappschalter – spring bolt switch
Landeklappenschalter – landing flap switch
Überdruckventil – high-pressure relief valve, 50kg/cm² (711 lb/in²)
Kühlerschalter – cooler switch
Handpumpe – hand pump
Windkessel – (pump) air regulator

Inset:

Sporneinfahrzylinder – tailwheel retraction cylinder
Überdruckventil – high-pressure relief valve, 65-80kg/cm² (853-1029 lb/in²)

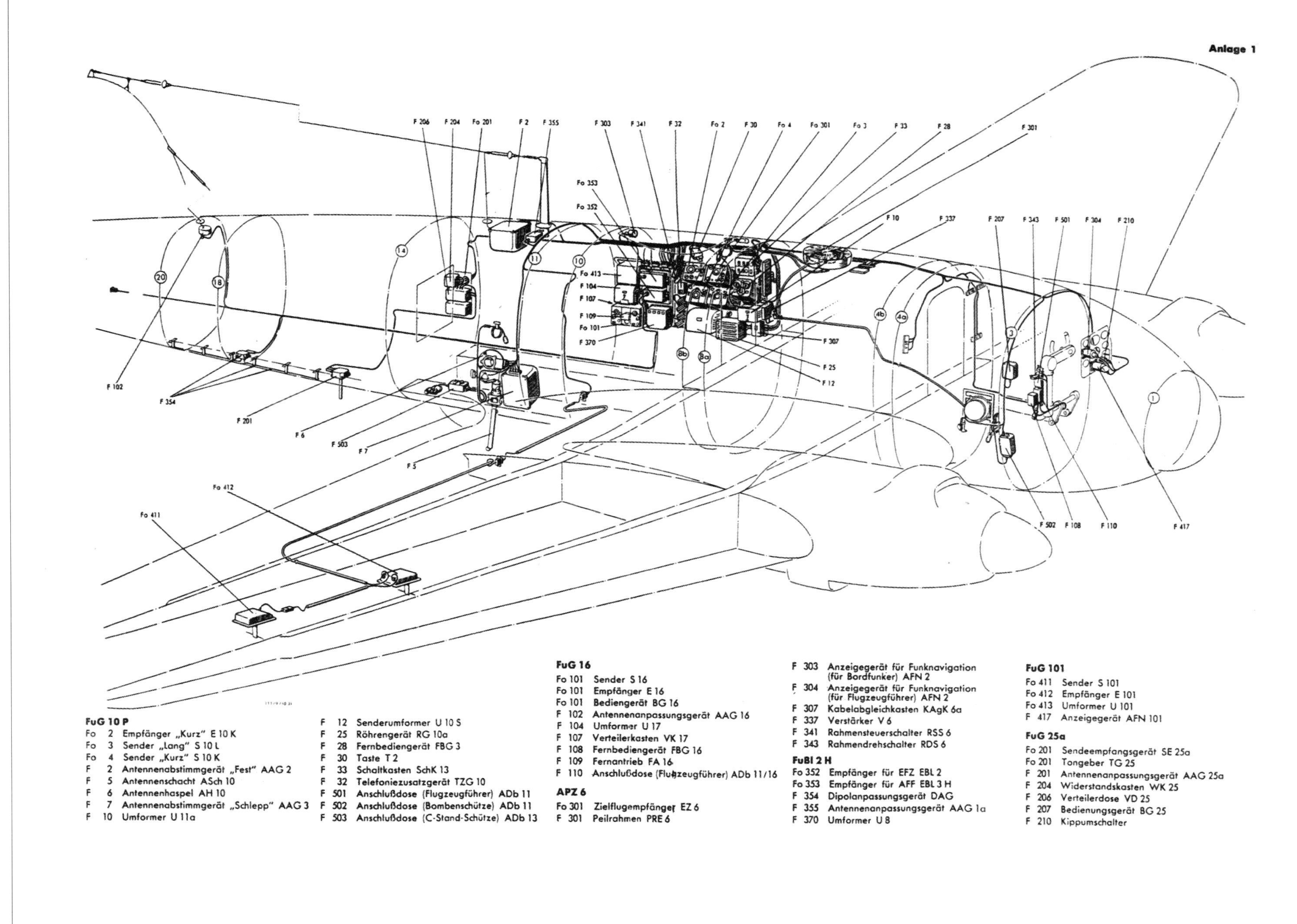
Anlage 1
FuG 10 P
Fo 2 Empfänger „Kurz" E 10 K
Fo 3 Sender „Lang" S 10 L
Fo 4 Sender „Kurz" S 10 K
F 2 Antennenabstimmgerät „Fest" AAG 2
F 5 Antennenschacht ASch 10
F 6 Antennenhaspel AH 10
F 7 Antennenabstimmgerät „Schlepp" AAG 3
F 10 Umformer U 11a
F 12 Senderumformer U 10 S
F 25 Röhrengerät RG 10a
F 28 Fernbediengerät FBG 3
F 30 Taste T 2
F 33 Schaltkasten SchK 13
F 32 Telefoniezusatzgerät TZG 10
F 501 Anschlußdose (Flugzeugführer) ADb 11
F 502 Anschlußdose (Bombenschütze) ADb 11
F 503 Anschlußdose (C-Stand-Schütze) ADb 13
FuG 16
Fo 101 Sender S 16
Fo 101 Empfänger E 16
Fo 101 Bediengerät BG 16
F 102 Antennenanpassungsgerät AAG 16
F 104 Umformer U 17
F 107 Verteilerkasten VK 17
F 108 Fernbediengerät FBG 16
F 109 Fernantrieb FA 16
F 110 Anschlußdose (Flugzeugführer) ADb 11/16
APZ 6
Fo 301 Zielflugempfänger EZ 6
F 301 Peilrahmen PRE 6
F 303 Anzeigegerät für Funknavigation (für Bordfunker) AFN 2
F 304 Anzeigegerät für Funknavigation (für Flugzeugführer) AFN 2
F 307 Kabelabgleichkasten KAgK 6a
F 337 Verstärker V 6
F 341 Rahmensteuerschalter RSS 6
F 343 Rahmendrehschalter RDS 6
FuBl 2 H
Fo 352 Empfänger für EFZ EBL 2
Fo 353 Empfänger für AFF EBL 3 H
F 354 Dipolanpassungsgerät DAG
F 355 Antennenanpassungsgerät AAG 1a
F 370 Umformer U 8
FuG 101
Fo 411 Sender S 101
Fo 412 Empfänger E 101
Fo 413 Umformer U 101
F 417 Anzeigegerät AFN 101
FuG 25a
Fo 201 Sendeempfangsgerät SE 25a
Fo 201 Tongeber TG 25
F 201 Antennenanpassungsgerät AAG 25a
F 204 Widerstandskasten WK 25
F 206 Verteilerdose VD 25
F 207 Bedienungsgerät BG 25
F 210 Kippumschalter

Aircraft Radio Installations

The illustration on the previous page provides detailed information on each equipment item and its associated components. The purposes of each of these are:

- FuG 10P: radio and crew intercom, and aircraft-to-aircraft communication.
- APZ 6: direction-finding (D/F) and target homing.
- FuBl 2H: blind-landing approach.
- FuG 101: electrical altimeter.
- FuG 25a: special-purpose radio communication.
- FuG16: aircraft-to-aircraft (together with FuG 10P).

Military Equipment

The defensive armament of the He 111 is concentrated in four locations and consists of:

- A-Stand (nose): one 20mm MG-FF/M cannon.
- B-Stand (dorsal fuselage): one 13mm MG 131.
- C-Stand (ventral fuselage): one 7.9mm MG 81Z twin machine-gun.
- D-Stands (two lateral positions): one 7.9mm MG 81 single machine-gun in each.

Weapon horizontal and vertical fields of fire (He 111H-16, Part 12A)

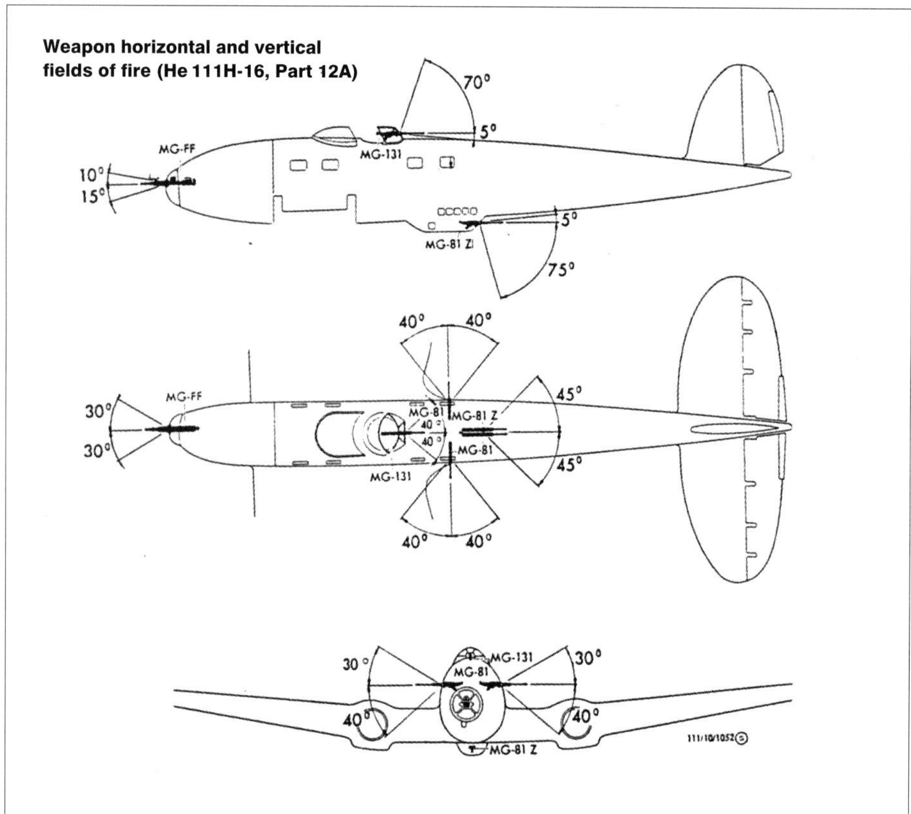

Opposite page, clockwise from top left:

The C-Stand 7.9mm MG 15 machine-gun.

The starboard D-Stand (lateral weapon). The Werknummer 4604 is just visible on the fuselage.

The Ikaria A-Stand (nose cupola) MG 15A gun-mount, traversable to +/- 60° vertically and 60° to either side.

The ESAC 250 (Electrische Senkrecht Aufhängung für Cylinderbomben) electrically operated vertical suspension canister for cylindrical bombs.

The Fieseler Fi 103 (V-1) flying-bomb was fired not only from ground catapults but also air-launched from specially equipped He 111H-22 aircraft. In operational use, the V-1 was launched from beneath the starboard side.

The MG 131 in close-up.

The ventral C-Stand with its single MG 15. Other weapons installed in this location were the MG 81 and the MG 131.

The five weapon positions (He 111H-16, Part 12A)

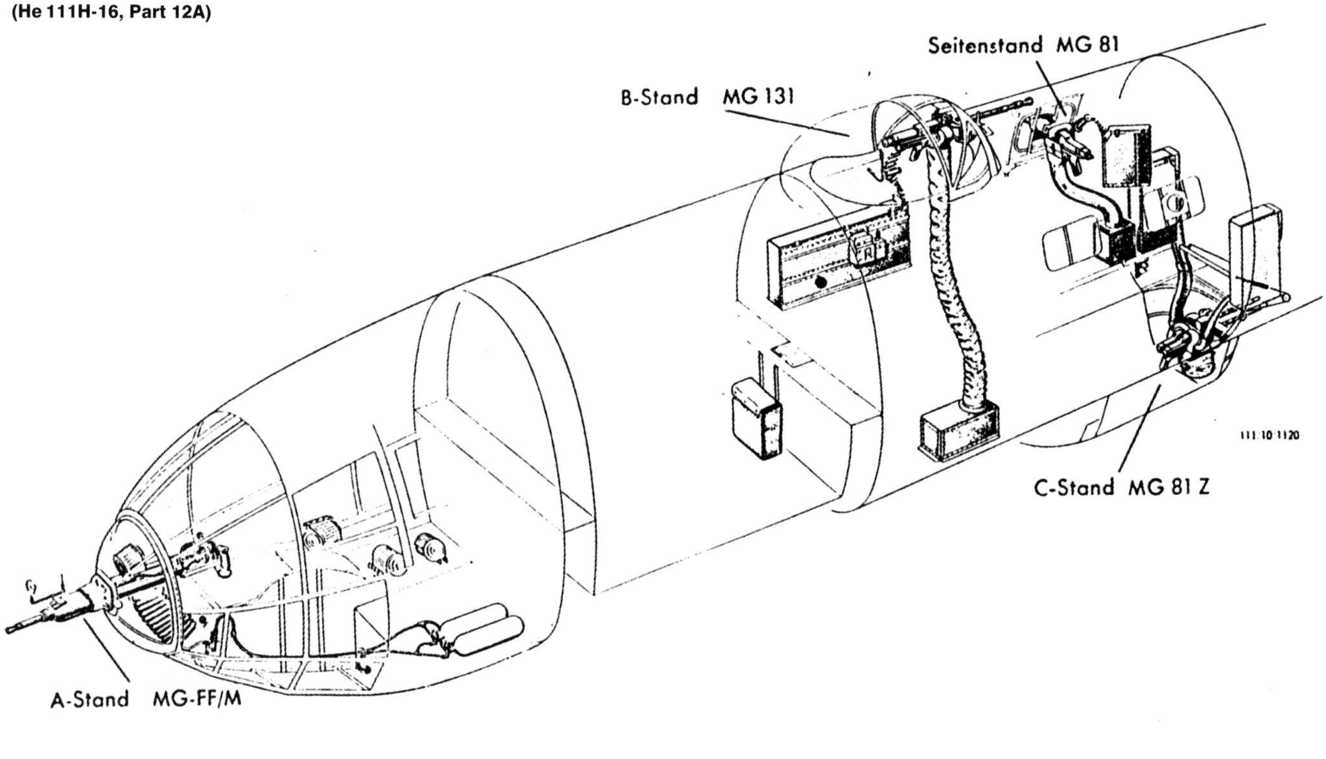

Seitenstand MG 81

B-Stand MG 131

C-Stand MG 81 Z

A-Stand MG-FF/M

111 10 1120

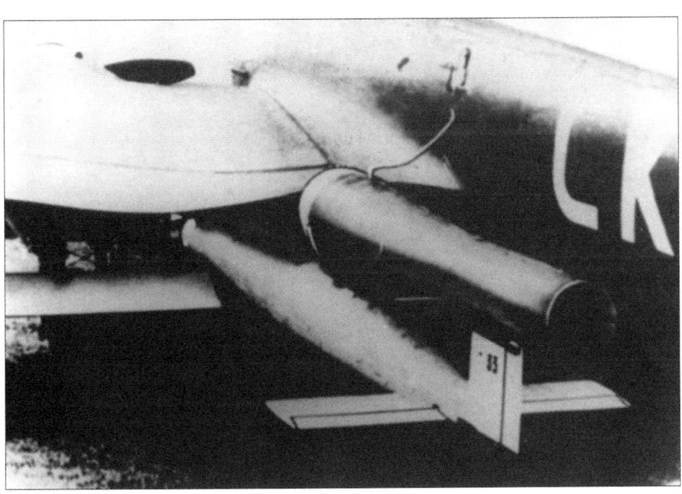

Weapons Technical Data Comparison

Weapon Type	MG-FF	MG 131	MG 81	MG 81Z	MG 15
Manufacturer	Licence-built Oerlikon-Becker	Rheinmetall-Borsig	Mauser	Mauser	Rheinmetall-Borsig
Calibre, mm (in)	20 (0.79)	13 (0.51)	7.92 (0.31)	7.92 (0.31)	7.92 (0.31)
Rate of fire (rounds/min)	540	930	1,600	3,200	1,050
Initial velocity, m/sec (ft/sec)	550-700 (1804-2297)	710-750 (2329-2461)	705-875 (2313-2871)	705-875 (2313-2871)	755 (2477)
Weapon weight, kg (lb)	35.70 (78.70)	19.70 (43.43)	6.50 (14.33)	12.90 (28.44)	7.2 (15.87) †
Total weapon length, mm (in)	1,338 (52.56)	1,168 (45.98)	993 (39.09)	915 (36.02)	1,078 (42.44)
Barrel length, mm (in)	822 (32.36)	546 (21.50)	475 (18.70)	475 (18.70)	600 (23.62)
Belt weight (100 rounds), kg (lb)	21 (46.3)	8.36 (18.4)	7.8 (17.2)	7.8 (17.2)	-
Belt length (100 rounds), mm (in)	-	2,385 (93.90)	-	-	-
Magazine (100 rounds), kg (lb)	33.10 (72.97)	-	-	-	-
Magazine (60 rounds)*, kg (lb)	20.30 (44.75)	-	-	-	-
Magazine (75 rounds), kg (lb)	-	-	-	-	4.24 (9.35)
Weapon width, mm (in)	155 (6.10)	233 (9.17)	114 (4.49)	234 (9.21)	134 (5.28)
Weapon height, mm (in)	135 (5.31)	123 (4.84)	183 (7.20)	183 (7.20)	185 (7.28) ‡
Projectile weight/sec, kg (lb)	0.810 (1.786)	0.527 (1.162)	0.308 (0.679)	0.616 (1.358)	0.202 (0.445)
Projectile type	M.Gr	Spr.Gr	SmK	SmK	SmK

* Weapon with magazine was 306mm (12.05in); † without drum; ‡ Data without gunsight; with gunsight = 315mm (12.40in).
M.Gr = Minengranate (literally, mine-type high-explosive shell); Spr.Gr = Sprenggranate (high-explosive shell); SmK = Spitzgeschoß mit Stahlkern (pointed projectile with steel core).

Principal Bombs Carried

Designation	Bomb type	Length x diameter	Weight	Tolerance	Explosive filling
SC 50	Minenbombe	1,100 x 200mm	50kg	+/- 4kg	25kg Fp 60/40
SC 250	Minenbombe	1,640 x 368mm	250kg	+/- 12kg	125kg Fp 60/40, Amatol, Trialen
SC 500	Minenbombe	2,010 x 470mm	500kg	+/- 20kg	260kg Fp 60/40, Fp 50/50 or Amatol 39 or 41
SC 1000	Minenbombe	2,580 x 654mm	1,027kg	+/- 34kg	590kg Fp 60/40 or Trialen 105
SC 1800	Minenbombe	3,500 x 660mm	1,832kg	+/- 65kg	1,000kg Fp 60/40 or 1,100kg Trialen 105
SC 2500	Großladungsbombe	3,895 x 828mm	2,500kg	+/-70kg	1,700kg Trialen 105
SD 50	Splitterbombe	1,090 x 200mm	50kg	+/- 4kg	16kg Fp 60/40, Amatol 39
SD 250	Splitterbombe	1,638 x 368mm	250kg	+/- 12kg	80kg Fp 60/40, Amatol 39
SD 500	Splitterbombe	2,007 x 396mm	480kg	+/- 23kg	90kg Fp 60/40
SD 1000	Splitterbombe	2,100 x 500mm	1,000kg	+/- 55kg	160kg Fp 60/40
PC 1000	Panzersprengbombe	2,100 x 500mm	988kg	+/- 50kg	152kg Fp 60/40
PC 1400	Panzersprengbombe	2,836 x 562mm	1,408kg	+/- 55kg	320kg Fp 60/40
PC 1600	Panzersprengbombe	2,812 x 536mm	1,600kg	+/- 50kg	230kg PMF 109
SB 1000	Großladungsbombe	2,650 x 660mm	1,000kg	-	735kg Fp 60/40, or 800-850kg Trialen 106, PMF 109
SB 2500	Großladungsbombe	3,693 x 785mm	2,500kg	+/- 70kg	1,710kg Fp 60/40, or Trialen 105, 106 or 109

Air-Dropped Weapons

The He 111 was able to carry a wide variety of air-dropped weapons. These were contained in the bomb-bay as well as externally beneath the wing centre-section. The accompanying photographs show two of these possibilities.

The He 111 could carry some 35 types of bombs, either internally or externally. These ranged from the SD 10 – a 10kg (22 lb) Splitterbombe (fragmentation bomb) – to the SC 2500 Max Großladungsbombe (high-explosive bomb with a high percentage of explosive weight). The table above lists some of the principal bombs carried.

In addition to the bombs listed above, various other types were carried, eg Brandbomben (incendiary bombs), Hohlladungsbomben (hollow-charge high-explosive bombs) and small Splitterbomben (anti-personnel or fragmentation bombs) not included here for space reasons – Author.

Translator's Note:
In the above data table, Minenbombe = standard thin-walled high-explosive (literally mine) bomb with around 50% high explosive (h.e.) weight; Großladungsbombe = thin-walled high-explosive bomb with up to 70% h.e. weight; Panzersprengbombe = thick-walled armour-piercing high-explosive bomb with up to 20% h.e. weight. Fp = Füllpulver (filling powder) explosive and other mixtures consisted of the following chemicals:

- Fp 02 = 100% TNT (trinitrotoluol).
- Fp 50/50 = 50% Fp 02 plus 50% Ammonsalpeter (ammonium nitrate).
- Fp 60/40 = 60% Fp 02 plus 40% Ammonsalpeter.
- Amatol 39 = 50% Dinitrobenzol plus 35% Ammonsalpeter plus 15% Hexogen (hexanitrodiphenylamine).
- Amatol 41 = 52% Ammonsalpeter plus 30% PH-Salz (ethylene diamine nitrate) plus 10% Hexogen plus 6 % Kalksalpeter (calcium nitrate) plus 2 % Montanwachs (mining industry wax) for storage stability.
- Trialen 105 = 70% Hexogen plus 15% Hexogen plus 1 % Aluminium powder.
- Trialen 106 = 50% Hexogen plus 25% Hexogen plus 25% Aluminiumsalpeter (Aluminium nitrate).
- Trialen 109 = 50% Trialen 105 plus 50% PMF 109.
- PMF 109 = 80% Hexogen plus 20% Aluminiumpyroschliff (Aluminium shavings).

For more details on the range of German bombs and explosives, see W Fleischer's *German Air-dropped Weapons* (Midland Publishing, 2004).

He 111H Series Variants

The most diverse of the H-series variants ranged from the He 111H-1 to the H-23. For space reasons, the following data lists each variant in tabular form, concentrating principally on their major differences.

He 111H-1 (Bomber)
- Powerplants: two Jumo 211A-1s driving VDM airscrews.
- Two 4 ESAC 250 vertical bomb magazines in bomb-bay.
- Defensive armament: three MG 15s (one each in A1-, B- and C-Stands).
- In an unknown number of aircraft, the armament was supplemented by four MG 15 and one MG 17 machine-gun.
- Unprotected fuel tanks replaced by self-sealing tanks.
- Radio equipment: FuG IIIaU, later FuG X.
- Crew of four.
- Not fitted with catapult capability.
- Flight-testing commenced June 1939 (pre-production aircraft).

He 111H-2 (Bomber)
- Powerplants: two 1,200hp Jumo 211A-3s.
- Coolers as He 111H-1.
- Armament as He 111H-1.
- Radio equipment: FuG X.
- Aircraft designated H-2/R1 had long-range navigational equipment.
- Aircraft designated H-2/R2 had two lateral fuselage D-Stands, each with one MG 15.
- Not fitted with catapult capability.
- Flight-testing commenced May 1939.

He 111H-3 (Bomber)
- Powerplants: two 1,200hp Jumo 211Ds.
- Two 4 ESAC 250 vertical bomb magazines in bomb-bay.
- Could carry external weapons.
- Defensive armament: five MG 15s, one each in A-Stand (could also have one MG-FF), B-, C1-, C2, and D-Stands, plus one MG 17 in tail. MG 17 data: calibre 7.92mm (0.31in), length 1,175mm (46.26in), width 156mm (6.14in), height 159mm (6.26in), weight 10.2kg (22.49 lb), rate of fire 1,200 rounds/min.
- Servo-tab power unit reconfigured.
- Undercarriage area strengthened.
- Crew of five.
- Catapult capability installed.
- Radio equipment: as H-1 variant. When different, was designated H-3/R1.
- Flight-testing commenced in first half of 1939. Entered large-scale production in November 1939.

He 111H-4 (Bomber, Torpedo-bomber)
- Powerplants: initially Jumo 211D-1; later Jumo 211H-1 or F-1.
- Equipped with PVC rack for external loads up to 1,800kg (3,968 lb). In latter case, had two PVC 1006L racks also suitable for carrying torpedoes (PVC 1006B).
- Defensive armament: six MG 15s distributed over A1-, A2-, B-, C1-, C2- and D-Stands plus one MG 17 in tail.
- Maximum two 4 ESAC 250 vertical bomb canisters in bomb-bay.
- A few H-4s had provision for the X-Leitstrahl-verfahren (guide-beam system), recognisable by additional antenna on dorsal fuselage.

He 111H-5 (Long-Range Bomber, Torpedo-bomber)
- Powerplants: two Jumo 211Ds or Hs.
- From 80th aircraft, ETC 2000 introduced for SC 2500 bomb.
- Range increased by auxiliary fuel tanks in bomb-bay.
- Defensive armament: one MG-FF in A-Stand, one MG 15 in each of A2-, B-, C1-, C2- and D-Stands plus one MG 17 in tail.
- Due to higher weight, mainwheels had tyres measuring 1400 x 410mm (55.11 x 16.14in).
- Possibility for installing cameras.
- Use of VDM airscrews.
- Two torpedoes could also be carried if required.
- Armour-plating strengthened.

He 111H-6 (Bomber, Torpedo-bomber)
- Powerplants: two 1,340hp Jumo 211F-1s or F-2s.
- Used Junkers VS 11 airscrews.
- Cooler installation changed.
- Fuel quick-release system altered.
- According to load condition, fuel capacity varied from 3,450 litres to 4,285 litres.
- Crew raised to five.
- Defensive armament: one MG-FF in A-Stand, one MG 15 in each of A1-, A2-, B-, C2- and D-Stands plus one MG 17 in tail. An MG-FF was also often installed in the nose.
- He 111H-6/R2 had coupling for load-carrying glider towing.
- Radio equipment: FuG X, later FuG 16 and FuG 28. A few aircraft were equipped with FuG 202.
- Possibility existed of carrying two torpedoes.

He 111H-7 (H-6 Night Bomber variant, not built)
- Powerplants: two Jumo 211F-1s intended.
- Was to have been a 'skimmed' version for night operations, on which the tail MG 17 was dispensed with.
- Lateral weapon stands eliminated as well as a forward-firing MG 15.
- Planned to dispense with ventral gondola.
- Armour-plating was to be likewise reduced.

He 111H-8 (Bomber, re-build from H-3/H-5)
- Powerplants: two Jumo 211D-1s or F-1s.
- Defensive armament: one MG-FF in C1-Stand, one MG 15 in each of A1-, A2-, B-, C2- and D-Stands.
- Specialised variant with balloon cable deflectors, which, due to weight, required counterweight in rear fuselage.
- Above cumbersome frame later replaced by so-called Kuto-Nase (cable cutters) in wing leading-edge.
- Later modification planned to include Starrschlepp (rigid-tow) for gliders.

He 111H-9 (Trainer, modified H-1)
With regard to this variant, considerable differences exist in published accounts. In some the H-9 is described as a Schulflugzeug, while in others it is classified as a modified H-6 fitted with a Kuto-Nase (balloon cable-cutter nose).

- As Schulflugzeug (training aircraft), would have had dual controls.
- New arrangement of cockpit instruments.
- Powerplants: two Jumo 211A-1s or D-1s.
- Defensive armament removed, likewise jettison gear in bomb-bay.

He 111H-10 (Trainer, modified H-2/H-3)
In this case, too, the opinions of various authors disagree widely. Some say this variant was to have had strengthened armour protection, Kuto-Nase, reduced bombload, full defensive armament, MG 131 and MG 81Z installed, and two Jumo 211F-2 powerplants.

- Powerplants: two Jumo 211A-1s or D-1s.
- As Schulflugzeug, would have had dual controls.
- New arrangement of cockpit instruments.
- Defensive armament removed.
- Most probably armour-plating also removed.

He 111H-11 (Bomber/Torpedo-bomber, based on H-6)
- Powerplants: two Jumo 211F-2s.
- Optimised arrangement of cockpit instruments.
- Equipped as level bomber, torpedo-bomber and minelayer.
- Kuto-Nase as series installation.
- Defensive armament: one MG-FF in A-Stand, one MG 131 in B-Stand, one MG 81Z in C2-Stand and one MG 81 in each D-Stand. MG 17 in tail deleted.
- Additional armour protection for B-Stand.
- Sliding canopy roof could be closed.
- Newly configured canopy glazing to reduce former dazzle effects.
- Unknown number of H-11s were equipped with tow coupling.

He 111H-12 (Trials & Training aircraft for pilotless missile operations, based on H-6)
- Powerplants: two Jumo 211F-2s.
- Defensive armament reduced to one MG 15 in A-Stand and one MG 131 in B-stand; C-Stand position removed.
- Underwing stations for two Henschel Hs 293 glide-bombs; alternatively, two PC 1400 X (Fritz X) guided bombs could be carried.
- Missile radio guidance system: FuG 203 Kehl III transmitter; corresponding antennas installed between fuselage and tailplane.
- Aircraft heating installation expanded with Kärcher heater.

He 111H-13

This sub-type designation was not allocated.

He 111H-14
(Bomber/Pathfinder, based on H-3)

- Powerplants: two Jumo 211F-2s.
- Defensive armament: one MG 15 in each A- and B-Stand (supposedly also MG 151/20 in individual cases), one MG 81Z in C2-Stand and one MG 81 in each lateral D-Stand.
- Air-dropped weapons installation consisted of two 4 ESAC 250 vertical containers, alternatively one 4 ESAC plus one ETC 2000 for externally suspended loads.
- Transmission equipment: FuG 16, FuMB 4 Samos radio monitoring receiver, Peil G V with APZ-5 and FuG 351 Korfu.
- For missions on Eastern Front, aircraft were later equipped with glider tow coupling.

He 111H-15 (Bomber)

The suggestion that this variant was a bomber intended to launch the Blohm & Voss BV 246 unpowered glide-bomb cannot be established with certainty. On this subject, author Heinz Nowarra wrote: 'Since [the BV 246] had not reached production maturity, it was used as a night bomber equipped with normal PVC.' The He 111H-15 is also mentioned in literature as a Pathfinder fitted with additional radio equipment and strengthened armament (one MG-FF, one MG 131, one MG 81 and two MG 15s). Exactly which H variant served as the basic model has not been established at the present time.

He 111H-16 (Bomber, based on H-14)

This was the fourth large-scale series-produced H variant, whose principal features were:

- Powerplants: two Jumo 211F-2s.
- Fuel capacity of 4,285 litres, equal to that of H-6.
- Defensive armament: one MG-FF in A-Stand, one MG 131 in B-Stand, one MG 81Z in C2-Stand and one MG 81 in each lateral D-Stand. In some A-Stands MG 131 with roller gun-mount was fitted.
- Armour-plating installed was detachable and could be jettisoned to reduce weight.
- When equipped with the appropriate radio equipment, H-16 could be used as target-finder, in which case armour protection was increased and weapon jettison gear reduced (H-16/R3).
- Radio equipment: FuG 16, FuG 10P, including APZ-6. Various aircraft also had FuG 101A.
- Rüstsätze (field equipment sets) included load-carrying glider tow coupling (H-16/R2).

He 111H-17 (Trainer)

War-weary He 111H aircraft used as Schulflugzeuge are reported to have appeared under this designation, but unfortunately this cannot be confirmed. Whether such variants actually existed is not known. Principal features were:

- Dual controls with corresponding alterations to instruments arrangement.
- Removal of defensive armament and weapons jettison gear.

He 111H-18 (Night-bomber/Pathfinder/ Torpedo-bomber, based on H-16)

- Powerplants: two Jumo 211F-2s equipped with flame dampers.
- Defensive armament: one MG-FF in A-Stand, one MG 131 in B-Stand, one MG 81Z in C2-Stand and one MG 81 in each D-Stand. Lateral stands only partially fitted.
- Had possibility of carrying heavy calibre bombs or torpedoes externally.
- Internal bombload was contained in one or two 4 ESAC containers according to Rüstsatz fitted.
- Radio equipment: FuG X, FuG 16, FuG 101 and FuG 227. A few aircraft were fitted with FuG 200.

He 111H-19 (Trainer, based on H-16)

This Schulflugzeug with dual controls and suitably modified instrument arrangement was derived from He 111H-16s that could no longer be operationally employed. It had its armament and jettison equipment removed and altered radio installations.

He 111H-20 (Bomber/Transporter)

In contrast to the He 111H-11 and H-16, modifications consisted of new radio and weapons jettison equipment. The principal features were:

- Powerplants: two Jumo 211F-2s, partially with flame dampers.
- As military transport, could carry 16 soldiers and auxiliary equipment as well as crew of four.
- Alternatively, as well as crew of four could carry 15 paratroopers released from parachute release line.
- As bomber, carried crew of five.
- B-Stand armour protection removed.
- According to H-20 handbook of May 1944, defensive armament consisted of one MG 131 in WL/BR gun-mount in A-Stand, one DL 131/1C or E rotatable gun-mount in B-Stand, one WL 131/AL or CL gun-mount in C-Stand, and one LG 81Z/2B gun-mount in each lateral D-Stand. Installed later were MG 131 in WL 131/BR, BL, CL or CR-Walzenlafetten roller gun-mounts.
- Bomb jettison equipment: two 4 ESAC 250 or two ETC 1000.
- Externally fitted with two ETC 1000, or load-carrying suspension plate that was suitable for carriage of bombs or provisions containers.
- Rüstsatz 1, consisting of 835-litre fuel tank combined with 120-litre lubricant tank, housed in bomb-bay between vertical frames 4 and 8.
- Radio equipment: FuG 10, TZG 10 and FuG 16Z. D/F and target-finding accomplished with Peil G6 and APZ6, and blind-landing with FuBl 2H.
- Target approach assisted by FuG 16 coupled with ZVG 16, installed between fuselage frames 5 and 6. For special tasks, FuG 25A was available.
- Improved Kuto-Nase (balloon cable-cutter nose) installed.
- Original 500 x 180mm (19.7 x 7.1in) tailwheel replaced by one measuring 560 x 200mm (22.05 x 7.87in).
- Optical communications system installed, consisting of signal lamps in various colours on both sides of fuselage.
- Equipped with Starrschlepp (rigid-tow) equipment only; not able to be catapulted.
- Variants were H-20/R1 Transporter, H-20/R2 Starrschlepp, H-20/R3 Night-bomber and H-20/R4 Bomber with 20 50kg (110 lb) bombs as external load.

He 111H-21
(High-Altitude Bomber, based on H-20)

- Powerplants: two Jumo 211F-2s equipped with Hirth TK-9 exhaust-gas turbo-superchargers (retroactively installed).
- Jumo 213E originally planned for series installation had to be abandoned due to low availability.
- Defensive armament: one MG 131 in A-Stand, one MG 131 in B-Stand, one MG 81Z in C-Stand and one MG 81 in each D-Stand.
- Bomb jettison equipment presumably corresponded to He 111H-20.

He 111H-22 (Fi 103, V-1, Launching-craft)

Some 100 examples of the H-16, H-20 and possibly the H-21 were modified as mothercraft for air-launching Fieseler Fi 103 flying-bombs. For this purpose, the following modifications were necessary:

- Powerplants: two Jumo 211F-2s, since Jumo 213E still not available in sufficient quantities.
- Fi 103, suspended on starboard side on PVC 1006 beneath wing centre section, resulted in speed loss of around 20km/h (12mph). First air launch made on 10th December 1942 (from Focke-Wulf 200). First operational air-launch against UK identified by British on 8th July 1944.
- Installation of connection box and ignition equipment for missile.
- Due to heat emission from pulse-jet exhaust, affected parts of tailplane and fin additionally protected with sheet-metal covering layer.
- Normal bomb jettison equipment discarded on V-1 weapon carriers.
- Defensive armament reduced to one MG 131 in A-Stand, one MG 131 in B-Stand and one MG 81Z in C-Stand. A-Stand weapon often removed.

He 111H-23 (Military Transport)

This variant, derived from the H-20, served as a paratroop-drop or provisions carrier for Kommando operations; it could carry eight paratroops or two supplies containers. Powerplants were likewise Jumo 211F-2s in place of the planned but lacking Jumo 213A-1s. It was fitted with long-range radio equipment.

Since aircraft from other quarters were available in sufficient quantities for special operations, the H-23 machines envisaged for this purpose were to have been modified as night bombers.

This section concludes with technical data of specific He 111H models followed by a detailed listing of the structural details, dimensions, weights, performance and equipment of the He 111H-16, and the other powerplants that were installed in the He 111.

Technical Data Comparison

Heinkel Model	He 111H-1	He 111H-3	He 111H-6	He 111H-20	He 111H-22
Powerplant					
Type	Jumo 211A-1	Jumo 211D-1	Jumo 211F-1/F-2	Jumo 211F-2	Jumo 213E-1*
Take-off power, hp	1,000	1,200	1,340 (F-2)	1,340	1,750
Dimensions					
Wingspan	22.60m (74' 1¾")	22.60m (74' 1¾")	22.60m (74' 1¾")	22.60m (74' 1¾")	22.60m (74' 1¾")
Length	16.40m (53' 9⅝")	16.40m (53' 9⅝")	16.40m (53' 9⅝")	16.40m (53' 9⅝")	16.40m (53' 9⅝")
Height	4.00m (13' 1½")	4.00m (13' 1½")	4.00m (13' 1½")	4.00m (13' 1½")	4.00m (13' 1½")
Wing area, m^2 (ft^2)	87.60 (942.90)	87.60 (942.90)	87.60 (942.90)	87.60 (942.90)	87.60 (942.90)
Weights					
Empty weight, kg (lb)	6,740 (14,859)	7,200 (15,873)	8,680 (19,533)	8,680 (19,533)	10,500 (23,148)
Take-off weight, kg (lb)	12,600 (27,778)	13,120 (28,924)	14,000 (30,864)	14,000 (30,864)	15,930 (35,119)
Performance					
Maximum speed, km/h (mph)	410 (255)	440 (273)	440 (273)	440 (273)	475 (295)
Cruising speed, km/h (mph)	325 (202)	330 (205)	330 (205)	330 (205)	370 (230)
Range, km (miles)	2,000 (1,243)	2,300 (1,429)	2,300 (1,429)	2,250 (1,398)	2,900 (1,802)
Service ceiling, m (ft)	6,500 (21,325)	8,000 (26,245)	6,500 (21,325)	6,500 (21,325)	10,000 (32,810)
Military load					
Armament	3 x MG 15 1 x MG 17	5 x MG 15 1 x MG 17	6 x MG 15 2 x MG 81Z	3 x MG 131 1 x MG 81Z	2 x MG 131 1x MG-FF
Bombload, kg (lb)	2,000 (4,409)	2,000 (4,409)	2,000 (4,409)	(see text – opposite page)	3,000 (6,614)
(alternatively)	-	-	-	2 torpedoes	1 x Fi 103
Crew	4	4	5	3-4	5

*Planned version with Jumo 213 as a comparison to Jumo 211 engines.

Sectional view of the rescue/safety devices in the He 111H-20 (He 111H-20 Handbook). Key: 1 Waist belts; 2 First-aid pack; 3 First-aid bag; 4 Rear-view mirror; 5 Rescue dinghy; 6 Self-destruction explosive load.

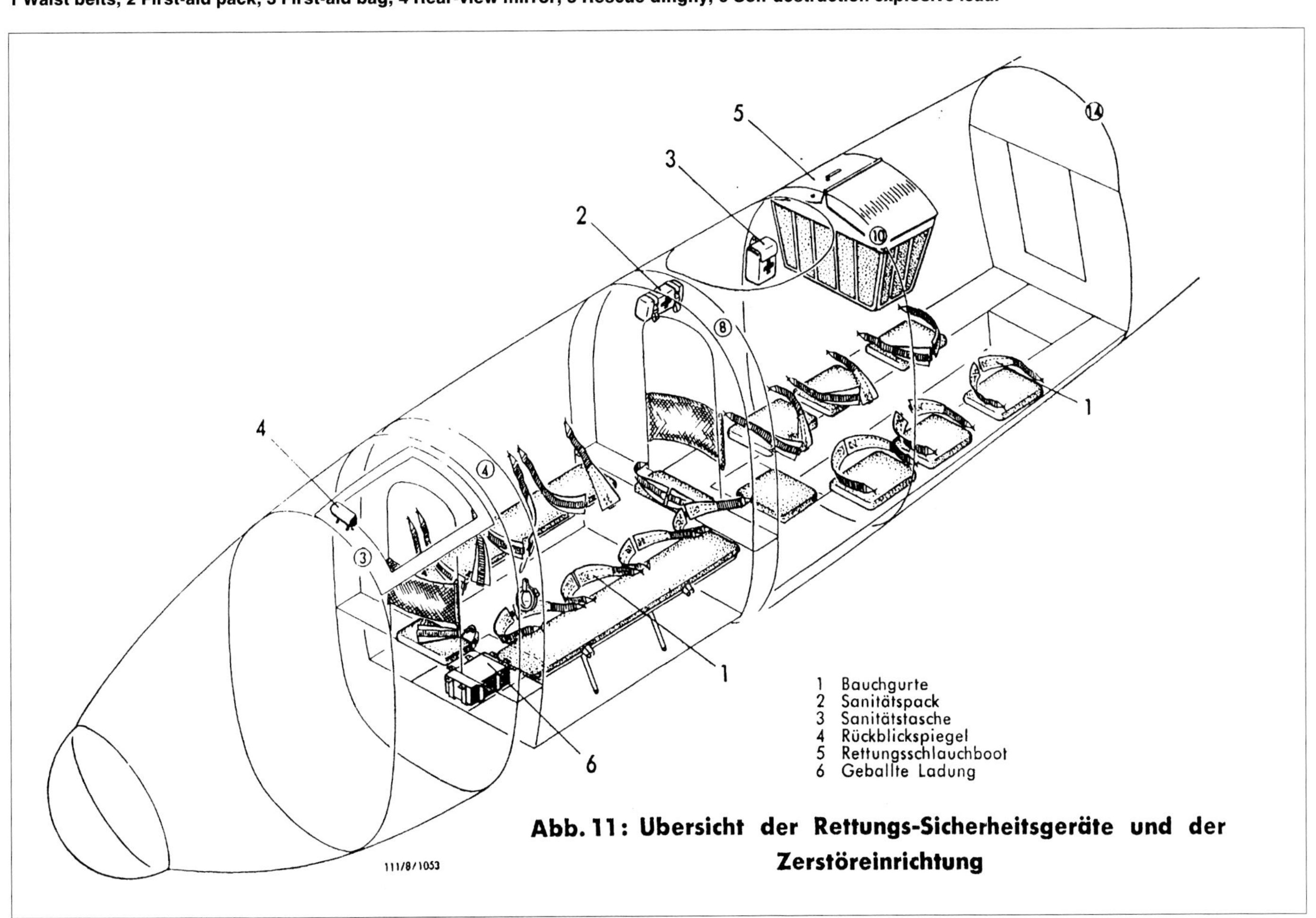

Opposite page, left column from the top:

Rear-quarter view of an He 111H-5.

Side-view of an He 111H-5.

An He 111H-6 Torpedo-bomber with practice torpedoes.

An He 111H-6 Torpedo-bomber during engine warm-up.

The balloon cable deflectors/cutters show this to be an He 111H-8. The Kuto-Nase later installed in the wing leading edge allowed this inconvenient structure to be dispensed with.

Right column from the top:

The aircraft underside was finished in RLM 65 Hellblau (light blue). Note the considerable blackening caused by the engine exhausts.

Despite the poor quality, this photo shows an He 111H-14 Pathfinder aircraft.

An He 111H-18 photographed in Rechlin.

An He 111H-21 (CI+IE).

An He 111H-22 carrying a Fieseler Fi 103 (V-1) flying-bomb beneath the starboard wing.

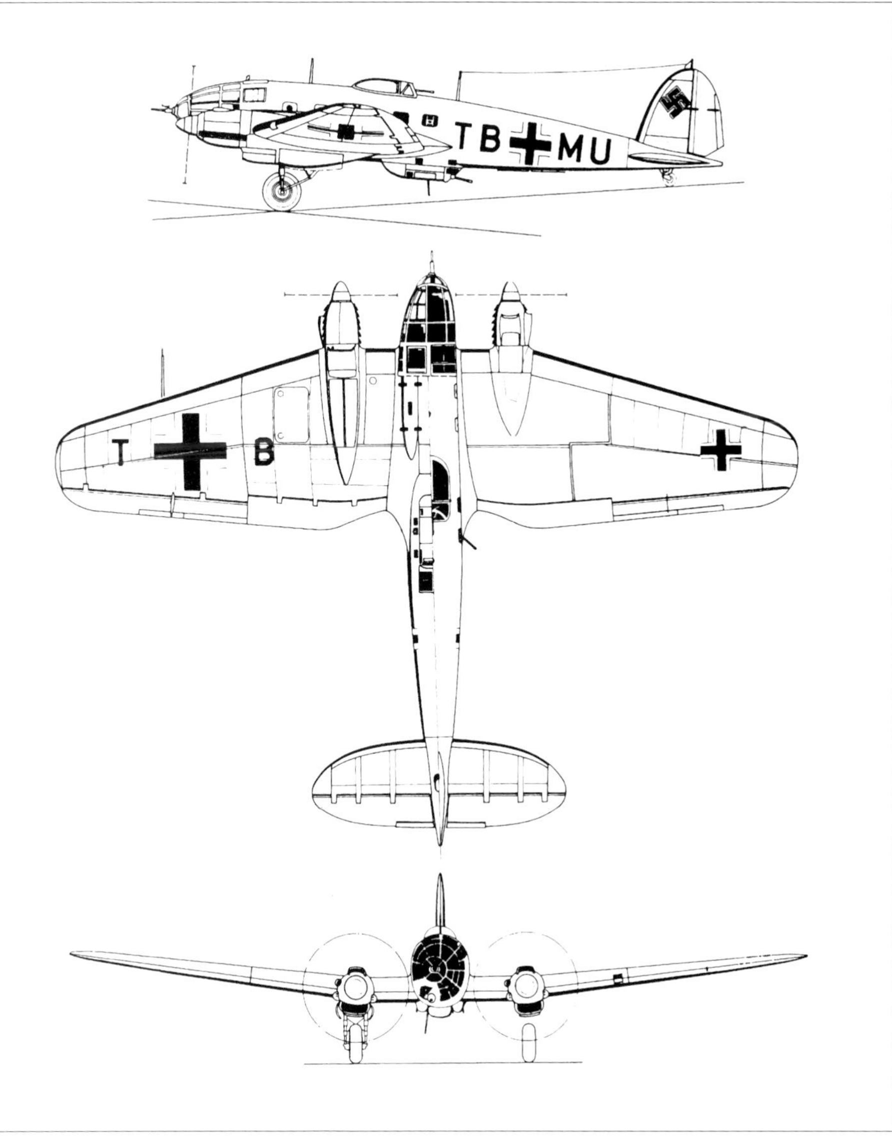

This page:

Three-view drawing of the He 111H-16.

An He 111H-16 in flight.

Technical Details of the He 111H-16

Fuselage

Overall length	16.4m (53ft 9⅝in) (Works drawing shows 16.2m, 53ft 1¾in)
Fuselage max width	1.675m (5ft 6in)
Fuselage max height	2.40m (7ft 10½in)
Number of longerons	4
Number of transverse frames	27
Type of construction	monocoque, stressed-skin, flush-riveted

Wing

Wingspan	22.6m (74ft 1¾in) (Works drawing shows 22.5m [73ft 9⅞in])
Wing area (geometric)	79.50m^2 (855.71ft^2)
Wing area (aerodynamic)	86.50m^2 (931.06ft^2)
Wing area (overall)	87.60m^2 (942.90ft^2)
Wing chord (max)	4.85m (15ft 11in)
Wing loading at a loaded weight of 14T (30,864 lb)	162kg/m^2 (33.18 lb/ft^2)
Outer wing dihedral	7°
Outer wing spars	2
Outer wing ribs	27
Type of construction	smooth sheet, flush-riveted

Ailerons

Attachment points	4
Number of spars	2
Number of ribs	25
Type of covering	fabric
Deflection range	25.5° up, 19.5° down (flaps at 0° setting)
Deflection range	25° up, 20° down (flaps fully extended)
Trim tabs	2 (inner tab for trim, outer tab as load relief)
Balance weight	1 (for outer trim tab)

Landing Flaps

Attachment points	3
Number of spars	1
Number of ribs	19 (mainly lattice-type)
Deflection range	15° at take-off, 64° for landing
Type of activation	hydraulic via control rods
Type of covering	smooth sheet, flush-riveted

Tailplane

Tailplane span	7.83m (25ft 8¼in)
Max chord (including rudder)	2.85m (9ft 4¼in)
Tailplane chord	1.97m (6ft 5½in)
Rudder chord	0.88m (2ft 10⅝in)
Number of spars	2
Number of ribs	15 (mainly lattice-type)
Variable setting range	-1.5° to +4.5°
Type of covering	stressed-skin, flush-riveted

Elevators

Max chord	0.88m (2ft 10⅝in)
Attachment points	4
Number of spars	2 (rudder/tab)
Number of ribs	15
Deflection range	25° up, 20° down
Trim tabs	1
Tab movement range	13° up, 9° down
Type of covering	fabric

Fin

Height	2.8m (9ft 2¼in) to fuselage axis
Max chord	2.545m (8ft 4¼in)
Number of spars	2
Number of ribs	10
Type of covering	stressed-skin, flush-riveted

Rudder

Attachment points	3
Number of spars	2 (rudder/tab)
Number of ribs	10
Deflection range	30° each side
Trim tabs	1
Deflection range	11° each side (max)

Undercarriage

Mainwheels	selectively, with oil-pressure-operated double servo-brakes of Elektronmetall or VDM firms
Mainwheel dimensions	1140 x 410mm (44.88 x 16.14in) (Works drawing shows 1100 x 375mm, 43.31 x 14.76in)
Undercarriage legs (each)	2 VDM-Faudi compressed-air legs
Tailwheel type	Kronprinz high-pressure tyres with deep-bed wheel rims
Tailwheel dimensions	500 x 180mm (19.69 x 7.09in) (Works drawing shows 465 x 165mm (18.31 x 6.50in))

High-Altitude Breathing Equipment

(Drawing shows old equipment)

Type of installation	Six hi-alt breathing apparata with dirt filter, oxygen pressure gauge and breathing tubes
Number of bottles	30 2-litre spherical steel bottles, five shut-off valves, 20 non-return valves and external filling connection

Radio Equipment

Radio and crew intercom	FuG 10P (600-300 KHz or 6000-3000 KHz)
Aircraft-to-aircraft comm	FuG 10 P8 and TZG 10 or FuG 16 (38.5-42.3MHz)
D/F and target-approach	FuG 10P with APZ 6
Radio landing aid	FuBl 2H (30.00-33.33MHz or 38.0MHz)
Electrical altimeter	FuG 101 (400-337MHz)
For special purposes	FuG 25a

Defensive Armament

A-Stand	1 x 20mm MG-FF cannon with six magazines or 180 rounds
Weapon mounting	cupola-type Lafette (gun-mount), L-FF 6 (V 41 gunsight)

B-Stand	1 x 13mm MG 131 B2 with 1,000 rounds (belt)
Weapon mounting	WL 131 AL rotatable gun-mount
C-Stand	1 x 7.92mm MG 81Z (each 850 rounds)
Weapon mounting	WL 81Z/3B gun-mount with Visier V 58 and Revi 16A reflector sight
D-Stands (lateral)	either MG 81 (500 rounds) or MG 81Z with 2 x 500 rounds
Weapon mounting	LK 140/80 Lafette for MG 81 or LK 81Z/2 Lafette for MG 81Z
Angular range of fire	see illustration on page 58 of this book

Air-Dropped Weapons

In bomb-bay	up to 8 ESAC vertical canisters for 250kg (551 lb) bombs in 2 x 4 ESAC arrangement
External suspensions	ETC 2000

Powerplants

Type	2 x Jumo 211F-2
Engine data	see Technical Data on page 68 of this book

Fuel system

Fuel type	B4 (87 octane), A2 (87 octane)
Fuel tank 1 (centre-section)	700 litres
Fuel tank 2 (centre-section)	700 litres
Fuel tank 3 (outer wing)	1,025 litres
Fuel tank 4 (outer wing)	1,025 litres
Fuel tank 5 (bomb-bay)	835 litres
Lubricant type	Aero-Shell medium, Mobiloil Rotring, Intava 100
Tanks 1 and 2 (centre-section)	2 x 120 litres

Propellers

Type	Junkers VS 11 three-bladed variable-pitch
Blade construction	light-wood Mantelblatt
Propeller diameter	3.50m (11ft 5¾in)
Pitch-change speed	12°/second
Item number	9-21624A
Setting/position indicator	none

Weights

Equipped weight	8,680kg (19,136 lb)
Fuel weight (normal)	2,425kg (4,962 lb)
Fuel weight (max)	2,550kg (5,625 lb)
Lubricant weight	190kg (419 lb)
Jettisonable load	2,000kg (4,409 lb)
Ammunition weight	205kg (452 lb)
Crew of five	500kg (1,102 lb)
Take-off weight	14,000kg (30,864 lb)

Component weights for transportation

Fuselage, including cockpit	1,900kg (4,189 lb)
Tailplane	108kg (238 lb)
Elevators (2)	52kg (114.6 lb)
Fin	27kg (59.5 lb)
Rudder	28kg (61.7 lb)
Landing flaps (2)	52kg (114.6 lb)
Ailerons	67kg (147.7 lb)
Outer wings (2)	930kg (2,050 lb)
Centre section	1,725kg (3,803 lb)
Main undercarriage	425kg (937 lb)
Powerplants (2)	2,020kg (4,453 lb)
Propellers (2)	395kg (871 lb)
Coolers (2)	176kg (388 lb)

Aircraft Performance

Mean cruising speed at max continuous power	
at low level	330km/h (205mph) at 2 x 910hp Range 1,950km (1,212 miles)
at 2,000m (6,560ft)	370km/h (230mph) at 2 x 1,025hp Range 1,930km (1,199 miles)
at 5,000m (16,400ft)	(3) 385km/h (239mph) at 2 x 900hp Range 2,060km (1,280 miles)
Mean cruising speed at cruising power	
at low level	285km/h (177mph) at 2 x 700hp, range 2,200km (1,367 miles) 330km/h (205mph) at 2 x 800hp, range 2,250km (1,398 miles)
at 5,000m (16,400ft)	365km/h (227mph) at 2 x 750hp Range 2,170km (1,348 miles)
Maximum speed	
at low level	350km/h (217mph) at 2 x 1,120hp
at 2,000m (6,560ft)	380km/h (236mph) at 2 x 1,220hp
at 6,000m (19,685ft)	405km/h (252mph) at 2 x 1,050hp
Times to height	
to 2,000m (6,560ft)	8.50min
to 4,000m (13,125ft)	23.5min
to 6,000m (19,685ft)	42.0min
Service ceiling	6,500m (21,325ft)
Range*	2,700km (1,678 miles) with 1,000kg (2,205 lb) external bombload 2,900km (1,802 miles) with 1,000kg (2,205 lb) bombload in bomb-bay 740km (460 miles) with 2,500kg (5,512 lb) external load + 750kg (1,653 lb) in bomb-bay

* with cruise and continuous power at take-off weight of 14,000kg (30,864 lb) at 5,000m (16,400ft)

The 12 cylinders of the BMW 6.0 Z were upright, as opposed to the inverted arrangement in the Jumo and DB engines.

The 'innards' of the BMW VI. With its 46.9-litre cylinder capacity, it was only able to develop a maximum of 750hp at take-off.

Above: **The Daimler-Benz DB 601 of 33.9 litres cylinder capacity delivered 1,100hp at take-off.**

Right: **Rear view of a DB 600, which had the same cylinder capacity as the DB 601, but whose take-off power of 850hp was noticeably lower.**

Technical Details of He 111 Powerplants

Powerplant type	BMW VI 6.0 Z	DB 600G	DB 601A-1
Number of cylinders	12, upright V	12, inverted V	12, inverted V
Cylinder volume	46.9 litres (2,862in³)	33.9 litres (2,069in³)	33.9 litres (2,069in³)
Volume per cylinder	3.908 litres (238.5in³)	2.825 litres (235.4in³)	2.825 litres (235.4in³)
Bore	160mm (6.3in)	150mm (5.9in)	150mm (5.9in)
Stroke	190mm (7.5in)	160mm (6.3in)	160mm (6.3in)
Compression ratio	6.0 (80 octane)	6.5 (87 octane)	6.9 (87 octane)
Reduction gearing	none	0.65	0.65
Take-off power	660hp at 2,200rpm	850hp at 2,300rpm	1,100hp at 2,400rpm
Cooling type	liquid	water	water

Opposite page:

A contemporary advertisement for the DB 600, as used in the Junkers Ju 90 V1 (D-AALU) above it and the He 111 at top right.

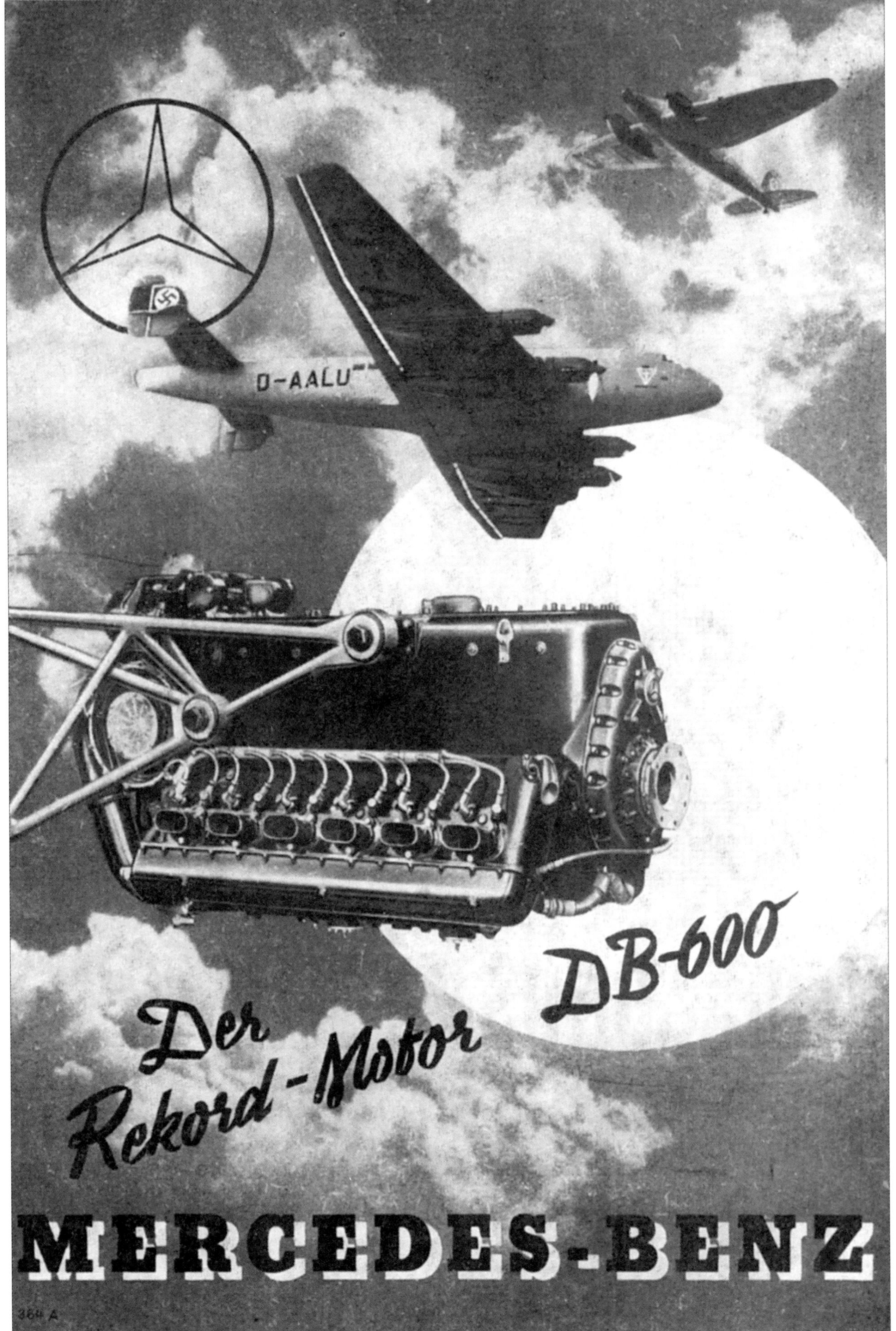
D-AALU
Der Rekord-Motor DB-600
MERCEDES-BENZ
364 A

Chapter Six

A 'One-Off'

The He 111Z Zwilling (Twin)

Background to the Origin of the He 111Z

The lack of a suitable towcraft for the giant Messerschmitt Me 321 load-carrying glider, first flown on 25th February 1941, led the Luftwaffe to adopt the Troika-Schlepp (triple-tow), which often resulted in tragedy. This emergency solution consisted of three Me 110s lifting their monstrous 'trailer' into the air by towing cables – an often hair-raising operation that was certainly not for inexperienced or timid pilots. Getting this large formation airborne in this fashion resulted in several losses even during the flight-testing and familiarisation phase, so much so that pressure was brought to bear on the authorities to find a completely different solution. This type of aerial acrobatics was regarded very suspiciously even by Generalluftzeugmeister Ernst Udet, who hoped to find a solution that could be brought about without too great an effort.

This took place at the beginning of 1941 when, during a visit to the Heinkel plant in Marienehe, he proposed the manufacture of a Zwilling (Twin) aircraft. At short notice, Heinkel commenced work on this project, and calculations showed that Udet's requirement could be achieved in a relatively short space of time. Realisation of this towcraft was simple in concept, as it was possible to make use of already tried and tested components; thus Heinkel Werke was able to create a suitable towcraft by using comparatively few materials in the process. The most noticeable new feature in its design was the tri-motor wing centre section that joined together the two He 111 fuselages.

Design drawings became available in August 1941 and the maiden flight of the prototype took place in the autumn of that year. The obligatory flight-test phase showed equally good results; even the emergency ditching of the next test prototype in the Müritzsee* in Rechlin did not prove a discouragement, as the aircraft was able to be quickly put back into operation. But despite the successful series of trials, only ten series-built aircraft followed. According to the original plan, ten per month were to have been completed from March 1943, but that remained only a proposal, and an order for 40 further examples was cancelled shortly afterwards.

The RLM was now pursuing other plans whereby the giant Me 321 was itself to be powered. The first prototype, equipped with six Gnôme-Rhône 14N engines and designated Me 323, raised itself into the air for the first time on 20th January 1942. The success of the ensuing trial confirmed the correctness of this decision, which led to the termination of He 111Z production after the two prototypes and ten series airframes had been built. The He 111Z series aircraft were originally to have been delivered during the period August to December 1942, but because of the precarious workforce situation, Heinkel had only been able to complete the first two aircraft by October 1942.

Ernst Udet and Ernst Heinkel looking at the speaker with questioning expressions.

* A Messerschmitt Leipheim report mentions that the He 111Z was built at the suggestion of the E-Stelle Rechlin. The very short interval between the release of design drawings and the first flight, quoted as 'autumn 1941' (but logically much later in the year, since the He 111Z did not enjoy top priority) has been questioned by a number of researchers, among them Heinkel historian Dr. Volker Koos and Christopf Regel (one of the authors of *German Secret Flight Test Centres to 1945*, Midland Publishing, 2002), the latter mentioning the crash site as not Müritz but Mütlitz near Rathenow in Brandenburg, but not ascribing it to the He 111Z V2. Details of the intriguing discussion and questions still unsolved on the history of the He 111Z are to be found in the Reader-Forum in the 5/03 (Oct/Nov 2003) and 1/04 (Jan-Feb 2004) issues of *Jet & Prop* – Translator.

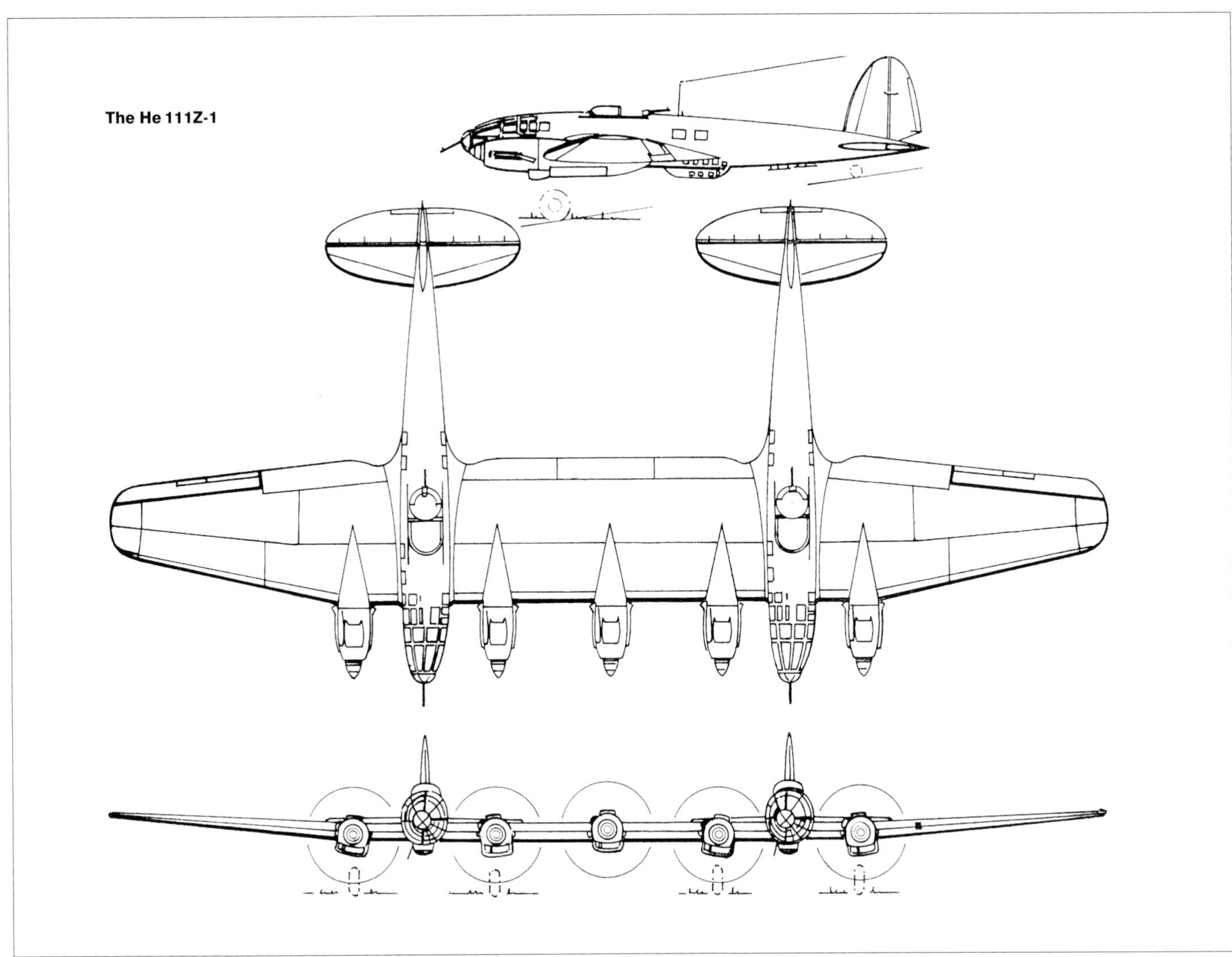

The He 111Z-1

We shall now take a closer look at the technical details of this unique Heinkel product.

The Configuration of the He 111Z-1

The He 111Z Twin was made up of two airframes of the He 111H-6 bomber version, although for some the H-16 was also used as a basis. In both cases the aircraft consisted of two normal fuselages taken from the production line but with all the bomber equipment discarded; however, defensive armament was retained. The most significant new component was the newly designed wing centre section that joined the two fuselages together.

This component, consisting of a normal dural monocoque with stressed-skin construction, was of rectangular section and had a span of 6.15m (20ft 2⅛in) and an area of 29.50m^2 (317.53ft^2). Connected to the normal fuselage attachment points, this assembly group of constant chord and thickness was relatively simple to manufacture. Measured from the fuselage datum lines, the fuselages were 12.8m (41ft 12in) apart; the overall span of the Twin thus reached the impressive figure of 35.2m (115ft 5⅞in), with a wing area of 147m^2 (1,582.26ft^2). Besides its lifting function, this centre section also housed a fifth engine and additional fuel tanks. With its five Jumo 211F-2 engines, the He 111Z had a total of 6,700hp (5 x 1,340hp). In published literature, the fifth engine is said to have been a BMW 801, but this was merely a project or at best an experimental installation. The centre section housed two fuel tanks, each of 1,025 litres capacity, bringing the total internal fuel capacity to 8,570 litres. On the He 111Z-1, additional fuel in the form of four 600-litre drop-tanks or other external loads was possible, carried on 4 ETC 2000 suspensions.

The cockpit with the pilot's operating and panel instruments was housed in the port fuselage, only the controls and most important instruments remaining in the spartan starboard cockpit. The crew of seven was made up of the pilot, first aircraft mechanic, radio operator and gunner in the port fuselage, and the observer, second mechanic and gunner in the starboard fuselage.

Since the He 111Z consisted of two He 111 fuselages mated together, the undercarriage was made up of four mainwheels and two tailwheels, effectively forming a 'six-point landing'.

Referring now to the towing system, the power of the five Jumo 211s was often barely sufficient to raise aloft a fully loaded Me 321. Where necessary, the Jumo engines were supplemented by so-called R-Geräte (RATO units), which themselves possessed considerable power. Two units were mounted beneath each fuselage with another beneath each outboard wing, adding 6 x 500kg (1,102 lb) thrust to the 6,700hp of the five engines. The Me 321 trailed on a steel cable 16mm (0.63in) in diameter and 150m (492ft) in length. This steel cabling converged from attachment lugs to the left and right of the wing centre section to a V-shaped fork some 8m (26.25ft) behind the wing centre section, thus almost completely avoiding damage to the inner tailplane halves as well as to the fins and rudders. The following towing combinations were planned:

- one Me 321 on a 150m (492ft) cable.
- two Go 242 gliders, the first on a 60m (197ft) cable and the second on a further 40m (131ft) cable behind the first. Some towing flights were even conducted with three Go 242s in tow.
- two DFS 230 gliders, the first on a Starrschlepp (rigid-tow), the second on a steel cable behind it.

The main theatre of operations for the He 111Z was the Russian front, where a few of the aircraft came to be used from January 1943 due to the lack of suitable landing grounds. Within

Above: **An He 111Z (DS+EQ) during preparations for a new towing flight.**

Left: **This He 111Z sports appreciably weather-worn winter sighting protection. Note the four large drop-tanks.**

Below left: **An He 111Z in winter camouflage.**

Lower left: **The He 111Z undoubtedly presented a most unusual sight.**

Bottom left: **A rare flying view of an He 111Z.**

Below right: **An He 111Z towing an Me 321 glider.**

Centre right: **A towed take-off of two Go 242 gliders.**

Bottom right: **An He 111Z motor parade. The four mainwheels were an unusual sight to the observer.**

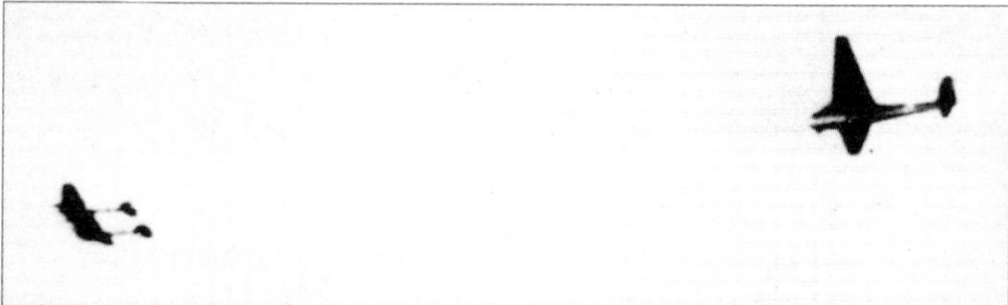

the scope of their limited use, the He 111Z also took part in supply flights to the Kuban bridgehead in the Soviet Union. Besides the vast stretches of Russia, it also appeared in the skies over France and Italy. However, the continually growing air superiority of the Allies throughout the war theatres turned supply flights of this nature into more of a Himmelfahrtskommando – a death-or-glory suicide squad. During the course of their operational use, all of the He 111Zs were destroyed.

The following are the most important events in the career of the He 111Z:

- Beginning of 1941: Ernst Udet suggests design of a 'twin' aircraft based on the He 111.
- August 1941: Plans completed.
- Autumn 1941: He 111Z V1 makes its maiden flight. The V1 was completed at Heinkel, the other machines at the Mitteldeutsche. Metallwerken in Erfurt on a licence basis.
- Autumn 1941: Commencement of the Rechlin series of trials.
- May 1942: He 111Z V1 is transferred to Leipheim and Obertraubling near Regensburg.
- October 1942: The first two series-built examples are delivered.
- December 1942: Completion of the last of ten series aircraft.
- January 1943: A few unsuccessful supply flights to Stalingrad are conducted, followed by supply flights to the Kuban bridgehead.
- July 1943: Sorties flown to Sicily.
- August 1943: Three machines have by now been lost, the remaining aircraft being damaged on the ground by enemy fire.
- Summer 1944: Because of Allied air superiority, the surviving He 111Zs are almost inoperative.
- September 1944: Almost all airborne troop units are out of action, by which time the Luftwaffe has only four He 111Zs left.

Not surprisingly, none of the few examples still available survived the exigencies of the war, thus bringing the story of a more than unusual aircraft to a destructive and catastrophic end. However, the history of the He 111Z would certainly not be complete without mention of the projects that were planned in 1942. These consisted of two variants that were designed to serve quite different operational purposes.

He 111Z-2

This variant was to have been employed as a bomber having a large payload and range. The competing aircraft in this category was the Junkers Ju 488, powered by the BMW 801. The He 111Z-2 was laid out to carry a bombload of four SC 1800 or six SD 1000 bombs and, as an alternative to these 'heavy rocks', could carry up to four Henschel Hs 293 glide-bombs, which would be guided to the target by the FuG 203b Kehl III transmitter installed in the starboard cockpit. With four Hs 293s, the He 111Z-2 had a calculated range of a moderate 1,094km (680 miles) at a speed of 314km/h (195mph). A further load variation was two LMA III air-dropped mines plus two SC 1800 bombs. The maximum bombload of the He 111Z-2 was 7,200kg (15,873 lb). The necessary power was to have been provided by five Jumo 211F-2 engines fitted with Hirth TK 11 turbo-superchargers. Defensive armament corresponded to twice that of the He 111H-6 variant, in addition to which an MG 151/20 was to have been mounted on a rotatable gun-mount in the wing centre section.

Heinkel's bomber design in this configuration possessed extremely unusual features, but could not display any convincing performance, so the He 111Z-2 remained only a project.

He 111Z-3

The same fate on the drawing-board was suffered by this long-range reconnaissance aircraft, which had roughly the same dimensions as the He 111Z-1 series version and the Z-2 variant. The He 111Z-3 was to have had a range of at least 4,945km (3,073 miles) at a speed of 476km/h (296mph) at 4,900m (16,075ft). To increase the range still further, four 900-litre drop-tanks were to have been carried, and a Typesheet even mentions two 1,200-litre drop-tanks. The maximum take-off weight with internal and external loads was 32,930kg (72,598 lb). Due to the lack of reliable documents, details concerning armament and other equipment are not possible at the present time.

Technical Data for the Z-1 and Me 321

	Heinkel He 111Z-1	Messerschmitt Me 321
Powerplant	Junkers	HWK
Type	Jumo 211F-2	109-500 (RATO)
Take-off power	5 x 1,340hp	up to 8 x 500kg thrust
Continuous power	5 x 1,120hp	-
Dimensions		
Wingspan	35.20m (115' 5⅞")	55.24m (181' 2¾")
Length	16.38m (53' 8⅞in)	28.15m (92' 4¼")
Height	4.53m (14' 10⅜in)	10.20m (33' 5⅝")
Wing area, m^2 (ft^2)	147.00 (1,582.26)	300.25 (3,231.79)
Wing loading, kg/m (lb/ft^2)	193.19 (39.57)	116.56 (23.87)
Weights		
Empty weight, kg (lb)	14,970 (33,003)	11,300 (24,912)
Equipped weight, kg (lb)	21,400 (47,178)	12,600 (27,778)
Fuel capacity (internal)	8,560 litres *	none
Fuel capacity (external)	4 x 600 litres	none
Take-off weight		
normal	-	35,000 (77,161)
maximum	28,400 (62,611)	39,400 (86,861)
Payload		
normal	-	22,400 (49,383)
at overload	-	up to 27,000kg (59,524)
Performance		
Maximum speed, km/h (mph)	435 (270)	230 (143) on tow
Cruising speed, km/h (mph)	392 (244)	-
Speed with one Me 321	219 (136)	-
Speed with two Go 242s	248 (154)	-
Landing speed, km/h (mph)	130 (81)	115 (71)
Range, km (miles)	2,000 (1,243)	Glide angle 1:16
Service ceiling, m (ft)	10,000 (32,800)	-
Defensive Armament †		
In nose loading doors	-	2-4 x MG 15
A-Stand	2 x MG 131	
B- and C-Stands	4 x MG 81	
D-Stand	2 x MG 81Z	
Radio equipment	FuG 17, FuG 101, Peil G6, FuG X, EiV crew intercom	
Crew	7-9	3-6

* Consisted of four 1,025-litre and four 700-litre wing tanks plus two 835-litre fuselage tanks; † Armament varied considerably and could consist of four MG 131s or two MG 81Zs plus four MG 81Zs. Use of the MG-FF in the nose has also been reported. These alterations were all undertaken by front-line [He 111] units – Author. In the Me 321, armament installation varied. In the Me 321 proposal of 3rd June 1942, powered by 12 x 300kg thrust or 24 x 150kg thrust Argus pulse-jets, provision was made for up to 17 MG 34s (a 7.9mm infantry weapon developed into the MG 81) – Translator.

Chapter Seven

He 111 Production and Prototypes

Heinkel's aesthetically pleasing Mehrzweckflugzeug (multi-purpose aircraft) was in production over a space of around eight years. From comparatively modest beginnings, when Arado, Dornier and Junkers also participated in its manufacture, He 111 production soon took on much larger dimensions. In order to satisfy the Luftwaffe's continually increasing needs, Heinkel Werk Oranienburg was erected from May 1936 onwards, and the first He 111 left the final assembly lines there in the following year, leaving just two further years to establish the Luftwaffe.

The historically significant date of 1st September 1939 marked the beginning of exhilarating but short-lived victories that undoubtedly led to misconceptions of Germany's capabilities and were soon reversed over the skies of Britain. In the first year of the war, a total of 452 He 111s and 69 Ju 88s were delivered, but 1940's production suffered extreme losses during the Battle of Britain, with 756 bombers lost. Meanwhile, the production figure for its closest rival, the Ju 88, climbed to 1,816 aircraft, some 26 times that of the previous year. While in 1940 Heinkel bombers bombarded targets in Holland, Norway, France and Great Britain, in 1941 the He 111 was encountered over Greece, the Balkans, North Africa and the Soviet Union. The curve of losses climbed sharply, and to compensate for it 950 He 111s left the production centres in 1941. For the Ju 88 the figure was even higher, with 2,146 bombers built. In 1942 the production figure for the He 111 stood at 1,337 aircraft, while production of the Junkers design in that year exceeded the 3,000 mark (of which 2,270 were bombers). In the penultimate year of He 111 production, 1943, only a small increase, amounting to 1,405 aircraft, could be achieved. With 2,160 examples, Ju 88 bomber production still remained uncontested at the peak. In that year American air power was shaping up, together with British bomber formations, with the aim of carrying out the so-called Combined Bomber Offensive; this division of tasks took the form of nocturnal raids by the RAF, and daylight 'precision raids' by the USAAF.

Meanwhile, not only was the long-suffering German civilian population in the target sights of the Allied bomber fleets, but also in increasing measure the infrastructure and industries of importance for the war, among them, of course, the aircraft factories. During the 'Big Week' of 20-25th February 1944, the aircraft industry became the particular object of attack, but despite the immense Allied efforts to largely eliminate the production centres in Germany and the occupied territories, the German armaments industry was still able to achieve previously unattained production figures. Under these extremely adverse conditions, up to the end of the third quarter of 1944 Heinkel produced 756 He 111s, while up to the end of that year Junkers produced 3,013 Ju 88s, although this number included only 661 of the bomber version. The end of the third quarter of 1944 also irrevocably saw the last of the He 111 bombers leave the final assembly halls. During the most intensive production period, 1939-44, a total of 5,656 He 111s were completed, while in the same period no fewer than 9,122 Ju 88s of various bomber versions were completed. Comparative figures for both aircraft are shown in the accompanying illustration on page 77.

The Taktverfahren Method of Timed Sequence Production

Concerning production itself, the following extract is taken from a contemporary article that appeared in the magazine *Flugsport* of April 1941: '...On a number of machines the fitters, mechanics, electricians, plumbers, sheet-metal workers, sprayers, etc, relieve each other, and step by step complete the manufacturing process of the aircraft. After the wings and all coverings, the fuel tanks, propellers and all measurement and control devices have been installed, an exact functional test of all components is undertaken. The completed aircraft is then rolled out of the assembly hall and is ready for flight. An important factor in maintaining uninterrupted *Takt* (timed sequential production steps) is a well-organised availability of all constructional parts. It is absolutely imperative that the workman must be able to concentrate fully on his task and not be held up at his workplace by high losses of time, caused for example by long walks to the storage area or through long waiting times spent in the stores. The problem has been solved by the parts needed for insertion in each *Takt* being sensibly conveyed to the workplace on an electrically operated access carriage. The latter is positioned directly next to the workplace so that the construction worker has only to grasp those clearly visible parts necessary for installation. Timely transportation is effected by stores personnel. And now to the *Takt* itself. At the head of the assembly hall is a wall clock, visible to all, which indicates at what time the *Takt* has to be completed. When the *Takt* time

Opposite page:

Left: **Assembly building in the Heinkel Werk Marienehe.**

Right: **Assembly building in the Heinkel Werk Oranienburg in 1935/36.**

Above: **In this view, at least 20 He 111s are in various stages of manufacture.**

Below: **Dornier was one of the licence manufacturers. This photo shows the He 111E during final assembly at the Norddeutsche Dornier Werke (NDW).**

Completed He 111 fuselages and wings await mating.

The percentage of female employees grew year by year at Heinkel, to which was added a steadily increasing number of forced-labourers and concentration camp inmates. By contrast, the proportion of skilled personnel, many of whom were highly qualified, steadily decreased due to call-up for military service.

An He 111H (D-AYWQ) destined for Rumania.

An He 111 fuselage in the assembly jig.

Illustration on the opposite page:

Total annual production of the He 111 and Ju 88, with the left-hand shaded blocks representing the He 111, and behind them the darker Ju 88 figures. Total He 111 production was 6,456 aircraft plus at least 16 of the civilian models, giving 6,472 in all, without the Spanish licence-built aircraft. These figures are taken from Ernst Heinkel's book *Sturmisches Leben* (*A Stormy Life*), which states that some 800 examples were completed up to 1939, in which year 452 He 111s were rolled out. The figures quoted by Heinkel most probably refer only to those that were produced in his factories. The difference between his figures and those of author Georg Brütting (7,891) must certainly be those built by licence manufacturers.

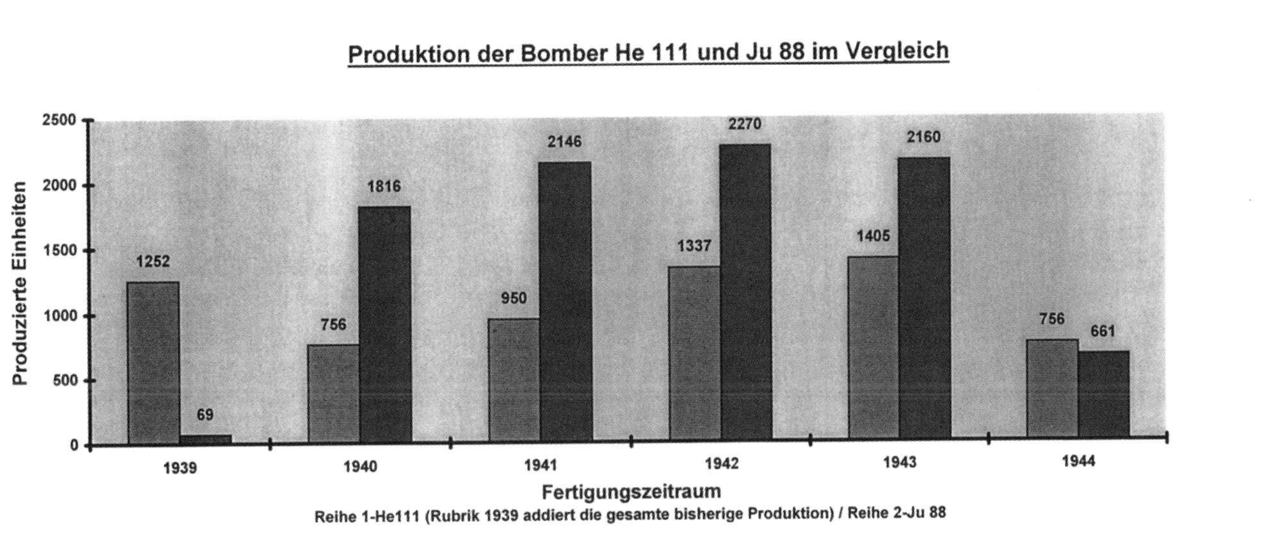

arrives, the work is interrupted by a siren, and working platforms, stairs, cables and compressed-air hoses are laid aside, the assembly hall doors are opened, and each one goes to the machine assigned to him. A second siren signals the pre-planned *Takt* sequence, in which each aircraft in the row is advanced so far forward until it reaches the position of the aircraft in front of it. Each aircraft is thus advanced to a workplace where it proceeds from one *Takt* to another. In short, it becomes "takted". A new He 111 stands proudly in front of the assembly hall.'

Another article in *Flugsport* in 1941 provides the following interesting information: '...The number of the individual *Takts* for the entire production effort is laid down according to the required production quantity (eg per month) and working time necessary for each aircraft, and is further influenced by the available assembly hall space and the type of aircraft construction. Clearly, only so many working hours can be predetermined for a particular *Takt*, depending on what a number of workers are able to achieve on the work object without getting into each other's way. This means, for example, that if a *Takt* has to be accomplished in 6 hours, and only three men are able to work in the cockpit at the same time without disturbing each other, the work distribution cannot exceed 3 men x 6 hours = 18 man-hours. Since work sequences of several more hours are available, the work must therefore be distributed over several *Takts*. It calls for an adroit organisation by the engineer to see to it that whatever the circumstances in all instances, mutual disturbances by the workforce or waiting times are avoided. It is thus intended that, as far as possible, installation elements are so prepared on the workbench that they merely need to be mounted on or installed in the airframe. For the designer, this forms an important area of a sophisticated series-production design. For him, it means combining the range of scientific and theoretical problems with those of economic requirements...'

He 111 Quarterly Production 1942-1944

Quarter	Year	Produced
First	1942	301
Second	1942	350
Third	1942	356
Fourth	1942	330
First	1943	462
Second	1943	340
Third	1943	302
Fourth	1943	301
First	1944	313
Second	1944	317
Third	1944	126
Fourth	1944	0

Total production by the German aircraft industry in September 1944 – the last production month for the He 111 – was 3,821 aircraft. Of this total, the following lists the comparatively small number of bombers produced, made up of:

- 2 He 111s – production terminating.
- 21 Ju 87s – production terminating.
- 74 Ju 188s – including 63 recce aircraft.
- 3 Ju 388s – pre-production aircraft.
- 18 Ar 234s – jet bombers.
- 0 He 177s – not produced since May 1944.

By far the most significant portion of production capacity was occupied by fighters: the Me 109 with 1,605 and the Fw 190 with 1,391 aircraft. Of the then high-tech developments – the Me 262 and Me 163 – production totals during September 1944 were 91 and 35 aircraft respectively.

He 111 Export Deliveries

Heinkel bombers did not only fly with the Luftwaffe Balkenkreuz insignia, as a small amount of production resulted from orders placed from abroad. In 1937 24 He 111F-1s were delivered to the Turkish Air Force, which also ordered an additional four He 111G-5s. The Chinese also issued a requirement for 12 aircraft, but in all only six He 111A-0s were delivered at a cost of RM 400,000 each, packed in crates and transported by sea. At the end of the Spanish Civil War, Spain incorporated 59 He 111 'survivors' into its air force, and in the period 1941-43 six new He 111s were added. To cover further needs, manufacturing licence agreements were concluded. Although this subject exceeds the scope of this narrative, which is limited to He 111 production within Germany, other user nations were:

- Bulgaria: One He 111H-16.
- Croatia: An application for purchase was made but rejected from the German side.
- Rumania: Procurement of various He 111s during the period 1939-44, comprising He 111E-3 (10), H-3 (32) and H-6 (10) aircraft.
- Slovakia: An uncertain number of He 111H-10/H-11s were flown here, reportedly consisting of two H-10 and three H-11s. One H-16 was taken over by Bulgaria.
- Hungary: According to the aircraft status as of 6th May 1941, Hungary had some 12 to 13 He 111s. A further 80 (He 111P) were ordered in 1944, but only 13 were delivered. Towards the end of 1944, the Hungarian Air Force received 12 (He 111H) aircraft from Luftwaffe stocks. In 1940 three He 111Bs were delivered.
- Japan: The Japanese Air Force intended to purchase a total of 44 He 111F aircraft, but the negotiations conducted in 1938 did not result in any agreement being concluded.

Development-series Prototypes

This section lists all the known He 111 prototypes, but with a number of gaps from the V26 to the V31 and from the V33 to the V45 due to the lack of complete documentation. The first line of each entry provides, where known, the Prototype Designation, Werknummer, Civil Registration and Version.

V1 713 D-ADAP He 111a
First flight 24.02.1935. Bomber, so-called 'multi-purpose aircraft'. Powerplants: BMW VI 6.0Z, wingspan 25m (82ft 0¼in), wing area 92.40m² (994.56ft²). Armament in B-Stand was mock-up; C-Stand armament not installed.

V2 715 D-ALIX He 111b
First flight in March 1935. Civil variant; airframe largely *Rostock*, similar to V1 but with non-transparent fuselage nose. BMW VI U powerplants, wingspan 23m (75ft 5½in) and wing area 88.50m² (952.58ft²). Used by Lufthansa, including route-testing. During mail-carrying flight on 12.03.1937 from Las Palmas to Bathurst, Gambia, crashed in fog on landing.

V3 714 D-ALES He 111c
First flight mid-1935. Bomber prototype. Transferred to Rechlin at beginning of 1936 for thorough testing. Trials of defensive armament unsatisfactory due to low performance. Powerplants: BMW VI U; wingspan 22.5m (73ft 9⅞in), wing area 87.60m² (942.90ft²). Airframe and armament later modified and corresponded to V5 prototype. Further trials with this aircraft related to engine testing.

V4 1968 D-AHAO He 111C-0
For Lufthansa. First flown in January 1936. On 10.1.36 *Dresden* was first publicly unveiled and with a claimed speed of 400km/h (248mph) attracted much comment from the press. (Not to be confused with He 111G-3, Werknummer 1885, D-ACDF *Dresden*.) Powerplants and airscrews as V2; wingspan 23m (75ft 5½in), wing area 88.50m² (952.58ft²).

V5 1440 D-AJAK, ex-D-APYS He 111B-0
In its later state, corresponded to V3 prototype except for DB 600C powerplants instead of BMW VI. Wingspan 22.6m (74ft 1¾in) and wing area 87.60m² (942.89ft²).

V6 1432 D-AXOH He 111-B-0
Similar to V5, but powered by DB 600C with VDM variable-pitch airscrews. Extended surface-cooling in wing nose section. Later re-engined with Jumo 210 and finally with Jumo 211A-1. Also served as first prototype for He 111E variant.

V7 1537 D-AUKY He 111B-1
Used in 1938 in He 111D development programme. In summer 1938 was equipped and underwent trials with full-view canopy. Also had new wings of He 111F and underwent trials as prototype for He 111P-series, being designated in this form as V19.

V8 1664 D-AQUO He 111B-1
Featured altered canopy and DB 600C installed in 1938. Powerplants were later exchanged for DB 600G and Ga respectively. Served as prototype for He 111P-series.

V9 1807 D-AQOX He 111D
Similar to V8. Around mid-1937 it was fitted with two DB 600Ga units for test purposes. As D-AQOX, served as prototype for He 111D series.

V10 1437 D-ALEQ He 111E
Originally an He 111B-0; after modifications served as He 111E prototype as D-ALEQ powered by DB 601s. ETC 500 bomb clasps later installed. Test-flown in 1940/41 with so-called safety controls developed by the Patin-Werke.

V11 D-ARCG He 111D
Used by Heinkel as test aircraft for DB 600C. Originally a B-series airframe from summer 1937, was also included in He 111D-series flight trials with altered coolers beneath engines and wing-mounted surface cooling. Also used in test programme for He 111F-1. Crashed during test flight as result of engine fire. Was at that time to have been fitted with oil-cooler for Jumo 211 for trials.

V12 2534 He 111G-0
Differed from V11 by having altered wing planform. Powerplants were likewise two DB 600Cs.

V13 2535 He 111G-0
Prototype completed towards end of 1936 with BMW VI engines. Otherwise similar to the V12.

V14 D-ACBS *Augsburg* He 111G-3
Unlike V13, was powered by DB 600, later replaced by BMW 132Dc motors.

V15 D-ADCF *Dresden* He 111G-3
Used in trials with various items of test equipment. Powered by two BMW 132H-1 motors.

V16 D-ASAR He 111G-4
Powered by DB 600, this aircraft served for long time as personal touring aircraft of Erhard Milch. Export variant was He 111G-5.

V17 D-ACBH He 111D-1
Originally belonging to He 111B series; served as experimental model for Torpedo-bomber variant. Also employed in trials for cooling system of He 111D-1.

V18 1003 D-ADUM He 111J-1
Originally one of He 111B series aircraft, powerplants were DB 600. Bearing unusual registration lettering split 'D-A+DUM', served as test machine for He 111J-1.

V19 D-APYS He 111H
Originally V7 prototype, a former He 111B-1, powered by DB 600C, replaced later by Jumo 211; served as He 111H prototype.

V20 No details available.

V21 1441
As opposed to other test prototypes, was equipped with auxiliary Flettner trim tabs.

V22 2314 D-AHAY He 111B-1
For reconnaissance purposes, this B-series airframe was used as Behelfsurkunder (auxiliary observation) machine with bombing equipment replaced by cameras and auxiliary fuel tanks.

V23 2343 He 111B-1
Used in equipment-related test series. In particular, aircraft heating system as well as ventral gondola was checked.

V24 No details available.

V25
Changes in defensive armament tested with this prototype, concerning installation of MG 17 in tail cone, MG-FF in nose and additional MG 15 in C-Stand.

V26-V31 No details available.

V32 2122 D-APZD
Served as engine and supercharger test prototype. In 1941 was powered by DB 601U plus TK-9 turbo-supercharger driving three-blade VDM airscrews with special Schwarz blades of 3.5m (11ft 5¾in) diameter. The 1,350hp DB 601U was largely similar to the DB 601T but differed in reduction gearing, modifications carried out by Weser Flugzeugbau in Bremen. Further trials conducted from end of 1942 with He 111 Werknummer 7880 fitted with Jumo 211F plus TK-9 turbo-supercharger. TK-9C was able to function at gas temperature of 1,100°C and at max speed of 22,000rpm. Was equipped with two-stage compressor whose hollow blading had so-called 'Christmas-tree' profile developed by DVL. Follow-on trials tested suitability of TK-11 and TK-15 turbo-superchargers.

V46-V48 He 111H-16
These three prototypes were based on the He 111H-16 and served for various trials with He 111H-20 series variants, among which were H-20/R1 paratroop transport, H-20/R2 freight and towing aircraft, H-20/R3 night bomber with flame dampers and reduced armament, and H-20/R4 Bomber.

Author Manfred Griehl in *Heinkel He 111* (Motorbuch Verlag, 1997) gives the prototype Werknummern as V11 (1432), V12 (1435), V13 (1438), V14 (1436) and V15 (1433) – Translator.

Right column:

He 111 V2 D-ALIX *Rostock* seen during maintenance work.

He 111 V3 D-ALES, the second bomber prototype.

He 111 V10 D-ALEQ was a prototype for the He 111E version.

Seen here is the former He 111 V7, which, after modification, became the V19 prototype for the He 111H series.

He 111 V32 D-APZD served as a turbo-supercharger test-bed.

Left column:

He 111 V4 D-AHAO, named *Dresden* by Lufthansa, made its maiden flight in January 1936. It was lost in an accident in April 1936.

He 111 V6 D-AXOH was powered by DB 600C engines.

He 111 V8 D-AQUO served as a prototype for the He 111P-series.

Chapter Eight

In War Service

A Pictorial History

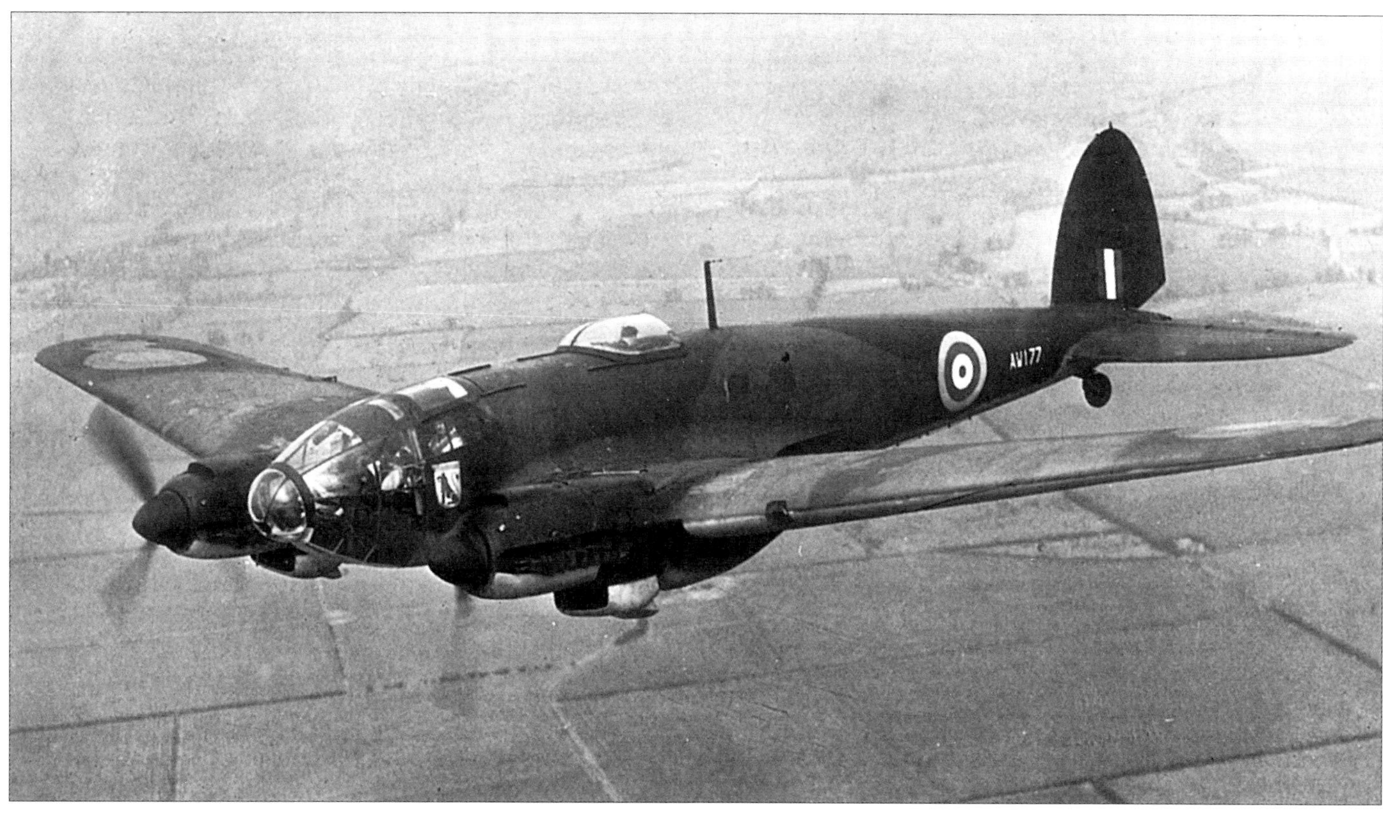

This He 111H, Werknummer 6853, coded 1H+EN of II./KG 26 Löwengeschwader, was forced to make an emergency landing near North Berwick on 9th February 1940. Suffering only slight damage, the British made it airworthy again and put the aircraft through a series of test flights. It was lost in a crash in November 1943.

This chapter is based on photographic material that depicts the He 111 in war service on all fronts far more authentically than words can convey.

According to a Report of the Luftwaffe Quartermaster-General dated 19th September 1938, the Luftwaffe had in its inventory a total of 1,235 bombers made up of the Do 17, Ju 86 and He 111. Of these, the He 111s comprised 272 He 111Bs, 171 He 111Es, 39 He 111Fs and 88 He 111Js, making a total of 570 aircraft.

A further Report of the Luftwaffe Quartermaster-General dated 2nd September 1939 lists a total of 1,179 bombers (together with a reserve of 30 Ju 86s), made up of Do 17s, 18 Ju 88s and 808 He 111s, the latter comprising 38 He 111E, 21 He 111J, 349 He 111P and 400 He 111H aircraft. See table, opposite page top.

According to this list of He 111 units, there were at least 726 operationally ready aircraft available. By May 1944, a few months before production was terminated, the He 111 was still to be encountered in the operational units given in the table on the opposite page, bottom left.

Because of their increasingly limited tactical potential, the number of bomber units continually decreased, and the pressure of the Allied offensives brought the unavoidable demise in an ever more drastic fashion. Just a few days before the date of this aircraft readiness status, American, British, Canadian and French troops stormed the Normandy beaches. Only a few months later, in January 1945, of the once so victoriously portrayed bomber pilots, there remained only legends. See the table on the opposite page, bottom right.

By April 1945 the bomber groups no longer existed. Their personnel had been scattered to the winds, and very often a member of a bomber group found himself as an infantryman again. Only a handful of Heinkel bombers still formed a part of Luftflotte 6 – to be more exact, of Stab/KG 4, I./KG 4, 8./KG 4 and 7./KG 53, consisting of 20 operationally ready He 111s. Solitary, still extant Gruppen of KG 51 and KG 76 at this time were equipped with the Me 262 or Ar 234 'wonder weapons', but these only represented in essence the proverbial 'drop in the ocean'.

He 111 Flying Units on the Morning of 1st September 1939

Luftwaffe unit	No flight-ready	Version	Location	Geographically nearest to
ObTdL ??				
10. See(F)/LG 2	?	?	Werder	Baltic coast
Westa 1./ObdL	?	?	Berlin-Staaken	18km W of Berlin
Luftflottenkommando 1				
(Air Fleet Detachment)				
Stab/KG 1	9	He 111H	Kolberg	Baltic coast (P)
I./KG 1	34	He 111E	Kolberg	
I./KG 152	34	He 111H	Pinnow-Plathe	10km ESE of Schwerin
Stab/KG 26	5	He 111H	Gabbert	70km WNW of Schneidemühl (P)
II./KG 26	3	He 111H	Gabbert	
I./KG 53	31	He 111H	Schönfeld-Crössinsee	
Stabkg 27	5	He 111P	Langenhagen/Werneuchen	26km NE of Berlin
I./KG 27	31	He 111P	Langenhagen/Werneuchen	
II./KG 27	32	He 111P	Wunsdorf/Neuhardenberg	30km NNE of Fürstenwälde
III./KG 27	33	He 111P	Delmenhorst/Königsberg/Nm	55km SSW of Stettin (P)
Stab (K)/LG 1	8	He 111H	Neuhausen	8km NE of Königsberg/East Prussia
II.(K)/LG 1	34	He 111H	Powunden	18km NNE of Königsberg
III.(K)/LG 1	32	He 111H	Prowehren	7km NW of Königsberg
Luftflottenkommando 2				
2.(F)/122	10	He 111H	Münster	
Stab/KG 54	6	He 111P	Fritzlar	26km SW of Kassel
I./KG 54	30	He 111P	Fritzlar	
II./KG 28	34	He 111P	Gütersloh	20km SW of Bielefeld
Stab/KG 55	6	He 111P	Wesendorf	36km W of Brunswick
I./KG 55	25	He 111P	Dedelsdorf	25km N of Gifhorn (nr Brunswick)
II./KG 55	2	He 111P	Wesendorf	36km N of Brunswick
III./KG 26	32	He 111H	Lübeck-Blankensee	
Luftflottenkommando 3				
Stab/KG 51	9	He 111H	Landsberg	50km WSW of Munich
I./KG 51	34	He 111H	Memmingen	40km SSE of Ulm
III./KG 51	33	He 111H	Memmingen	
Stab/KG 53	6	He 111H	Schwäbisch Hall	40km E of Heilbronn
II./KG 53	30	He 111H	Schwäbisch Hall	
III./KG 53	32	He 111H	Giebelstadt	15km S of Würzburg
Luftflottenkommando 4				
Stab/KG 4	6	He 111P	Oels	27km NE of Breslau (P)
I./KG 4	27	He 111P	Langenau	9km N of Breslau (P)
II./KG 4	30	He 111P	Oels	
III./KG 4	32	He 111P	Langenau	

(P) = In Poland after 1945.

He 111 Operational Units on 31st May 1944

Luftwaffe unit	Flight-ready	Luftwaffe unit	Flight-ready	Luftwaffe unit	Flight-ready
Luftflotte Reich		**Luftflotte 1**		**Luftflotte 7**	
III./KG 3	21	14./KG 5	8	II./KG 4	28
II./KG 27	12	Stab/KG 53	1	III./KG 4	26
IV./KG 27	33			IV./KG 4	22
IV./KG 53	21	**Luftflotte 4**		I./KG 27	37
IV./KG 55	17	I./KG 4	27	III./KG 27	33
I./KG 200	10	14./KG 27	7	I./KG 53	27
FAGr 123	?	1. Nachtaufkl. St.	?	II./KG 53	28
				III./KG 53	24
				I./KG 55	27
				II./KG 55	23
				III./KG 55	29
				TGr. 30	32

He 111 Operational Units in January 1945

Luftwaffe unit	Flight-ready
Luftflotte 3 (Air fleet)	
Stab/KG 53	1
II./KG 53	29
III./KG 53	24
Luftflotte 4	
Stab/KG 4	1
I./KG 4	22
II./KG 4	12
III./KG 4	11
Luftflotte 6	
IV./KG 55	10

The He 111 received its 'baptism of fire' in the Condor Legion.

Waiting was also part of the job, in this seemingly idyllic airfield scene.

A flypast of four Heinkel aircraft in pre-war markings. Second from left is an He 111, and third is an He 116.

On the way to a new mission.

Loading the deadly payload in its vertical containers.

Opposite page, clockwise from top left:

Hesitatingly employed on the front line for the first time in 1917 during the First World War, the life-saving parachute became standard equipment for military crews almost everywhere just a few years later.

This He 111 pilot is checking his parachute harness.

During the climb, each aircraft takes up its assigned position in the formation.

Climbing ever higher, the crew of this He 111 (TE+LQ) approach their target.

A well-known He 111 photograph over the Thames and London at the start of the Battle of Britain in September 1940.

A return flight in close formation. At the home airfield, many a crew will be awaited in vain.

This lucky homecomer is on his landing approach – but some of these ended tragically.

An He 111 (BO+PA) near a stack of bombs in the foreground.

Regular and thorough maintenance was already at that time a prerequisite for the high operational readiness of a unit.

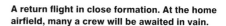

TE LQ

Left: **A martial 'snapshot' in typical War Reporter fashion.**

Bottom left: **View from the nose of a dangerously close neighbouring aircraft.**

Below: **Without adequate fighter protection, raids against England were anything but a cakewalk. With increasing Allied air superiority, year by year the situation deteriorated for the bomber crews.**

Below centre: **Such heavy 'rocks' could only be carried externally.**

Bottom right: **In enemy hands. This He 111H-16, Werknummer 8433, coded 2B+DC, BT+KV, was flown by a Hungarian pilot to San Severo, north of Foggia, Italy, on 14th December 1944, and surrendered to the Americans. At a later date, the aircraft was shipped to the USA and, bearing Foreign Equipment number FE 1600 (subsequently T2-1600), was test-flown in 1945/46 at Freeman Field, Seymour, Indiana.**

Top: **The Starrschlepp (rigid-tow) method of a DFS 230 (CB+ZB) behind an He 111 (RN+EE) towcraft, tested by the DFS in 1942.**

Upper left: **Two characteristic Heinkel designs pictured together. The He 100, the strongest competitor of the Me 109, was unsuccessful in the pre-war competition for the Luftwaffe's standard fighter.**

Upper right: **A wrecked He 111 from the unsuccessful Iraq operation.**

Lower left: **A Walter RATO unit in action.**

Lower right: **A torpedo-equipped He 111 with nose ship-detection radar.**

Right: **Even in close-formation flight, safety was often deceptive. The strengthened defensive armament introduced during the course of development was hardly able to match the often inadequate fighter protection.**

Chapter Nine

Modelling the He 111

In contrast to aircraft such as the Dornier Do X and Do 335, the modeller has a wide choice of He 111 kits, varying from the miniature 1/144th scale up to 1/48th scale, and satisfying all requirements. To represent the numerous kits, modeller Ralf Schlüter describes his experiences with those from Italeri and Airfix.

The accompanying photos show two of the several modelling kits, which unfortunately cover only one version – the He 111H series. The best reproduction in 1/72nd scale, in terms of dimensions, contours and details, is Italeri's. Exemplary in this kit is the precisely moulded defensive armament. The injection parts are perfectly designed and moulded, so that all parts fit exactly, although minor corrections to the inner wing root sections will result in a smooth fuselage-wing transition without any filler being necessary. This also applies to the rest of the kit. Despite the projecting sheet edges, it is a pleasure to complete the model, and a gentle filing off of these projections to provide a straight edge gives a respectable result.

The Airfix kit is an old well-known one, which, in the 1970s and 1980s, was slightly improved upon (the Airfix pilots were introduced), but basically it remains a familiar old Airfix 'bird'. In its dimensions and contours, the Airfix interpretation of the aircraft is more of a light caricature of the He 111C's features, but it produces a handsome overall impression. The deep rounded wings are a little too canted to the rear, the drop-shaped fuselage a little longer and hence more slender, and the transparent nose a little larger and more prominent than the rather under-dimensioned powerplants, which are less articulated due to the undersized airscrew blades. As already stated – a splendid caricature. Putting it together is much less fun than with the Italeri kit: the age of the model and its contours make this quite plain. The wing-fuselage transition has to be made compatible by first thoroughly removing all extraneous material to enable an upper surface transition without filler. The underside can then be joined by filing off. Details are rather rough, the wheels too small, and the transparencies – well... It is patently obvious that the Airfix engineers did not realise that the shrinkage factor of cooled transparent plastic is higher than that of the other components. A considerable amount of filing and widening of the two vertically separated fuselage halves is necessary in order to make the cabin fit the outer dimensions of the fuselage.

The finished product represents a late-model He 111H-20 with traversable turret. I was unfortunately unable to verify the accompanying markings in any documentary source. I built this kit from the box, but modified it to H-22 standard, which carried a large number of Fi 103 (V-1) flying-bombs, launching them over the North Sea against London. The livery represents the standard He 111 RLM 70/71 colours interposed with the RLM 76 wavy-line markings for nocturnal operations over water.

He 111 Surface Colours and Camouflage

Deutsche Lufthansa

The surface finish and camouflage patterns on the He 111 were many and varied. Beginning with the He 111C civil version of Deutsche Lufthansa, they consisted of:

- Fuselage and wings in dural grey.
- Fuselage cheat line from the nose in black.
- Engine nacelles and undercarriage doors in black.
- Fin swastika in black within a white disc, the whole enclosed in a red band.

Three-tone Segmented Camouflage

From 1936/37 the He 111 bombers were given a very pleasant three-tone camouflage, made up of the following colours:

- RLM 61 Dunkelgrau (dark green) upper sides.
- RLM 62 Grün (green) upper sides.
- RLM 63 Hellgrau (light grey) upper sides.

For the undersides, RLM 65 Hellblau (light or sky-blue) was used. The surface colouring described here was also used by Condor Legion aircraft.

Two-tone Segmented Camouflage

In accordance with Luftwaffe Dienstvorschrift (Service Regulation) LDv 521/I, a completely different surface colouring was introduced in 1938. Also of a segmented pattern, it comprised two shades of green for the upper sides, namely:

- RLM 70 Schwarzgrün (black-green) upper sides.
- RLM 71 Dunkelgrün (dark green) upper sides.
- RLM 65 Hellblau (light blue) undersides.

The Airfix Heinkel He 111H-20 kit. See also the colour pages.

The Italeri He 111H-6. Both models were built by Ralf Schlüter.

It should be noted that, from 1941 onwards, another shade of RLM 65 became available that tended more to a grey tone.

Night Camouflage

For nocturnal operations, different requirements had to be met, which the day schemes were only partially able to fulfil or else not at all. Here, two different colour tones were applied:

- A washable Mattschwarz (dull or matt-black) coating, designated Flieglack 7120.22.
- A durable Mattschwarz (dull or matt-black) coating with Zwischenlack (intermediate finish) 7123 and Decklack (surface finish) 7124.22. As a rule, the latter was only applied on highly stressed areas.

Winter Camouflage

In snowy weather the standard camouflage was obviously unsuitable, and for this purpose a washable snow camouflage was resorted to. Additionally, the possibility existed of treating highly stressed parts with resilient lacquer. The white Flieglack 7126.21 was applied roughly with scrubbing-brushes, large paint-brushes and even with brooms. A finer method was undoubtedly the spray-gun. The aircraft's upper call-sign lettering and that on the fuselage sides was to be painted round.

Tropical Camouflage

The camouflage requirements on the African continent were completely different and called for new solutions. In this case it was not green tones that dominated but brown and sand-coloured shades. Grün (green) was used in combination with the aforementioned shades only in the form of RLM 80 in a mottled pattern. The dominant colours in the African war theatre were:

- RLM 79 Sandgelb (sand yellow) upper sides.
- RLM 80 Olivgrün (olive green) upper sides.
- RLM 78 Hellblau (light blue) undersides.

Newly arrived aircraft were mostly given a locally suitable camouflage, since that which had been applied for the European theatre was completely useless. In instances where there were supply problems with German colours, recourse was made to those of the Italian ally.

War Theatre Markings

The aircraft markings relative to the war theatre concerned were denoted by various colours. In the Russian theatre RLM 04 Gelb (yellow) was used for the circular fuselage band and beneath the wingtips. RLM 21 Weiß (white), in the same places, was used in the African or Mediterranean theatre of operations, as well as in the southern sector of the Eastern Front. Photographs confirm that in the African and Mediterranean regions, engine nacelles were partly also given a white coat. The RLM 04 Gelb (yellow) Balkan theatre identifier was also applied to the engine nacelles and on the vertical rudder.

The following colours came to be used on various airframe components:

- RLM 04 Gelb (yellow) for example, the rudder, airscrew boss, call-sign lettering, fuselage bands, wingtips and engine nacelles.
- RLM 21 Weiß (white) for the outer Luftwaffe Balkenkreuz insignia, rudder, airscrew boss, engine nacelles, wingtips and call-sign lettering.
- RLM 22 Schwarz (black) for the inner Luftwaffe Balkenkreuz, airscrew boss and lettering.
- RLM 23 Rot (red) for the airscrew boss and call-sign lettering.
- RLM 24 Dunkelblau (dark blue) for the airscrew boss and call-sign lettering.
- RLM 25 Hellgrün (light green) for the airscrew boss and call-sign lettering.

Because of the complexity of this topic, it is not possible here to cover the entire spectrum of the various types of camouflage and markings. Those readers wishing to delve deeper into this subject (and familiar with the German language) are warmly recommended to consult Martin Ullmann's book, *Oberflächenschutzverfahren und Anstrichstoffe der deutschen Luftfahrtindustrie und Luftwaffe 1935-1945* (*Surface Protection Methods and Materials of the German Aviation Industry and Luftwaffe 1935-1945*), published in an expanded new edition by Bernard & Graefe Verlag (Bonn, 2003).

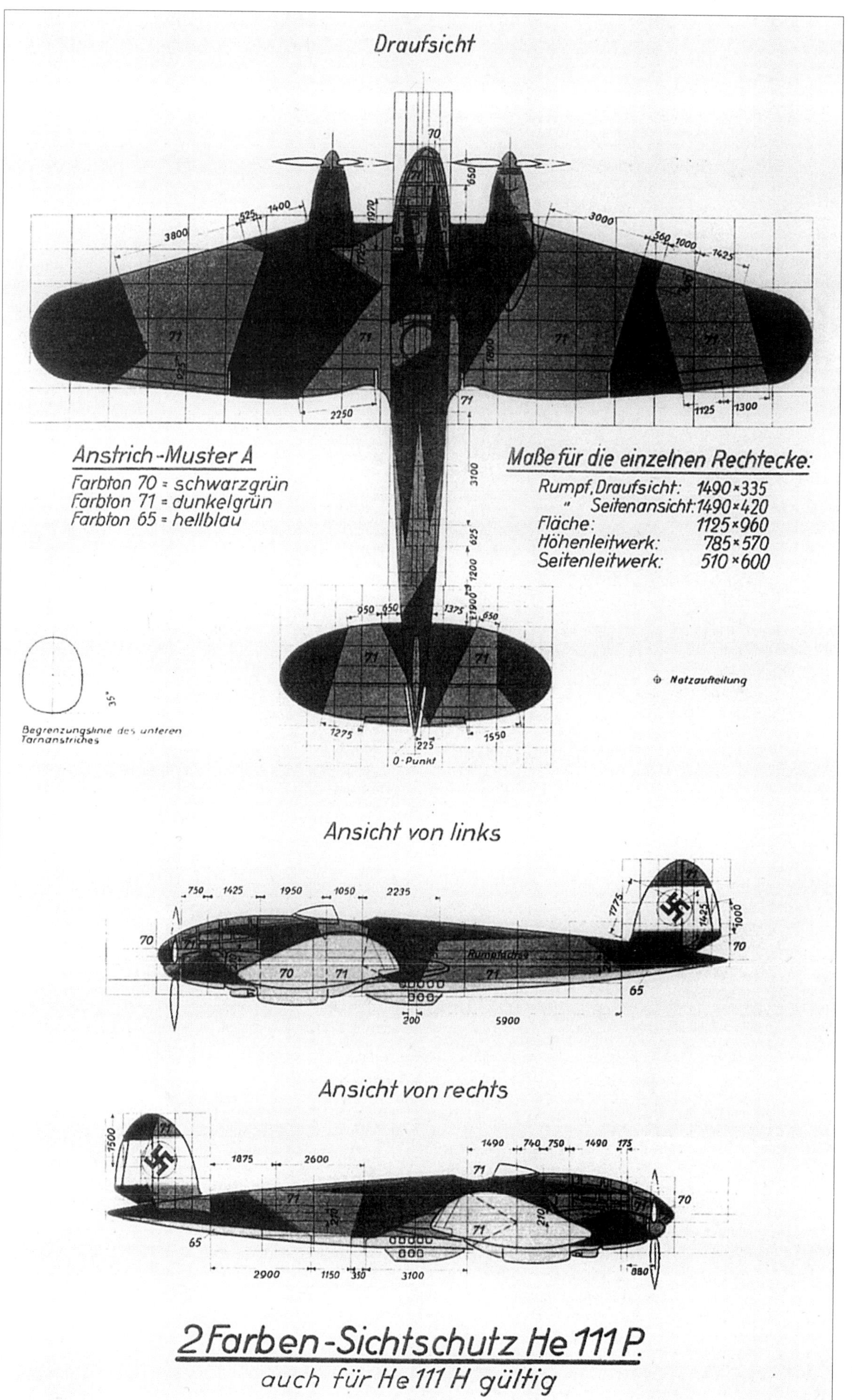

He 111P two-tone camouflage pattern (also valid for He 111H).

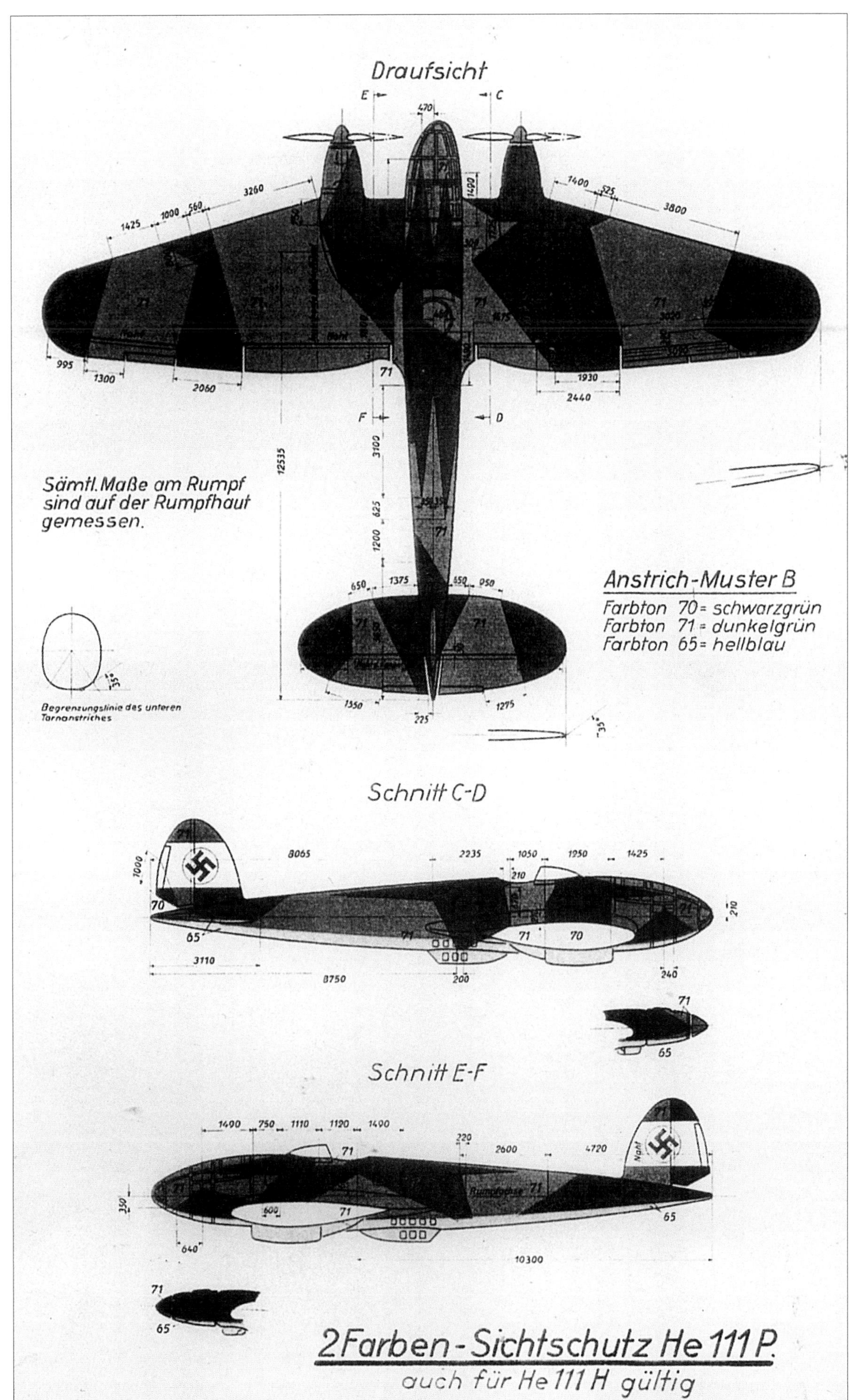

He 111P two-tone (reversed) camouflage pattern (also valid for He 111H).

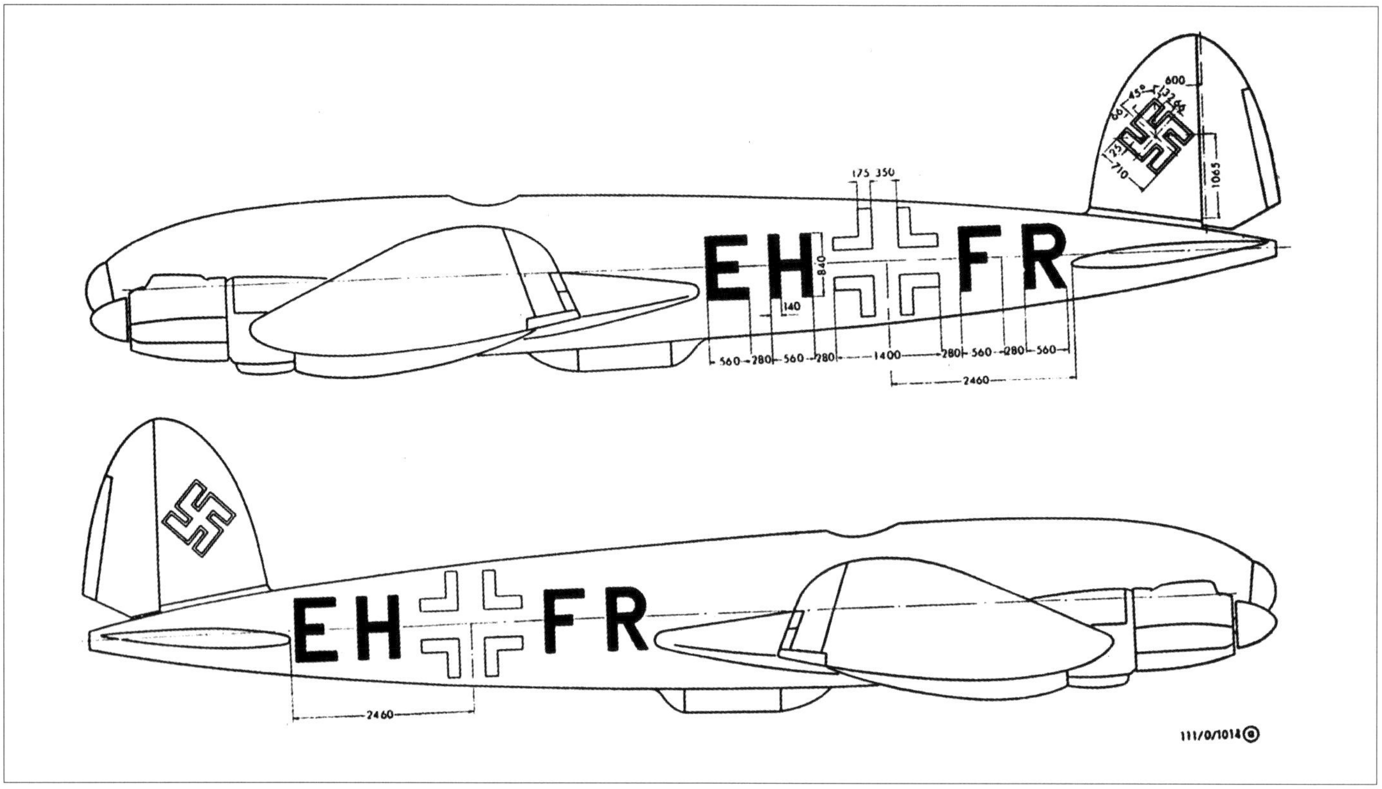

Dimensions specified for the fuselage and fin markings.

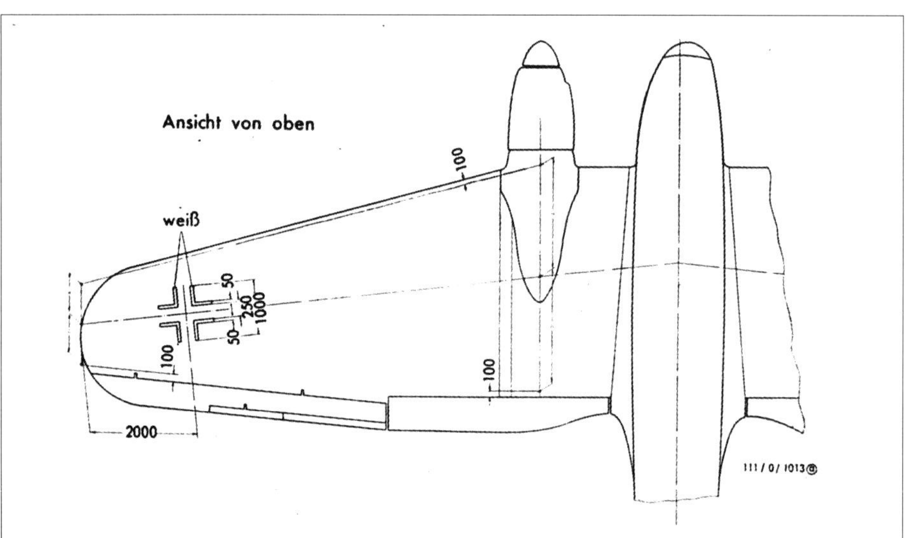

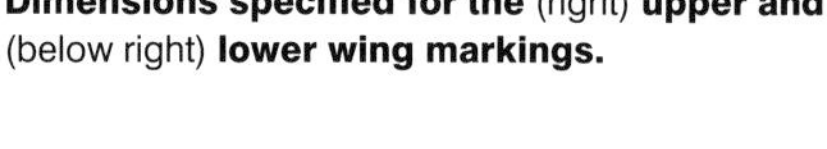
Dimensions specified for the (right) **upper and** (below right) **lower wing markings.**

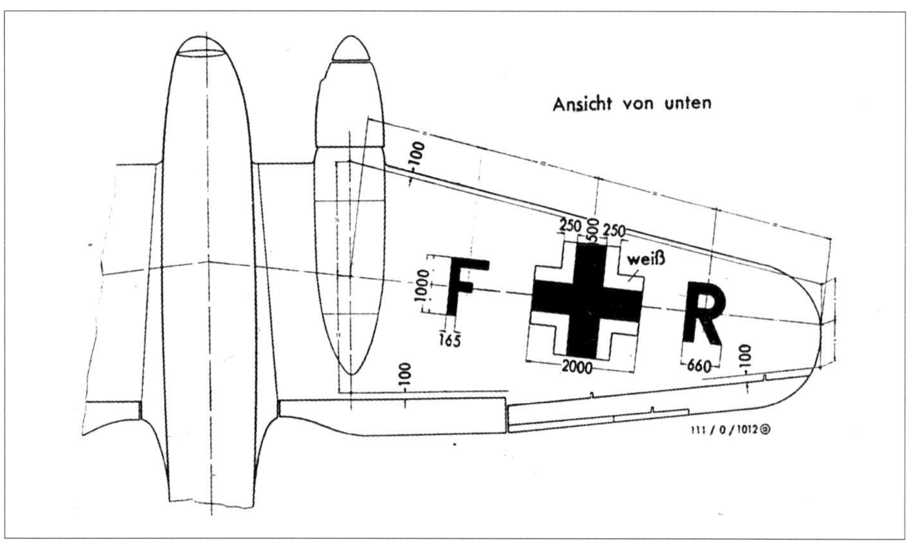

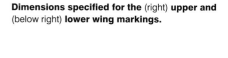

Photographs on the opposite page:

Views and details of the (left) Italeri and (right) Airfix models by Ralf Schlüter.

DA

1H
AH

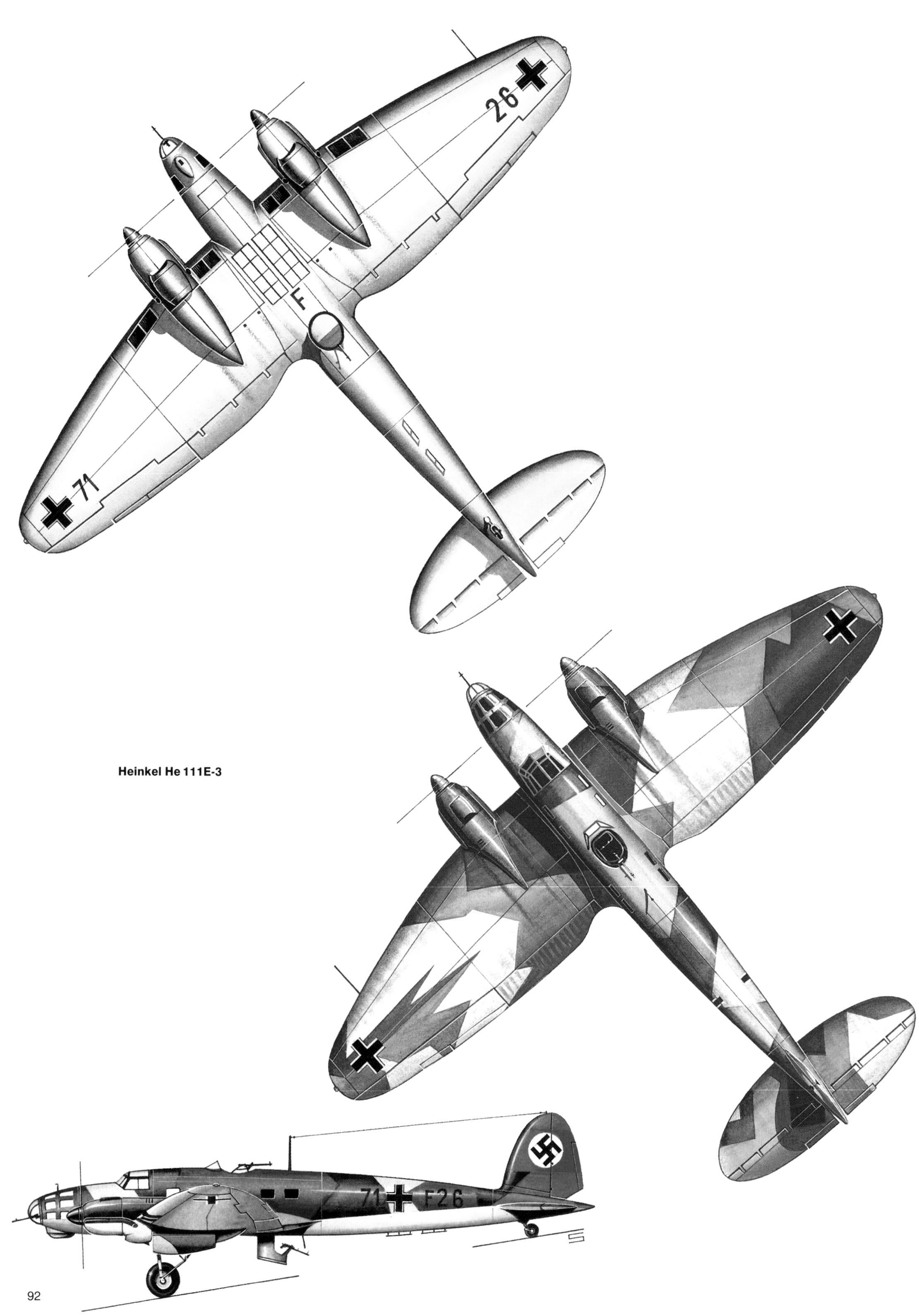

Heinkel He 111E-3

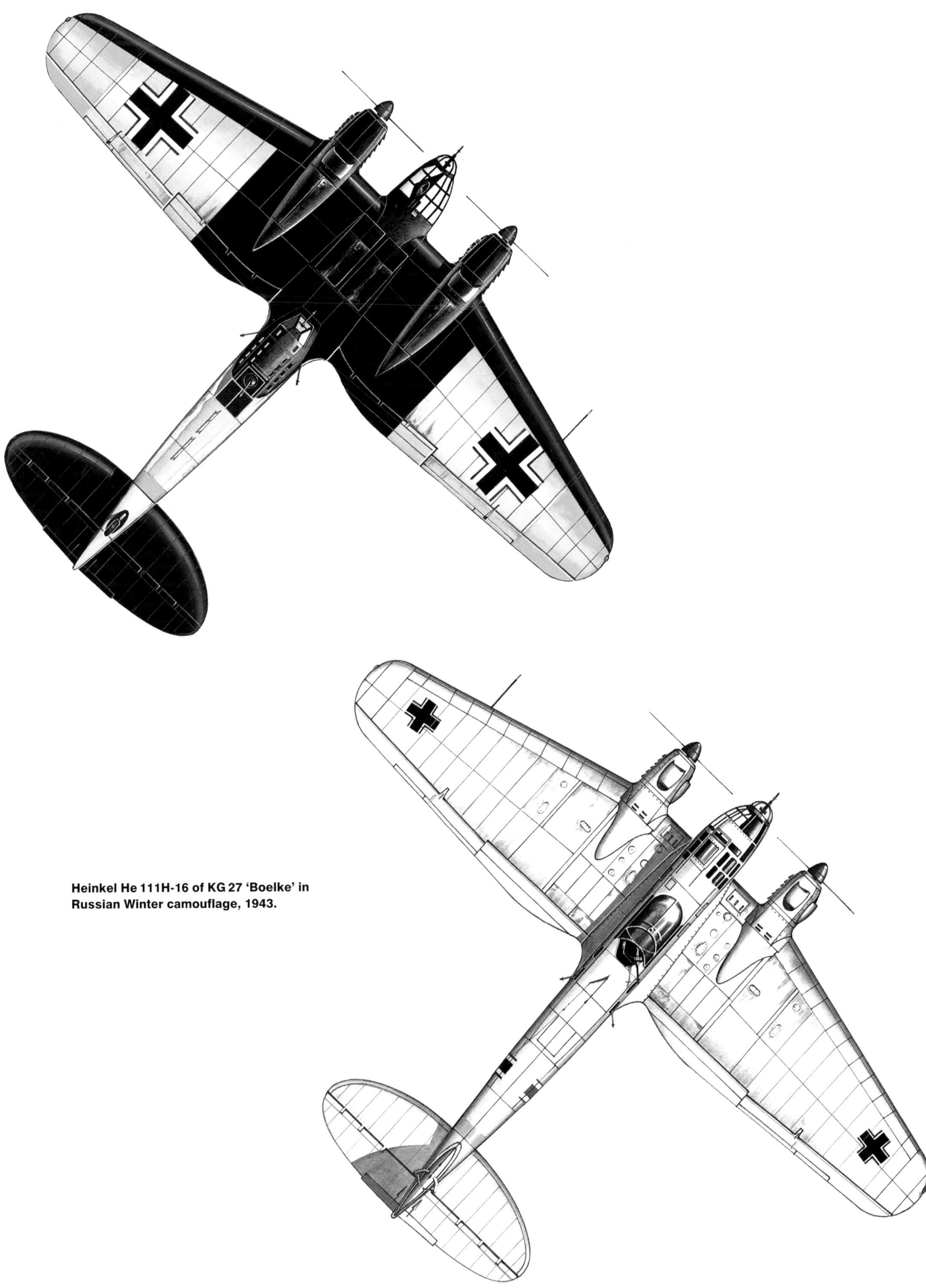

Heinkel He 111H-16 of KG 27 'Boelke' in Russian Winter camouflage, 1943.

Heinkel He 111H-16

Heinkel He 111H-22 with Fi 103

Sources and Acknowledgements

This book is based largely upon original documents, which enable a far more authentic account to be made than is possible with secondary literature. The latter were nevertheless consulted, and comprise extracts from the following reliable publications:

Die deutsche Luftwaffe series: Bernard & Graefe Verlag
Vol 2: *Flugmotoren und Strahltriebwerke;* Gersdorff/Grasmann/Schubert, 1981.
Vol 5: *Ernst Heinkel – Pionier der Luftfahrt;* H Dieter Köhler, 1983.
Vol 7: *Bordfunkgeräte – Vom Funksender zum Bordrada;* F Trenkle, 1986
Vol 9: *Typenhandbuch der deutschen Luftfahrttechnik;* Bruno Lange, 1986.

Flugzeugindustrie und Luftrüstung in Deutschland: Lutz Budraß; Droste Verlag, 1998.
Geschichte der deutschen Kriegswirtschaft 1939-1945, Vol 3: Dietrich Eichholtz; 1996
Deutsche Geheimwaffen 1939-1945 – Flugzeugbewaffnungen: Fritz Hahn; Erich Hoffmann Verlag, 1963
Stürmisches Leben: Ernst Heinkel; Mundus Verlag, 1953; Aviatik Verlag, 1998
Flugzeugbewaffnung: Hanfried Schliephake; Motorbuch Verlag, 1977
Markierungen und Tarnanstriche der Luftwaffe im Zweiten Weltkrieg, Vols 1 to 4: Karl Ries
Das Deutsche Reich und der Zweite Weltkrieg: Militärgeschichtliches Forschungsamt, Potsdam

The majority of the photographs are from the author's archives, the collections of the various individuals mentioned below, and from the Bernard & Graefe Verlag. Written material, identified as original documents, has been reproduced in facsimile form from original aircraft Handbooks, which, because of their condition, were unsuitable for direct reproduction.

Finally, I should like to express my sincere thanks to all those individuals and institutions without whose friendly support this monograph would not have been possible. Special thanks in this regard go to Messrs Baumann, Siemon and Schuller, as well as to Ralf Swoboda who prepared the colour illustrations, and to Ralf Schlüter who built the scale models referred to.

Karl-Heinz Regnat

LUFTWAFFE SECRET PROJECTS
Fighters 1939-1945

Walter Schick & Ingolf Meyer

Germany's incredible fighter projects of 1939-45 are revealed in-depth – showing for the first time the technical dominance that their designers could have achieved. With access to much previously unpublished information the authors bring to life futuristic shapes that might have terrorised the Allies had the war gone beyond 1945. Full colour action illustrations in contemporary unit markings and performance tables show what might have been achieved.

Hbk, 282 x 213 mm, 176pp, 95 colour artworks, c160 dwgs and c 30 photos
1 85780 052 4 **£29.95**

LUFTWAFFE SECRET PROJECTS
Strategic Bombers 1935-45

Dieter Herwig and Heinz Rode

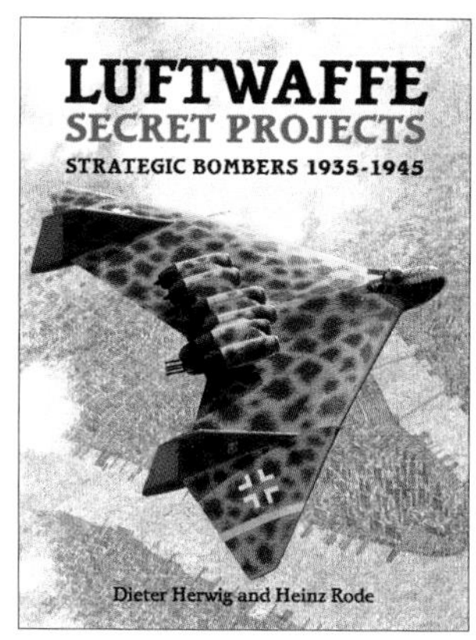

In this companion to the enormously popular volume on fighters, Germany's incredible strategic bomber projects 1935-45 are revealed showing the technical dominance that their designers could have achieved if time had allowed. The authors bring to life futuristic shapes that might have terrorised the Allies had the war gone beyond 1945. Careful comparison with later Allied and Soviet aircraft show the legacy handed on, right up to today's stealth aircraft.

Hbk, 282 x 213 mm, 144pp, 100 colour artworks, 132 b/w photos, 122 dwgs
1 85780 092 3 **£24.95**

LUFTWAFFE SECRET PROJECTS – Ground Attack & Special Purpose Aircraft

Dieter Herwig and Heinz Rode

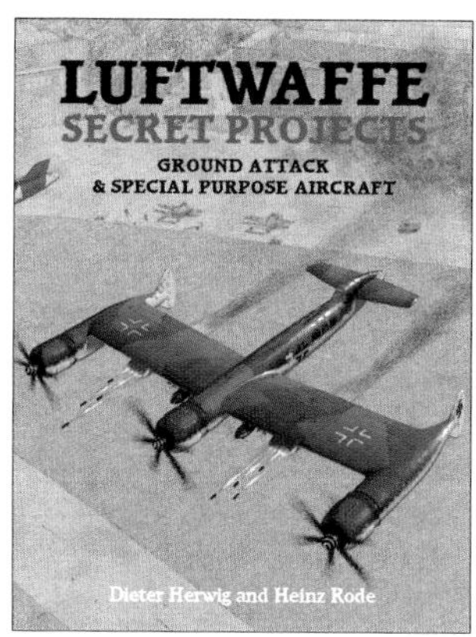

This third volume in the series takes a close look at a varied range of about 140 ground attack and special purpose aircraft types including Kampfzerstörer (multi-purpose combat aircraft), multi-purpose and fast bombers, explosive-carrying aircraft intended to attack other aircraft, air-to-air ramming vehicles, bomb-carrying gliders and towed fighters, and airborne weapons and special devices (rockets, cannon, flamethrowers etc).

Hbk, 282 x 213 mm, 272pp, 154 colour illustrations, 168 b/w photos, 196 dwgs
1 85780 150 4 **£35.00**

GERMAN AIR-DROPPED WEAPONS TO 1945

Wolfgang Fleischer

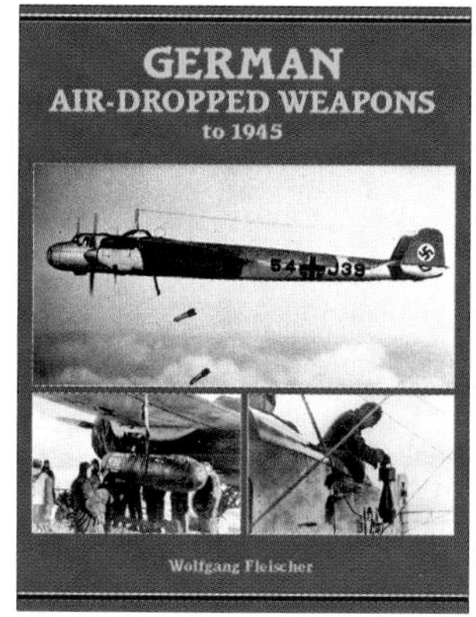

This traces the development of German air-dropped ammunition from the crude, 'aeronautical artillery' of WW1 to the advanced remote-control bombs of WW2. Major topics within the book include demolition bombs, incendiary bombs, special dropped ammunition, sea-dropping ammunition and dropping containers. A comprehensive illustrated listing gives information on 100 different bombs, 22 canisters and 50 of the most important bomb fuses.

Hbk, 282 x 213 mm, 240pp, 200 b/w photographs with over 200 drawings
1 85780 174 1 **£24.99**

KAMPFFLIEGER Bombers of the Luftwaffe Volume One: 1933-1940

J R Smith and E J Creek

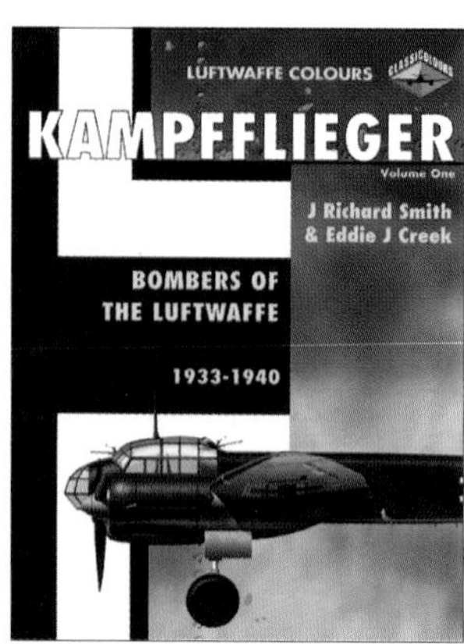

This, the first of four volumes, begins with an outline of the clandestine German bomber development following the end of World War One up to the birth of the new Luftwaffe under the Nazi Party in 1933 and the evolution of the German bomber force. The Luftwaffe's debut in the Spanish Civil War and the formation of the new Kampfgeschwader is covered. Also includes the invasion of Poland, the birth of Blitzkrieg and concludes with the eve of the invasion of the West.

Softback, 303 x 226mm, 96 pages c230 photos, 15 col profiles, maps
1 903223 42 3 **£16.95**

MESSERSCHMITT Me 163 VOLUME TWO

S Ransom & Hans-Hermann Cammann

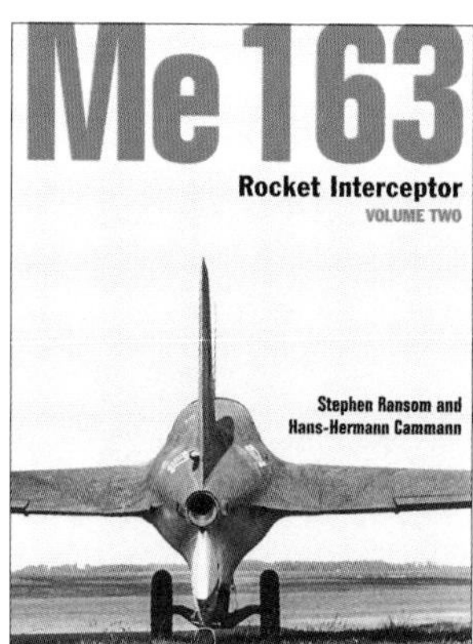

Following years of detailed research, this is the second volume in a two volume study of the Luftwaffe's legendary Messerschmitt Me 163 rocket-powered interceptor.

The authors have found incredible new documentary material and previously unpublished photographs, receiving co-operation from many former pilots who flew this radical and daunting aircraft, as well as Allied pilots who encountered it in combat.

Hardback, 303 x 226 mm, 224 pages, c300 photos, 20 colour artworks
1 903223 13 X **£35.00**

ON SPECIAL MISSIONS
The Luftwaffe's Research and Experimental Squadrons 1923-1945

J R Smith, E Creek and P Petrick

The story of the Verschuchsverband, the Trials and Research Unit of the Luftwaffe High Command, one of the most intriguing, clandestine and rarely-covered elements of the Luftwaffe before and during World War Two.

Using unpublished recollections from pilots who flew secret, long-range recce and spy-dropping missions, as well as hundreds of rare and fascinating photos, the book recounts the history, operations and aircraft of the unit.

Hardback, 303 x 226 mm, 128 pages, c360 b/w photos, 15 colour artworks
1 903223 33 4 **£19.95**

HELICOPTERS OF THE THIRD REICH

S Coates with J C Carbonel

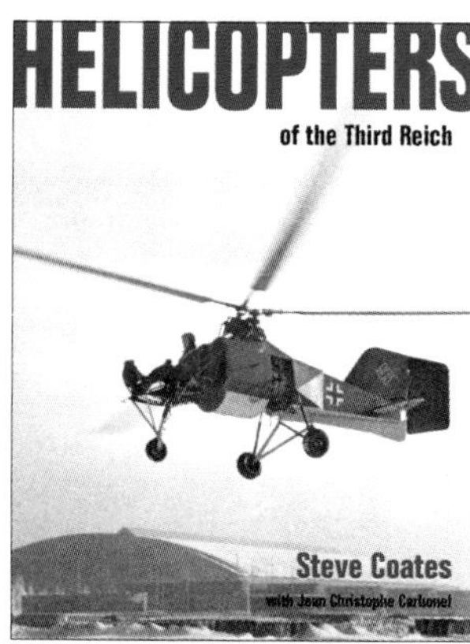

By the end of the Second World War, the Germans were, despite minimal funding and bitter inter-service rivalries, technologically ahead of their American counterparts in the development of rotating-wing aircraft. This book is the first comprehensive account of the development of auto-gyros and helicopters in Germany during 1930 to 1945 and sheds light on an unjustly neglected area of considerable aeronautical achievement.

Hardback, 303 x 226 mm, 224 pages, 470 b/w and colour photos, plus dwgs
1 903223 24 5 **£35.00**